HOW TO
WRITE
SONGS
on Guitar

Rikky Rooksby

EPIGRAPH: *"THE NEXT BIG THING IS A GOOD SONG."* BRIAN EPSTEIN

How to Write Songs on Guitar

A guitar-playing and songwriting course

Rikky Rooksby

A BALAFON BOOK

First British edition 2000

Published in the UK by Balafon Books, an imprint of Outline Press Ltd,
115J Cleveland Street, London W1P 5PN, England.
www.balafon.dircon.co.uk

ISBN 0-87930-611-4

Printed in Hong Kong

Art Director: Nigel Osborne
Design & production: Phil Richardson
Editor: Jim Roberts

Print and origination by Colorprint Offset Ltd, Hong Kong

00 01 02 03 04 5 4 3 2 1

As I write these words in January 2000, a young man has just strode past in the rainy street outside. He was singing the wordless refrain to America's 1972 hit 'Horse With No Name', a song that was recorded probably before he was born. Somehow, that says something significant about the popular song.

The popular song, commercially distributed on vinyl, tape or CD, is a marvellous art form. For 50 years it has woven itself into the fabric of the lives of millions of people across the world. The hit record, originally on the hallowed 45rpm, has focused the emotions we've lived and given us glimpses of those we have not, could not, should not or perhaps one day will, live. After the sense of smell, nothing evokes another time and place more than a song. Despite its ubiquitous cultural presence, the craft of the writers, performers and engineers who have captured these musical visions continues to be lamentably under-estimated. This is the magic medium in which whole worlds of experience and feeling are conjured up in a mere two or three minutes. In part, this is a book about the craft that goes into popular song at its best.

Mainly, this is a book for songwriters, guitarists and people who write songs on the guitar. It is also a book for anyone fascinated by popular song and will enhance your listening pleasure through awareness of what goes on in a record. It explains all the important parts of songwriting, shows how these concepts work on the guitar and illustrates them with references to recorded songs. There has probably never been a songwriting book with such a wide range of examples. This is not for the musically narrow-minded. Within these pages, you will find singers and bands from many styles of music from The Beatles to Nirvana, from Jimi Hendrix to Andy Williams, from Kate Bush to Bruce Springsteen, from The Sex Pistols to Madonna. You can learn some aspect of songwriting from absolutely everyone who has written a memorable song. ● RIKKY ROOKSBY, OXFORD MARCH 2000

Like all great musicians, great songwriters are probably born, not made. No tutor, no book, no course, can make you write songs that embed themselves in the memory of a generation and achieve critical as well as commercial acclaim. Only a few people will ever compose songs of the stature of 'Good Vibrations', 'Strawberry Fields Forever', 'Walk On By' or 'Like A Rolling Stone'.

Some of us grew up being told these were just pop songs, disposable artefacts to enjoy today and throw away tomorrow. Thirty years on they aren't looking quite so disposable, and we are beginning to appreciate that the artists who wrote and performed them are maybe not as common as was once assumed.

Craft

Even so, you can learn to write good songs, songs that will not only please yourself and your friends but may also please the ears of people in the music industry who need songs for their artists. If you already write songs, there's always something new to be learned about the craft, an insight or trick to help you improve or try a new avenue.

Inspiration cannot be turned on like a tap. All songwriters with any experience know the difference between writing when inspired and writing to meet a deadline. It can be the difference between sailing a boat with the wind in your sails and rowing the damn thing. But there are certain tricks you can use to try to encourage inspiration, by cultivating a fertile expectancy. This could be a way of putting yourself in the mood, perhaps by listening to music that affects you.

A good songwriter should be able to write a song on order. This can be done purely from craft, even if there isn't any inspiration at the start. And sometimes a song started in the spirit of trying to bolt one together without a strong inspiration can be transformed and become truly inspired halfway through the process.

Unconscious and Conscious Elements

When a song is taking shape, it is a delicate entity. For many writers it starts as a mood, a feeling. This feeling attaches itself to a chord, a chord sequence, a melody or a rhythm, or a phrase. Suddenly what was ordinary is "ensouled" in some way, like a charged battery. At this point a thousand possibilities hang about the embryonic song. As it is shaped, many subtler choices – some conscious, some unconscious – are made. These choices are part of the craft, and in this area knowledge about songwriting can make a vital difference to the finished song.

A songwriter plays a curious mixture of roles, and different writers identify with these roles in differing amounts. In one way, the songwriter acts as a midwife, bringing into existence something that subjectively feels as though it already has an existence of its own. This is why songwriters, when interviewed, often express the feeling that in some way the song is not really theirs. They speak of trying not to get in the way, of listening for what the song wants, and of not imposing on it and forcing it to take on a form that is alien to it. It is as though the songwriter is a medium or "channel" for the song.

In another way, the songwriter is someone who practises a craft, as a sculptor takes a block of stone and carves it away until a form is realised. This also has its truth. Looked at from this angle, knowledge of songwriting technique is a positive thing because it enables you to surpass your limitations. It will keep you from writing the same song over and over.

You need an awareness of both roles. The "midwife" role will keep you in a frame of mind that is open and prevent too much conscious interference; the "sculptor" role will take a good inspiration and make it better. That's what this book is about.

The better informed you are, the better able you are to make these choices. This means that instead of doing something too obvious, you come up with a better idea. This is craft, this can be learned, and absorbed so that its operation becomes intuitive. You bring it to bear before the song sets in the mould. Making changes at a later stage can be difficult but listening to great cover versions can be a good guide to the ways in which songs can be changed. Think of Hendrix's 'All Along The Watchtower', Joe Cocker's 'With A Little Help From My Friends', Nilsson's 'Without You', or Tori Amos' 'Smells Like Teen Spirit'. Compare Marvin Gaye's 'I Heard It Through The Grapevine' to the earlier version by Gladys Knight or The Beatles' 'Something' with Shirley Bassey's.

This book states, or implies, many musical rules. It is good to know them before you break them, but always remember:

Rule 1: There are no absolute rules. A great song may break a rule.

Rule 2: When rules dominate, formula results. Too much formula is the enemy of invention.

Mystery

At its core, all great music has a profoundly mysterious quality. This is especially true of great popular songs   be they pop, rock, folk, blues or soul. In large-scale works such as the symphony, there is usually an immense amount of architectural design and much development of ideas. Popular song is almost entirely about statement there is no time or desire or expectation of development. Most songs are between two and five minutes long. Because of its relative harmonic simplicity (though often nowhere near as simple as "serious" music criticism assumes) and its lack of development, popular song generally stands or falls on the level of inspiration in its initial material.

Take, for example, a chord sequence such as G D Am, G D C. How many songwriters in 1971 sat with a guitar or at a piano playing those chords at some time or other? How many thousands actually finished songs in which those chords appear roughly in that order? How many made it to live performance or recording? Probably hundreds yet only Bob Dylan wrote 'Knockin' On Heaven's Door'. And if you or I sit down to write a song on that sequence tomorrow, the mood our song captures will be different. It is as if the chords of a song are like the guy-ropes that keep a balloon in place; they aren't the balloon itself. In the same way, Tracks Of My Tears' may consist mostly of G C and D, but its spirit goes far beyond that. In this way, the elements of a song can be classified as more or less central, depending on how special they are. The most individual element is the performance, then the sound of the arrangement, then words and melody, then harmony, then rhythm, then tempo.

This facet of songwriting is worth remembering because it is encouraging. Songwriters who have been writing for a while sometimes find it hard to write songs with simple harmonic sequences because they don't spark any ideas. As a result, they search for more unusual or more complicated sequences. Remembering that harmony is always re-invigorating itself reminds you that there are always great songs to be written with the simplest of means.

What Kind of Song

For the purposes of this book, we need to define the kind of song you're trying to write. Songs come in all shapes, sizes, forms and styles, from the 12-minute extravaganza of a Meatloaf hit to the two minutes of a classic Elvis tune from the

1950s. From an artistic point of view, there is no such thing as a right or wrong form. If all songs were written to commercial formulas, we would all die of boredom. The dullest periods in the history of the singles chart were the ones when formulas dominated and eliminated the diversity of popular music.

For practical reasons, a book such as this needs to be based upon certain assumptions. It assumes you want to write songs that come in under the five-minute mark and use a traditional verse/chorus format, and that are approachable rather than avant-garde. You may have other musical ambitions, but even so there will be plenty here you can adapt and use.

Throughout the book, something like 1,500 popular songs from the 1950s to the present illustrate specific techniques of songwriting. A large number were hits on one or both sides of the Atlantic. I am not implying that they are all great songs, even if they were hits – some are, some aren't. Our interest in them is structural and technical. From Dusty Springfield to Led Zeppelin, from The Four Tops to The Sex Pistols, from Madonna to Catatonia, from Bob Marley to Oasis, there is quite a range of artists. If a song wasn't a single, you'll probably find it either on a "Best Of" compilation or a well-known album. The Beatles are well represented, not only because they were outstanding but because most people are familiar with their work. A copy of *The Beatles Complete Chordbook* (Wise, 2000) is invaluable from a songwriting point of view. If you don't find your favourite song or artist, don't get mad. After all, I couldn't consult the entire history of Western popular music in time for the deadline!

Have All the Great Songs Been Written?

Sometimes it can feel as though all the great songs exist and the best ideas have been used but there are always great songs waiting to be written. If it helps, think of them as hovering in the ether. It is true that the musical forms of a particular period cannot again have the same impact as when they were first heard. But locate yourself at any year in pop history, look at the next year's charts, and think about the songs no one had yet written. There were probably songwriters in the Brill Building in New York in 1962 chewing on their pencils, staring at the piano keys and blank manuscript paper, thinking that there were no more good tunes. Yet within a couple of years Lennon & McCartney, Holland-Dozier-Holland, Bacharach & David and Asher & Wilson would be producing classics by the bagful. Furthermore, how come it took rock music 40 years to produce 'Smells Like Teen Spirit', a decade after it was widely believed that guitar rock was dead? How was it that The La's 'There She Goes' was written in 1989 instead of 1968? How come no one wrote Travis' 'Why Does It Always Rain On Me' before 1999?

The Challenge of Today

Many feel that the period from 1960 to 1980 was a "golden era" for popular music, when more memorable songs were released, especially as singles, than in later periods. Is this true? Or is it merely rose-tinted memories of the music heard when young? Will those who grew up in the 1980s and 1990s feel the same way about their era?

Actually, there are objective factors that point to a decline in the quality of commercial songwriting – that is, the music that fills the airwaves and the Top 40 and Top 100. Lyrically, popular song has grown insular and afraid to address the world, while at the same time it is more pretentious, confusing obscurity with profundity. When it comes to banality, what difference is there between the next record that tells you to "shake your body" and 'Sugar Sugar' except that the former will hide its vacuousness beneath a tough, metallic production?

If there is a decline in popular music, the cause is not hard to find. It is the misuse of technology. Note I do not say technology itself. Human beings are easy to tempt, and technology is a seductive thing. When cost-cutting, a ticking clock, and laziness link up, it is not surprising if technology is made to serve these purposes in ways that are detrimental to music.

In the hands of the unmusical, digital technology all too often dehumanizes music. The charts are full of "virtual music" created entirely on computer-music that has never moved a molecule of air. Anything programmed has no expression at the point of execution, even if it has expression of design. Our minds are much more sophisticated in hearing music than many believe; we register the difference. The triumph of the silicon chip over the human spirit is nowhere better heard than in the chopped-up sampling of a singer's voice, done so a single vocal phrase can be manipulated on a keyboard. Sampling replaces the old crime of plagiarism with a new, more thorough-going one: the stealing not only of an idea but the performance and real-time expression of that idea. Musicians' actual performances are thus coerced into new musical contexts without their express permission. Instead of taking the time to find a great drum sound, why not sample a 1970s rock album? Suddenly, 50 other people go for the same sample. The ability to play an instrument is itself devalued. Sampling is theft.

Craftsmanship is replaced by a cut-and-paste ethic: the montage is everything. Why bother to paint when you can combine bits of other artists' pictures? Recordings no longer capture the sound of a group of musicians, perhaps highly talented, playing together at a moment in time. The arrangement no longer benefits from the excitement that such recording generates and is swathed in sterile perfection. Click tracks and drum machines impose a rhythmic tyranny in which an unrelenting beat is perfectly in time. The groove is lost, and techniques such as the crudest sudden division of the beat into smaller units to create pneumatic-drill snare-rolls and a twist of e.q. replace the continual invention of a good drummer. Rhythm is exalted over melody, harmony, time, tempo and key changes.

More than anything else, today's popular music is sick with repetition. In the past, bad pop records overstayed their welcome by repeating a hook or a chorus for what seemed countless times. Now it's worse, because each repetition is not a re-performing (with tiny human variables) but the exact recycling of two bars of music. Why sing a chorus more than once when you can copy your performance onto the second and the third? It's cheaper and quicker, but another opportunity for expression is lost. Why record a I VI IV V or a I V II progression when you can sample a couple of bars from 'Every Breath You Take' or 'Knockin' On Heaven's Door', copy them identically, sing something different over the top, and pass it off as a "song"? Why create a mood when, with an act of musical vampirism, you can suck one from a record that already exists in collective memory? Have all writers and performers grown so cynical? Is this all they think a popular song can be? Do they really believe in this soul-less vision? Or do they go home after every TV promotion and listen to Aretha or Al Green with a sense of relief?

I think the popular song is capable of much more than this impoverished parody of itself. That's one reason why I wrote this book. From these pages I hope you will take new ideas and new inspiration. This is a handbook of songwriting technique, so don't feel that you have to read it in sequence. Dip into different sections and play with ideas. There's no requirement to tackle the whole lot at once.

There are great songs waiting to be written.

SONGWRITING METHODS

ABBREVIATIONS

Roman numerals I VII
indicate chord
relationships within a key.

m *minor*

maj *major*

Song sections:

br *bridge*

c *coda*

ch *chorus*

hk *hook*

i *intro*

pch *pre-chorus*

v *verse*

Most of the chord-sequence examples
are standardized for comparison
into C *or* A *minor.*
Famous songs referred to in C *major*
or A *minor are not necessarily in*
the key of the original recordings.

What's involved in writing a song?

A song has four basic elements: words (the lyric) are sung to a tune (melody) that is supported by chords (harmony) and played to a certain combination of beat and tempo (rhythm).

a song = lyric + melody + harmony + rhythm

In different styles of music the balance of importance between these elements will change. In recent dance music the lyric is often reduced to a line or two, sampled and repeated; melody and harmony are also simplified, but rhythm is everything. Rap dispenses with melody and significant harmony but emphasises the lyric. MOR music stresses melody and a non-dissonant harmony but downplays rhythm. Rock and soul stress rhythm but not necessarily at the expense of the other elements. If you have been writing songs for a while, you may feel stronger on some of the four elements than others.

Even famous songwriters are often better at certain things than others. Bob Dylan's early music was harmonically conservative, coming as it did out of the American folk tradition, and his style of singing is hardly conducive to bringing out the contours of a beautiful melody, yet the attitude of his vocal style and his lyrics revolutionized popular music.

Where should I start?

There is no set way of writing a song. You do not have to do things in any fixed order. Some writers have a preference for working in one method, while others find that songs arrive in many different ways. John Lennon liked to put a lyric sheet on a piano and poke around on the keys, looking for a chord sequence. Paul McCartney has related how 'Yesterday' – the most covered song of all time – came to him in a dream. If you are lucky, you can sometimes have an original song come together in your mind, with words, melody, chords and rhythm.

A song can be composed in any of the following ways:

1 Start with a lyric and then set it to music.

Some people prefer this method because the subject matter may suggest certain things about the mood of the music. The rhythm of the words can evoke a tune. Some find it easier to have words to sing instead of humming or using nonsense lyrics when constructing a melody. It's good to keep a book of lyric ideas, even if they're not finished. You need only one verse and a chorus to get the basic structure of a song – extra verses can be written later.

2 Start with a melody and then harmonize it.

I call this "top-down" songwriting. Much recent music suggests this has become a less common technique, and songwriting has suffered as a consequence. All too often, melodies are constructed *after* the chord sequence; the melody can be constrained or neglected as a result. In the mid 20th century, popular songwriters paid more attention to the melody at an early stage in composition. The beauty of this technique is that it will encourage you to compose an effective tune. If the tune works on its own – if it has an expressive quality, some pleasing movement and a catchy "hook" – it will sound even better when everything else is in place. Think of a melody such as 'I Only Want To Be With You' – it's delightful even when sung unaccompanied.

3 Start with the harmony.

Construct a pleasing chord sequence and then try to find a melody. I call this composing "from the middle out". This is a common approach, especially among guitarists. Strumming your way round a chord sequence does not require much technique, and it allows the mind to play with words and melody. Chord sequences can be inspiring and suggest an emotion or mood that can be focused later through a lyric and melody.

The disadvantage of this approach is that the chords can prevent the melody from developing a shape of its own – the melody becomes an afterthought. It is all too easy to sing a couple of steps up or down as the chords change, moving from a note that fits with one chord to one that fits with the next. The result is a highly linear or "horizontal" tune that is squeezed into a narrow range – usually less than an octave – and often monotonous. Male singer-songwriters/guitarists are prone to this approach because they are usually less able or less prepared to write a melody with a wide range. Women songwriters often write melodies that have a greater span and more vertical "jumps" because their voices can deliver them. Compare the "vertical" melodies composed by Tori Amos or Kate Bush with some of Jackson Browne's or Bruce Springsteen's songs.

Another problem of composing the chord sequence first is that it may artificially chop the melody into phrases that are only as long as the time spent on a chord. Listen for songs where each melodic phrase starts on the second beat of the bar (or thereabouts) and ends just before the next chord change. The verse in Texas's 'Summer Son' is an example. This can be a sign that the melody was composed after the chord progression: the writer is waiting for the chord change in order to pitch the next melodic phrase against the new chord.

4 Start with a rhythm track.

It could be a drum pattern or loop, and a tempo. I call this "bottom-up" composing. If you are writing music in any genre in which rhythm is a major component, this makes sense as a creative procedure. Any music intended for dancing needs a strong rhythm. One common fault of singer-songwriter material is that it lacks rhythmic interest, and this is a way to avoid that trap. Try singing against a drum rhythm to give your melodies greater rhythmic presence. If you have not done so before, try writing songs with a drum machine, an approach used by Kate Bush for her albums *The Dreaming* and *Hounds Of Love*. This can make you more aware of rhythm.

For a further refinement of the "bottom-up" approach, add a bassline. The bass should reinforce the rhythm, and it will also suggest a harmony. You will, however, be free to treat the bass notes as the foundation of major or minor chords or their inversions, since a single note in the bass can imply a number of different chords. (There will be more about this later.)

If one of these methods doesn't work for you, then try another. Or, to stop yourself from writing the same kind of song over and over, deliberately choose a different method.

Other Strategies for Songwriting

Here are some other stratagems you may find helpful:

1 Compose away from your instrument. This stops you from falling back on familiar patterns. Listen to the music in your mind and shape it in your imagination. When you have an idea firmly in place, then go to an instrument .

2 Try a different instrument. Guitarists have a tendency to use chord sequences and keys that are easy to finger. Try composing on a keyboard instead. You don't have to be able to 'play' the piano in any technical sense. All you need to work out simple sequences is the ability to play major and minor triads.

3 Borrow a structure. This is a bit like keeping the scaffolding but changing the building inside. Take a song you like and write down the basic structure. Eliminate the chords but keep the same form, tempo and length. Then write a new song using the same structure.

4 Arbitrarily choose some limits – a key, a tempo, a time signature, a theme, a style – and write a song to fit. Experiment with different genres. Set yourself a challenge by writing a song:

- that is only two minutes long
- that starts with a chorus
- where the verse is in A and the chorus in F
- that is in any time signature other than 4/4
- that changes from 4/4 to 6/8 and back
- that has an odd number of bars in the verse or chorus
- that increases in tempo
- that does not have a turnaround
- where the structure is verse, verse, bridge, verse, and the "hook" is in the verse
- that is a sad song with only major chords
- that has no minor chords
- that begins with some effective rhymes picked from a dictionary and used to generate a lyric.

5 Pastiche. Write in the style of a singer or band you admire. Many songwriters begin this way, writing songs that sound like their favourite music. It is also a useful exercise for more experienced writers, even when they have worked through the initial phase of strong influence by one particular artist or group.

6 Read a book or magazine, see a film, go for a walk. Imagine and observe. Listen to conversations on the bus or in the shopping queue. Then put it down in a song.

7 Visualize. Sit in a silent room and close your eyes. Imagine a box of 45rpm singles, each one an unwritten classic. Choose one, visualizing the coloured bag and label. Take it out, put it on a turntable, lower the stylus onto the grooves, and listen to the crackle of vinyl and the low-level rumble of the turntable. Keep your mind passive and allow the music to start. You may get a song from your memory. You may get something new – and even if it's only a few bars, it could be enough to start a new song.

The first of the four key terms that we are going to examine is harmony, and this means discussing chords.

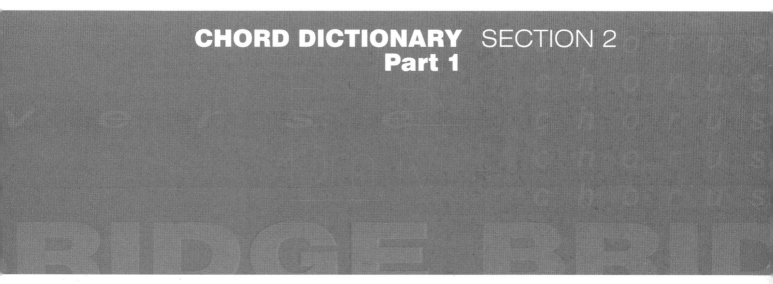

CHORD DICTIONARY SECTION 2
Part 1

In this section, we will look at the function of harmony in songs. Harmony is supplied by chords, and learning chords is how most people start on the guitar. One thing that makes the guitar popular as an accompaniment instrument is that it is relatively easy to learn some chord shapes, strum them and sing. Many professional performers have got by for years with little more than this.

The basic chords presented here will give you all the chords you need to start writing songs. Section nine comes later and deals with more complex chords in part two of the Chord Dictionary.

What is a chord?

A simple major or minor chord comprises three notes and is called a triad.

The four types of triad

Notes	Scale		Name
	Degrees	Gaps	
C E G	1 3 5	2+1½	C major
C E♭ G	1♭3 5	1½+2	C minor
C E♭ G♭	1♭3♭5	1½+1½	C diminished
C E G♯	1 3 ♯5	2+2	C augmented

ABBREVIATIONS

Roman numerals I VII
indicate chord
relationships within a key.
m *minor*
maj *major*
Song sections:
br *bridge*
c *coda*
ch *chorus*
hk *hook*
i *intro*
pch *pre-chorus*
v *verse*
Most of the chord-sequence examples are standardized for comparison into C *or* A minor.
Famous songs referred to in C *major or* A minor *are not necessarily in the key of the original recordings.*

What is a chord?

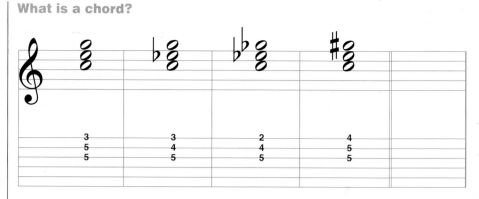

Of these four, it is major and minor chords that concern the songwriter most. The major/minor fluctuation, along with the possibility of key changes, is one of the glories of the Western musical tradition. Diminished and augmented chords are less important, having only specialized applications. Most of the basic chord shapes that guitarists strum take these three notes and double or triple them for a fuller sound.

Triad shapes

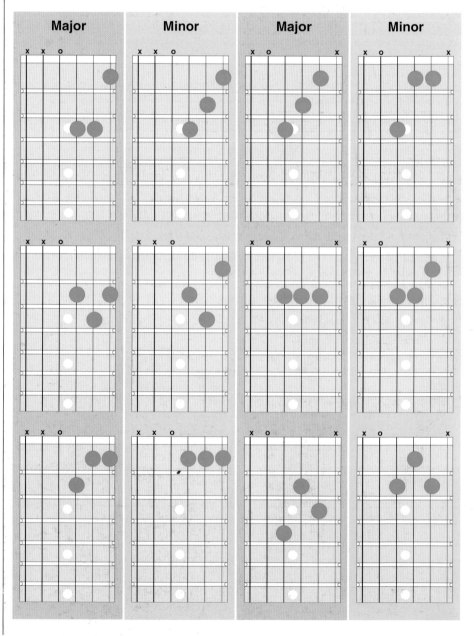

How notes are duplicated in guitar chords

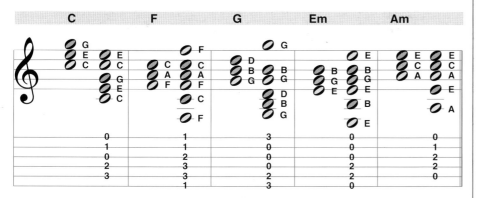

A single chord like A major is capable of many different voicings.

Contrasted A chords

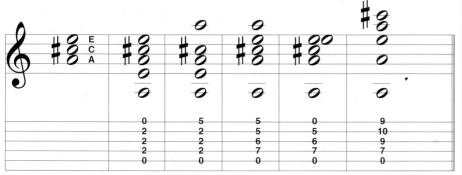

Major Chords

Major chords are the most important in songwriting; everything else revolves around them. They are the most flexible in conveying the widest range of moods. By setting and arrangement of how they are played, a huge variety of emotions can be expressed. Compared to minor chords, major chords are often said to sound positive, upbeat or happy. Even so, it is possible to express sadness with them.

Guitar chords can be broadly divided into those that have open strings and those that do not. Open-string chords have a more resonant quality than fully fretted chords. The chords of A, C, D, E and G on the guitar have effective open-string shapes, and the other major chords are derived from these shapes. If a chord has no open strings in it, with or without a barre, it is a movable shape and can be positioned up and down the fretboard.

Major chord shapes

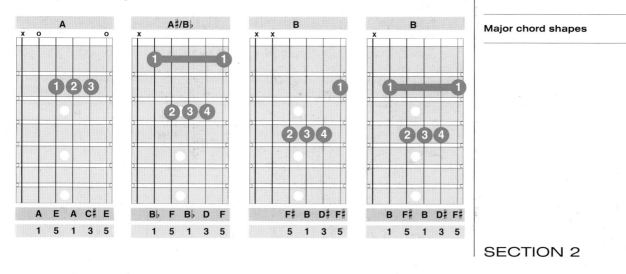

Major chord shapes continued

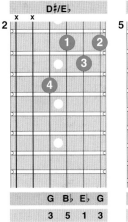

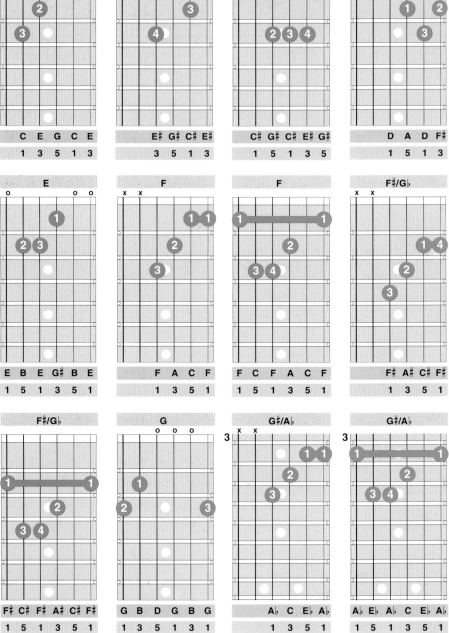

C				
C	E	G	C	E
1	3	5	1	3

C#/Db			
E#	G#	C#	E#
3	5	1	3

C#/Db				
C#	G#	C#	E#	G#
1	5	1	3	5

D			
D	A	D	F#
1	5	1	3

D#/Eb			
G	Bb	Eb	G
3	5	1	3

D#/Eb				
Eb	Bb	Eb	G	Bb
1	5	1	3	5

E					
E	B	E	G#	B	E
1	5	1	3	5	1

F			
F	A	C	F
1	3	5	1

F					
F	C	F	A	C	F
1	5	1	3	5	1

F#/Gb			
F#	A#	C#	F#
1	3	5	1

F#/Gb					
F#	C#	F#	A#	C#	F#
1	5	1	3	5	1

G					
G	B	D	G	B	G
1	3	5	1	3	1

G#/Ab			
Ab	C	Eb	Ab
1	3	5	1

G#/Ab					
Ab	Eb	Ab	C	Eb	Ab
1	5	1	3	5	1

Minor Chords

Minor chords sound sad, unhappy or melancholic. A song written entirely in minor chords will accentuate this. A comic song, though, might deliberately mismatch the theme of the lyric with the harmony – imagine a tragic lyric set to a series of major chords at a quick tempo, or a happy lyric set entirely in a minor key at a slow tempo.

In most chord progressions, minor chords are combined with majors. This causes a subtle alternation of mood and tone that can be aesthetically and emotionally stimulating. Some types of music do not have chord sequences in this sense; in Indian music, for example, there are long scale sequences that are mono-chordal, without chord or key changes.

The chords of Am, Dm and Em have effective open-string shapes.

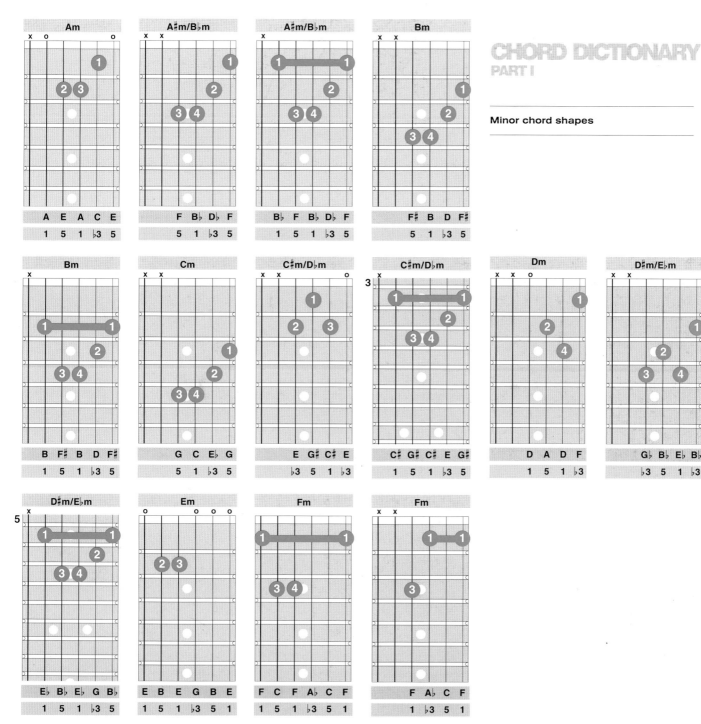

CHORD DICTIONARY
PART I

Minor chord shapes

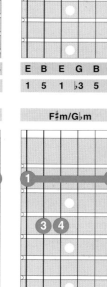
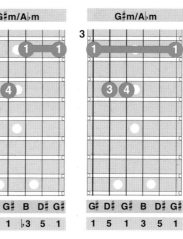
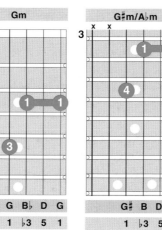

Dominant Seventh Chords

A different type of chord can be created by adding another note to a triad. This note is often identified by a number that indicates its scale degree.

Here is the scale of C major:

1	2	3	4	5	6	7
C	D	E	F	G	A	B

The triad of C major (chord I) is made by putting together the notes C, E and G (1-3-5). The dominant seventh chord is formed by adding the note one tone (one full step) below the root: C major C E G becomes C E G Bb. It is called the "dominant" seventh because in traditional harmony the fifth note of the scale (the dominant) is the only one on which a dominant seventh chord will occur if you build a chord upon it. In the key of C, for example, G is the dominant; G dominant seventh is G B D F. Notice that the fourth note of the chord, F, is one full step below the root, G.

In the blues, however, a dominant seventh chord can occur on chord I or chord IV as well as chord V, and in popular music the seventh note of the scale is often flattened.

The chords of A7, B7, C7, D7, E7 and G7 can be played in first position as open-string shapes.

The dominant seventh chord has a hard, bluesy sound. Use it to toughen up a chord sequence, as it does in songs such as 'Caught By The Fuzz', 'When I Get Home', 'Baby's In Black' and 'Hard Day's Night'. It is also used to establish a new key – there is more about this in section ten on key-changing.

Dominant seventh chord shapes

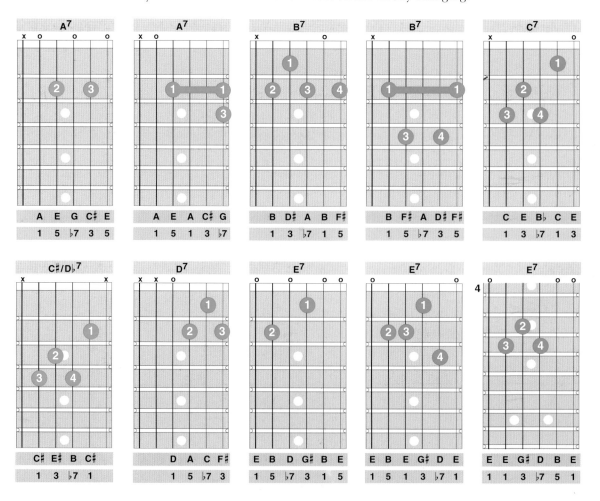

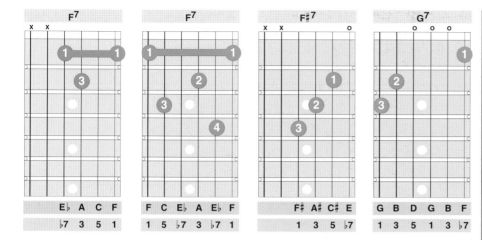

E♭ A C F	F C E♭ A E♭ F	F♯ A♯ C♯ E	G B D G B F
♭7 3 5 1	1 5 ♭7 3 ♭7 1	1 3 5 ♭7	1 3 5 1 3 ♭7

Dominant seventh chord shapes continued

Major Seventh Chords

This chord is formed by adding the note one semitone (half-step) below the root. C major C E G becomes C E G B. In traditional harmony, it occurs on chords I and IV. Another way of thinking of a major seventh is to think of it as major and minor triads superimposed (C E G = C major; E G B = E minor).

In contrast to the dominant seventh, the major seventh has a romantic quality. For this reason, it is excellent for expressing gentle, intimate emotions, which is why it is often used in ballads, soul, pop and MOR. The major seventh is central to the work of composers such as Burt Bacharach. It works better at medium to slow tempos because at speed the nuance of the chord is easily lost. At quicker

Major seventh chord shapes

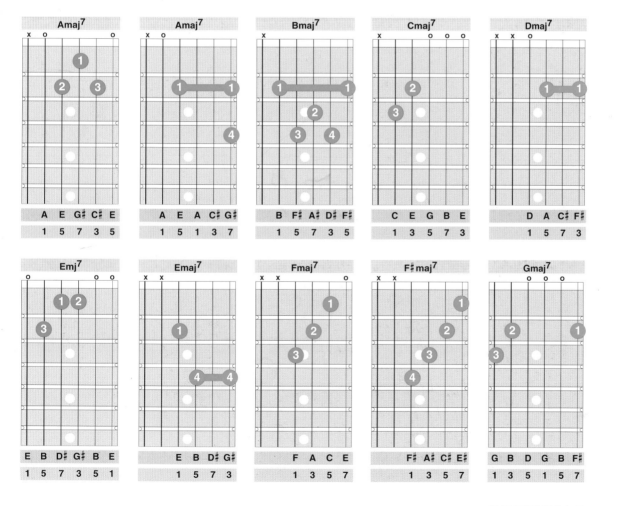

A E G♯ C♯ E	A E A C♯ G♯	B F♯ A♯ D♯ F♯	C E G B E	D A C♯ F♯
1 5 7 3 5	1 5 1 3 7	1 5 7 3 5	1 3 5 7 3	1 5 7 3

E B D♯ G♯ B E	E B D♯ G♯	F A C E	F♯ A♯ C♯ E♯	G B D G B F♯
1 5 7 3 5 1	1 5 7 3	1 3 5 7	1 3 5 7	1 3 5 1 5 7

tempos it can be heard in Latin-influenced material. There is a string of five major seventh chords in the bridge of Aztec Cameraís 'Oblivious'. It is not so common in hard and heavy rock, punk, etc, though Jimmy Page has used them occasionally, as in 'Carouselambra' and 'Ten Years Gone' where all the chords in the A D G C bridge sequence are major sevenths. He also used an Amaj7 Em7 change to devastating effect on the bridge of The Firm's 'Fortune Hunter'. The major seventh is a delightful chord to climax a crescendo, as in 'Tears Of A Clown', where the hook is D B Em Cmaj7.

Open-string major sevenths can be played for Amaj7, Cmaj7, Dmaj7, Emaj7, Fmaj7 and Gmaj7.

Minor seventh chord shapes

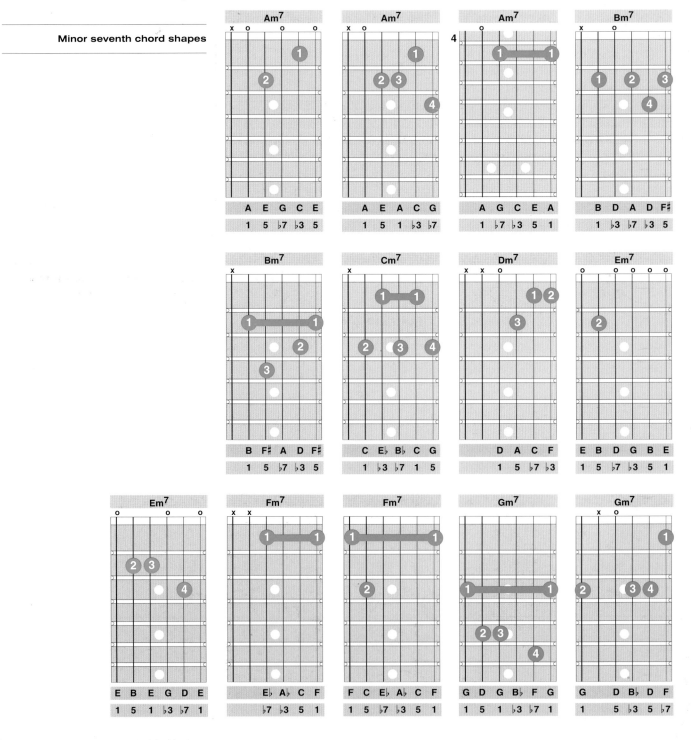

Minor Seventh Chords

Adding the note that is one tone (full step) below the root of a minor chord produces a minor seventh. C minor C Eb G becomes C Eb G Bb. In traditional harmony it occurs on the I, IV and V chords if these are derived from the natural minor scale, and on chords II, III and VI of a major scale. Another way of looking at a minor seventh is to think of it as a major triad superimposed on a minor triad (C Eb G = C minor; Eb G Bb = Eb major), the opposite of the major seventh.

The minor seventh is a diluted version of the minor chord. It has a sad quality but is not as sad as the straight minor. Use it where you feel the minor would be too depressing, and for combining with majors. A song written entirely in minor sevenths would be less depressing than one written entirely in minors. Minor sevenths combine nicely with major sevenths – a well-known trick in soul music. Try an ascending I II III IV sequence like C Dm Em F and then play it like this: Cmaj7 Dm7 Em7 Fmaj7.

There are open-string minor sevenths for Am7, Bm7, Dm7, Em7 and Gm7

The Minor/Major Seventh Chord

This chord is formed by adding the note that is one semitone (half-step) below the root of a minor chord. C minor C Eb G becomes C Eb G B. This is a tense chord with a strange sound that is not exactly sad or happy – more like threatening. In pop songs, it is usually found only as a passing chord between the minor and the minor seventh: try Cm Cm/maj7 Cm7. On the guitar, this is most easily done from Am, Dm or Em. Minor/major sevenths tend to crop up in soundtrack music for horror and thriller films. John Barry used them in the soundtracks of the 1960s James Bond films. You will find one in the coda of 'That Means A Lot'.

Minor/major seventh chord shapes

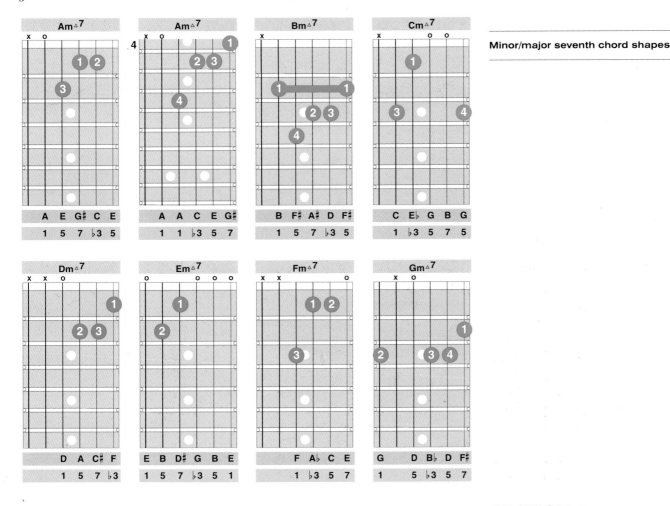

Suspended fourth chord shapes

Suspended Fourth Chords

Having dealt with the sevenths, we move to several chord types that inhabit a strange musical "neutral zone". We'll begin with the suspended fourth, which is formed by replacing the third with the fourth of the scale. C major C E G becomes C F G. Since the only difference between C major and C minor is the third (E or Eb), if it is removed you cannot tell whether the chord is major or

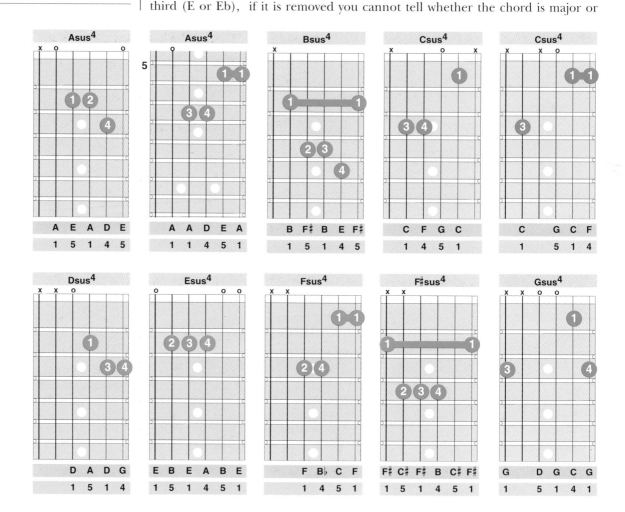

minor. The suspended fourth is therefore neither major nor minor, but neutral. Csus4 can occur in the keys of C major or C minor.

This is a very tense chord. The fourth wants to resolve by dropping back either a semitone (half-step) to a major chord or a tone (full step) to a minor chord. Therefore you should use it when you wish to build momentary tension. Pop songs tend to use sus4s at transition points to build excitement – for example, from the end of a verse into a chorus, or at the end of a chorus into a repeat of the chorus. They are popular in rock music because of their tension. 'Two Hearts Are Better Than One', 'She's The One', 'Jean Genie', 'Pinball Wizard' and 'Can't Keep It In' all feature prominent sus4s.

Effective open-string sus4 are available for Asus4, Dsus4, Esus4 and Gsus4.

Suspended Second Chords

Brother of the sus4, the sus2 is formed by replacing the third with the second of the scale. C major C E G becomes C D G. Like the suspended fourth, the suspended second is neither major nor minor. It is not quite as tense as the sus4, having more ambiguity and space. It is good for atmospheric songs, especially if you want to convey emptiness, and the sus2 works well with (or as a substitute for) minor chords.

The sus2 combines nicely with the sus4, as a finger is added, taken off, etc. John Lennon used this on 'Happy Christmas (War Is Over)' and you'll also find it in 'Needles and Pins', 'So Sad About Us', 'I Need You', 'I'll Feel A Whole Lot Better', 'Summer Of 69' and 'Brass in Pocket'.

You can play effective open-string versions of Asus2, Csus2, Dsus2, Fsus2 and Gsus2.

Suspended second chord shapes

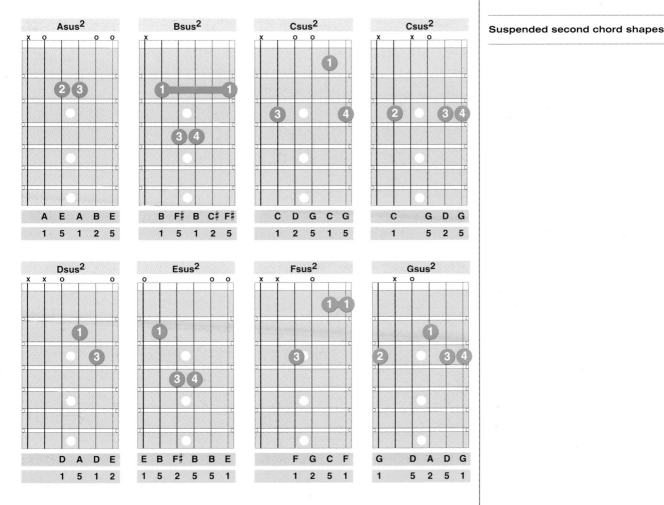

Fifth Chords

This type of chord is related to the sus2 and sus4 because, once again, the third has been removed. C5 is C G. A C5 chord could be played in C major or C minor. You can solo over it using a number of different scales and there won't be a clash -possibly *The* Clash, but not *a* clash. This harmonic neutrality makes it suitable for hard rock.

Open any book of rock transcriptions and you'll see loads of these. They come in two basic forms. There's the "power chord" fifth (C G), possibly with the root doubled an octave higher (C G C), usually played on the bottom three strings of the guitar with any quantity of distortion. This is for aggressive music, be it punk, grunge, hard rock or HM. No matter how different their politics, lyrics or haircuts, Green Day, Nirvana, Queen, Guns 'N Roses and Metallica are all united in using fifths. For this type, there are open-string shapes for A5, C5, D5, E5 and G5.

In the other form of this chord, the two notes are doubled or tripled across the strings. Hence the G5 favoured by Noel Gallagher, which goes from bottom to top G x D G D G (A-string muted), and Pete Townshend's A5 (A E A E A) from the A-string up. With a stark, bold tone, this type of chord sounds good strummed in moody and aggressive acoustic stuff.

Fifth chord shapes

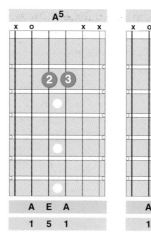
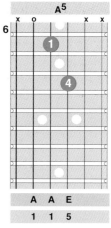
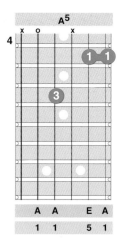

A⁵	A⁵	A⁵	A⁵
A E A	A E A E A	A A E	A A E A
1 5 1	1 5 1 5 1	1 1 5	1 1 5 1

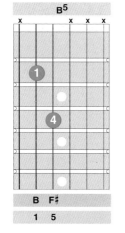
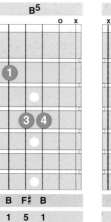

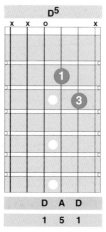
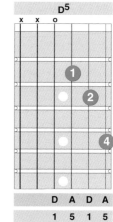
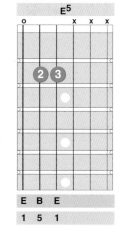

B⁵	B⁵	C⁵	D⁵	D⁵	E⁵
B F#	B F# B	C G C G	D A D	D A D A	E B E
1 5	1 5 1	1 5 1 5	1 5 1	1 5 1 5	1 5 1

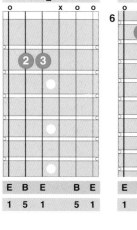
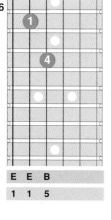

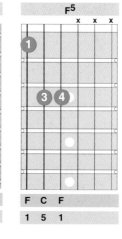
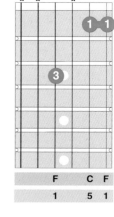

E⁵	E⁵	E⁵	F⁵	F⁵	G⁵
E B E B E	E E B	E E B E B E	F C F	F C F	G D G D G
1 5 1 5 1	1 1 5	1 1 5 1 5 1	1 5 1	1 5 1	1 5 1 5 1

Fifths (any position)

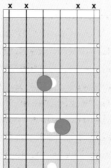

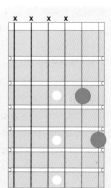

24

SECTION 2

The fifth chord will toughen up a progression. You can sing a minor or major melody over the same fifth chord – it makes no difference. On a recording with multiple guitar tracks, it combines nicely with full major or minor chords.

Dominant Seventh Suspended Fourth

This is quite a popular chord, an amalgam of a dominant seven and a sus4. In C this would C F G Bb. This chord is neither major nor minor. It can resolve either to C7 or Cm7, depending on whether the F drops to E or Eb. The presence of the seventh makes this chord not as tense as the straight sus4.

There are open string shapes for A7sus4, D7sus4, E7sus4 and G7sus4.

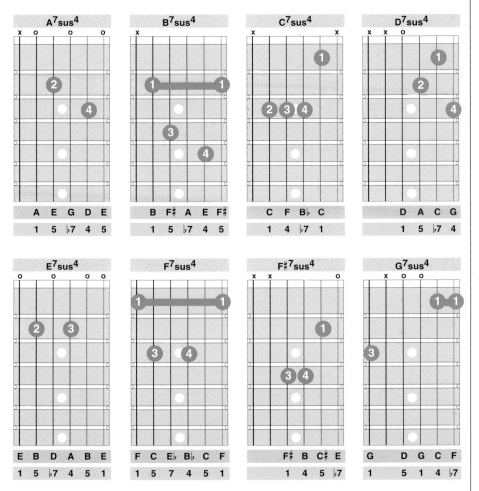

Dominant seventh suspended fourth chord shapes

Major Sixth Chords

The major sixth is formed by adding the sixth note of the scale to the major chord. C major C E G becomes C E G A. It is a slight dilution of the major chord, just as the minor seventh is a dilution of the minor chord. In fact, C E G A are the same notes that make up Am7 (A C E G). In many guitar chordbooks and sheet music, you will find chords shown as major sixths that are really inverted minor chords. It is essential for the major sixth that all four notes be sounded.

In most pop contexts a major sixth will lend a mildly "jazzy" sound, and it is heard in Latin American music. The verse of 'No Reply' has two major sixths, giving it a slightly Latin quality. It is associated with The Beatles, who sang a major sixth in the last chord of 'She Loves You'. Roxy Music's 'Love Is The Drug' is one of a number of songs that alluded to this by ending on a similar major sixth.

Major sixth chord shapes

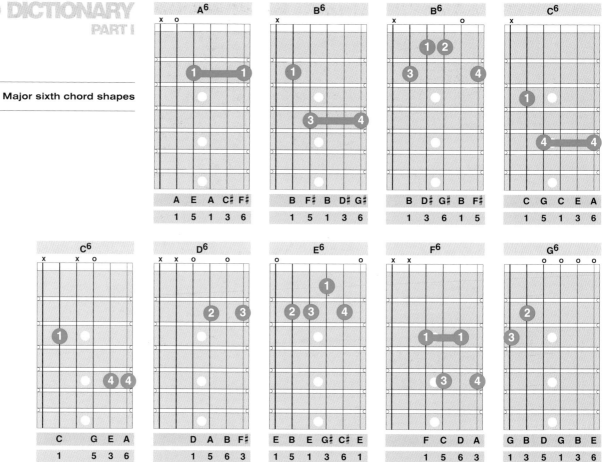

Minor Sixth Chords

The minor sixth has two forms. This is because there are several different minor scales. It is formed by adding the sixth note of the natural minor scale or Aeolian mode (A B C D E F G) to the minor chord, and it also occurs on the harmonic minor scale (A B C D E F G#). A minor A C E becomes A C E F – the same notes as Fmaj7 (F A C E) but in a different order.

This minor sixth is mildy dissonant because of the minor second between the fifth and sixth notes of the scale. Most guitar shapes will not place these notes next to each other, so the dissonance will be muted. Nevertheless, the dissonance acts as an intensifier of the minor chord. Use this minor sixth when you want to make a minor more tense and unsettling. It is rare in pop music, though there is

Minor sixth chord shapes

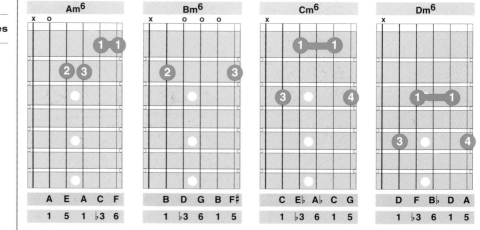

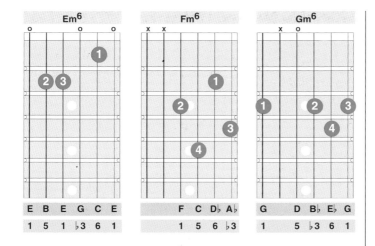

a fleeting one just before the chorus of 'Run To You' by Bryan Adams.

Minor Sharp Sixth Chords

The other type of minor sixth chord is formed by adding the sixth of the melodic minor scale (A B C D E F# G#) or the Dorian mode (A B C D E F# G) to the minor chord. A minor A C E becomes A C E F#. This chord is quite close to D7 (D F# A C) and a second inversion D7 (A D A C F#) where the open A string is deliberately strummed will sound similar.

The minor sharp sixth has an angular quality because of the dissonant augmented 4th between C and F#, as is found in the dominant seventh, but it is not as depressive as the minor sixth. It is slightly easier to find shapes for the

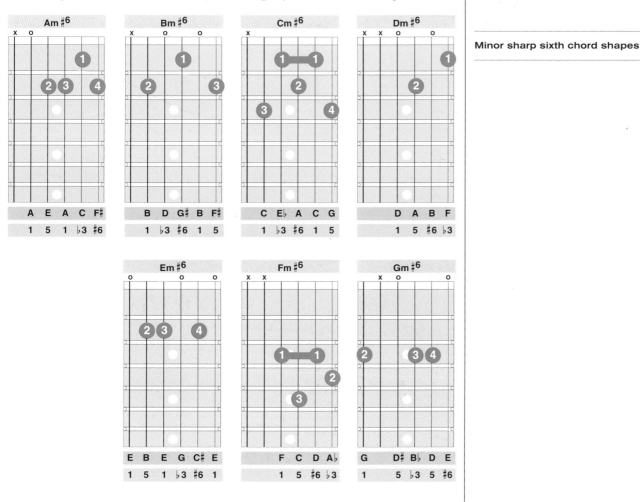

Minor sharp sixth chord shapes

minor sharp sixth than the minor sixth. It is not a common chord, though around the time of the 'White Album' Lennon became fond of it, as can be heard in the verses of 'Happiness Is A Warm Gun'. It is effective to use this chord when a song features a change from the minor form of chord IV to I. In C major, this would be Fm (F Ab C) to C; try Fm#6 (F Ab C D) instead of Fm. Try playing Am G C and then Am#6 G C and notice the change in feeling.

Augmented Chords

To complete Part 1 of the Chord Dictionary, we'll look at two chord types that have occasional uses. The augmented chord is a major triad where the top note (the fifth) is sharpened: C E G becomes C E G#. In traditional harmony, it does not occur on the major scale but is found on the harmonic minor scale as chord III (C E G# in A harmonic minor).

This chord is tense sounding and never played for more than a beat or so. It is usually found as a passing chord between a major and a minor or a major and a major sixth. Try changing from D to D+ to Bm, or D to D+ to D6. Chuck Berry famously put an augmented chord at the start of the classic song 'No Particular Place To Go' to imitate a car horn. You can catch the augmented strutting its funky stuff in 'All My Loving' (ch: VI bVI+ I in E), 'Ask Me Why' (ch: IV V I I+) and 'From Me To You' (end of bridge). It is an essential part of the riff in 'Kashmir' – recently given a down-market re-fit and renamed the good ship 'Come With Me' by Puff Daddy. There are augmented chords in 'It Won't Be Long', 'Michelle', 'Fixing A Hole', 'I'm Happy Just To Dance With You', 'Mamma Mia' and 'Just Like Starting Over'. An E+ kicks off 'Oh Darling', and the chorus of 'Hey Bulldog' has the hypnotic climbing sequence Bm Bm+ Bm6 Bm7,

Augmented chord shapes

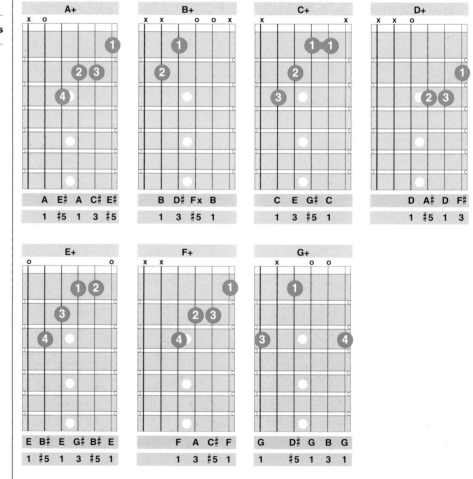

followed by the same sequence starting from Em. Notice that an augmented chord is made up of two intervals of two tones (full steps) each. If you try to add another one, you come full circle: in C, the note two tones above G# is ... C. Therefore, the augmented chord cannot be added to by the method which increases the complexity of other chords.

Diminished/Diminished Seventh Chords

The diminished triad (C Eb Gb) is almost never used on its own. Instead, another note one-and-a-half tones above is added to create a diminished seventh: C Eb Gb Bbb (B double-flat = A in pitch). In sound, this is close to a dominant seventh chord. If we change C Eb Gb Bbb enharmonically (using alternate names for the same notes) to C Eb F# A, the Eb has to drop only one semitone (half-step) to D to make a D7 chord. That's why this chord has a highly ambiguous quality.

As with the augmented chord, you don't want to stay on a diminished seventh for long. It is the musical equivalent of one of those strange particles in sub-atomic physics – the sort that are in six different places and/or six different times at once. The diminished seventh is a mutant offspring of the minor chord, whose main employment is as a doorway between different keys.

Each note in a diminished seventh can be regarded as the root, so each shape has multiple names. Bizarre, isn't it? I guess you won't be surprised if I tell you that the number of hit singles with diminished sevenths is pretty small. It sometimes turns up in Meatloaf numbers, to assist that air of faded grandeur. David Bowie put several in the chorus of 'Quicksand', thus causing a generation of guitar tyros to gnash their teeth because they could not figure out what the hell was going on. But it is popular in jazz. You have been warned. . . .

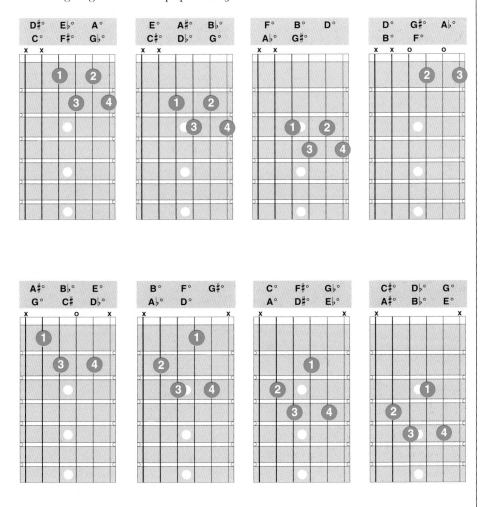

Dimished seventh chord shapes

ABBREVIATIONS

Roman numerals I VII
indicate chord
relationships within a key.

m *minor*

maj *major*

Song sections:

br *bridge*

c *coda*

ch *chorus*

hk *hook*

i *intro*

pch *pre-chorus*

v *verse*

Most of the chord-sequence examples
are standardized for comparison
into C *or* A minor.
Famous songs referred to in C *major*
or A *minor are not necessarily in*
the key of the original recordings.

Many guitarists write songs but don't necessarily know the theory behind the chords – they simply use their ears. Sometimes a melody or a riff will suggest an unusual chord change, and you may later discover that you have included a chord that is not strictly "in key". If it works in the context of the song, that's fine. The history of music is littered with broken rules.

Chords in a major key

In fact, though, there is a simple formula for working out which chords fit together best. Let's look at it in a guitar-friendly key, C major. The notes of the C major scale are: C D E F G A B. They are separated by a set pattern of intervals: tone, tone, semitone, tone, tone, tone, semitone (full step, full step, half-step, full step, full step, full step, half-step). In frets, the pattern is: 2 2 1 2 2 2 1. This pattern governs all major scales, regardless of the starting note. You can test this by choosing any note on any string and going up the string playing the notes in the 2 2 1 2 2 2 1 pattern. You will always get a major scale.

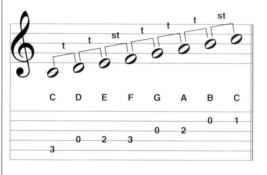

Scale of C major

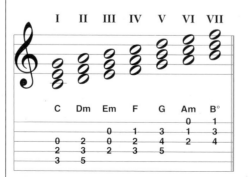

Chords of C major

The chords of C major are formed from the seven notes of the scale: D F A (2 4 6), E G B (3 5 7), F A C (4 6 1), G B D (5 7 2), A C E (6 1 3) and B D F (7 2 4). The sequence of chords is the same for every major key: major, minor, minor, major, major, minor, diminished.

The chords that combine well in C major are C Dm Em F G and Am. The seventh chord, B diminished, can be ignored as it is rarely used. We can get an acceptable substitute by flattening the seventh note and turning it into a major chord. In C major, this would mean flattening B to Bb.

Chords in a minor key

Minor keys are slightly more complicated because there are different versions of the minor scale. A natural minor (also known as the Aeolian mode) is A B C D E F G A. The pattern of intervals is tone, semitone, tone, tone, semitone, tone, tone (full step, half-step, full step, full step, half-step, full step, full step). In frets this is 2 1 2 2 1 2 2. The chords formed from the seven notes of this scale generate a sequence true for every natural minor key: minor, diminished, major, minor, minor, major, major.

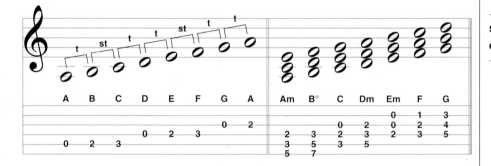

Scale of A natural minor

Chords of A natural minor

Another possibility is the harmonic minor scale, which has a raised seventh. A harmonic minor is: A B C D E F G# A. The pattern of intervals is: tone, semitone, tone, tone, semitone, tone and a half, semitone (full step, half-step, full step, full step, half-step, step and a half, half-step). In frets: 2 1 2 2 1 3 1. The chords formed from the harmonic minor scale are: minor, diminished, augmented, minor, major, major, diminished. In songwriting this is almost never used. In this example, the G# would turn chord V into a major, but the other chords would remain as they were in A natural minor.

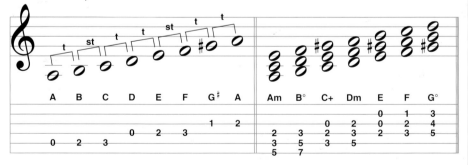

Scale of A harmonic minor

Chords of A harmonic minor

The Roman Numeral System

There is a handy way of notating and thinking about chord progressions without specifying the key. This is possible because the *internal* chord relationships of all major keys are identical. The same is true of all minor keys as long as they are based on one type of minor scale. The system has been used for hundreds of years in classical music. This is how it works.

There are seven notes in a major scale. Each one is given a Roman numeral: I, II, III, IV, V, VI, VII. In C major this means I = C, II = Dm, III = Em, IV = F, V = G, VI = Am, and VII = B diminished. Notice the sequence of chords: major, minor, minor, major, major, minor and diminished, the same for all major keys. Therefore we can write a chord sequence purely in these Roman numerals: I VI IV V. Regardless of the major key in which we play this it will always comprise a major chord followed by a minor and then two majors. Their relationship to each other is constant whatever the key. Compare these examples:

I	VI	IV	V
C	Am	F	G
G	Em	C	D
Eb	Cm	Ab	Bb
B	G#m	E	F#

These can all be described as I VI IV V. The *pitch* changes (and perhaps the ease of playing on the guitar) but the *effect* of the progression is the same in each case. The Roman numeral system is a very useful way of describing chord progressions. Once you get familiar with using it and thinking with it, you will find it an invaluable shorthand for understanding progressions.

In this book additional abbreviations sometimes add detail to the Roman numerals:

i first inversion (in C major, iIV = F with A bass; iVI = Am with C bass)

ii second inversion (in C major, iiIV = F with C bass; iiVI = Am with E bass)

m minor version of what would normally be a major chord. (In C major IVm = Fm instead of F)

maj major version of what would normally be a minor chord. (In C major IIImaj = E instead of Em)

b chord on the flattened note of the scale (bVII, bVI, bIII)

7 indicates a dominant seventh if the chord is major; minor seventh if it is minor (in C major, I7, IV7, V7, bVII7 = C7, F7, G7, Bb7; in C major, II7, III7, VI7 = Dm7, Em7, Am7; in C major, IVm7 needs the "m" because IV is normally major. This indicates Fm7.)

Not only does the Roman numeral system help you to understand keys and progressions, and to see how in different keys they mirror one another, but also to grasp how a single chord can have a different harmonic function according to which key it is in. There is a practical use, too. If you write out a chord sequence in Roman numerals, play it in a chosen key and discover the melody is too high for you to sing, it's easy to move it to another key without writing out all the chords again.

Which Chords Belong Together in Which Keys?
I devised this table to assist students to work out chord sequences from records. This can be time consuming and frustrating if you don't use a little knowledge to cut down the seemingly endless possibilities. A vast number of popular songs can

Table of chords and keys,
columns 1-12 (I-IV min)

	I	II	III	IV	V	VI	♭VII	♭VI	♭III	IImaj	IIImaj	IVmin
C♯ major	C♯	D♯m	E♯m	F♯	G♯	A♯m	B	A	E	D♯	E♯	F♯m
F♯ major	F♯	G♯m	A♯m	B	C♯	D♯m	E	D	A	G♯	A♯	Bm
B major	B	C♯m	D♯m	E	F♯	G♯m	A	G	D	C♯	D♯	Em
E major	E	F♯m	G♯m	A	B	C♯m	D	C	G	F♯	G♯	Am
A major	A	Bm	C♯m	D	E	F♯m	G	F	C	B	C♯	Dm
D major	D	Em	F♯m	G	A	Bm	C	B♭	F	E	F♯	Gm
G major	G	Am	Bm	C	D	Em	F	E♭	B♭	A	B	Cm
C major	C	Dm	Em	F	G	Am	B♭	A♭	E♭	D	E	Fm
F major	F	Gm	Am	B♭	C	Dm	E♭	D♭	A♭	G	A	B♭m
B♭ major	B♭	Cm	Dm	E♭	F	Gm	A♭	G♭	D♭	C	D	E♭m
E♭ major	E♭	Fm	Gm	A♭	B♭	Cm	D♭	C♭	G♭	F	G	A♭m
A♭ major	A♭	B♭m	Cm	D♭	E♭	Fm	G♭	F♭	C♭	B♭	C	D♭m
D♭ major	D♭	E♭m	Fm	G♭	A♭	B♭m	C♭	B♭♭	F♭	E♭	F	G♭m
G♭ major	G♭	A♭m	B♭m	C♭	D♭	E♭m	F♭	E♭♭	B♭♭	A♭	B♭	C♭m
C♭ major	C♭	D♭m	E♭m	F♭	G♭	A♭m	B♭♭	A♭♭	E♭♭	D♭	E♭	F♭m

be transcribed more easily if you first identify the key and then work with the chords on the table that belong in that key. For songwriters, the diagram is a handy guide to which chords sound good together. It will also help you to identify chords in common in different keys to facilitate key changes. This does not mean that you cannot introduce other chords into sequences, only that they may sound less natural. On the left you have the keys. C major is in the middle, with no sharps or flats. As you go down the table, the keys are increasingly flat; in the opposite direction, increasingly sharp. Notice that although there are only 12 notes there are 15 keys. This anomaly is explained by the fact that three keys are different ways of writing out the same notes. Which name is chosen depends on whether you are composing on the flat or sharp side of things.

SECTION 3

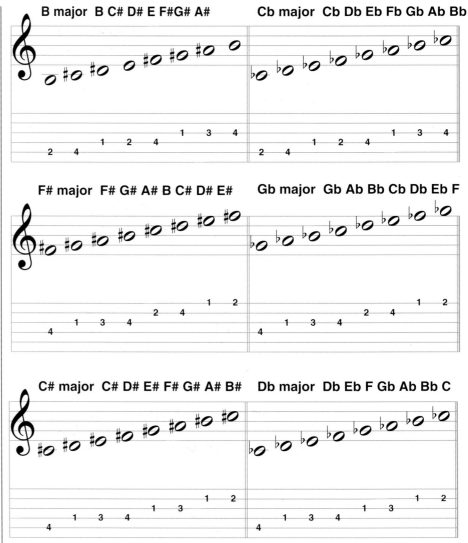

Let's look at this table in more detail.

Columns 1-6 show the six most important chords in songwriting. We're not concerned here with whether they are played in extended form as sevenths, sixths, suspensions, ninths, etc. All we need to think about is the root position major or minor form. As you look down the columns, notice that I, IV and V are always major chords, and II, III and VI are always minor.

Columns 7-9 are grouped. These are all major chords, and they are grouped because they are built on flattened notes of the scale: the bVII, the bIII and the bVI. Chord VII is given in its flattened form as a major, because VII is a diminished chord and therefore rarely used (as we discussed at the end of the previous chapter). The chord on the bVII is very common in popular music because of the influence of blues harmony and the resulting use of the Mixolydian mode (C D E F G A Bb) in many songs.

The bVII can be used to approach chord I instead of V. Compare these two sequences:

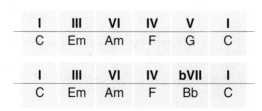

I	III	VI	IV	V	I
C	Em	Am	F	G	C

I	III	VI	IV	bVII	I
C	Em	Am	F	Bb	C

The latter occurs twice in the verse of 'Help'.

The bIII is a significant blues chord; the bVI is heard in blues and pop-rock. The bVI can also be found in a non-blues or hard rock context as in the verse of 'Hello Goodbye' or in the chorus of the 1920s pastiche 'Honey Pie'. There's a bVI in Foo Fighters' 'For All The Cows' (v) where we find the sequence E C B (I bVI V). A common sequence often heard at the end of a phrase is:

bVI	bVII	I
Ab	Bb	C

This is an alternative approach to I instead of via V. You can hear it in 'She's Electric' (just before the verse) and in the verse of 'Going For The One'. There is a fine use of the bVI at the end of the chorus in Boston's 'More Than A Feeling' – the music pauses on it before sliding by a semitone (half-step) to VI (Eb-Em in G major). The combination of a major-minor change with the half-step is very satisfying.

A Hard Rock Formula

The chords from columns 7-9 are often mixed up with columns 1-6 in songs that have a harder edge. A formula for writing hard rock songs in a generic Rolling Stones/Black Crowes/Bad Company style involves combining chords I, IV and V with these three flattened chords. Here are some examples:

I bIII IV: C Eb F
'Back In The USSR', 'I Am The Walrus', 'Sgt. Pepper's Lonely Hearts Club Band', 'Whippin' Piccadilly', 'One Big Family' ch, 'Life Is Sweet' v, and in reversed form as I IV bIII in 'Connection' ch.

I bIII IV V bVII: C Eb F G Bb
'Baby You're A Rich Man', 'Knock On Wood' i, 'In The Midnight Hour' i

I bIII IV bVI bVII: C Eb F Ab Bb
'Hey Joe', 'Trampled Underfoot'

I bIII IV V bVI bVII: C Eb F G Ab Bb
'Brown Sugar'

I IV bVII: C Bb F
'Another Girl' v, 'Get Back'

I IV V bVII: C F G Bb
'A Hard Day's Night', 'Jean Genie', 'Pretty Vacant' v, 'Sunshine Of Your Love'

I V bVII: C G Bb
'I'm a Loser' v, reversed to I bVII V in 'Misty Mountain Hop'

Reverse Polarity

Columns 10-12 make another group. These are what I call 'reverse polarity' versions of chords II, III and IV, where what was a minor chord turns into a major and vice versa. These are often used as substitutes in a chord sequence. Play these popular sequences:

I	II	IV	V	I	III	IV	V
C	Dm	F	G	C	Em	F	G

Now try the 'reverse polarity' trick:

I	II maj	IV	V	I	III maj	IV	V
C	D	F	G	C	E	F	G

The major version of II creates the momentary expectation of a key change to G minor or G. The move to F cancels this out. The expectation would be heightened if you played D7. The chorus of 'All You Need Is Love' has I IImaj V.

The major version of III creates the momentary expectation of a key change to A minor or A (as heard in chorus of 'Golden Slumbers'). Once again, the move to F cancels this out, and you can heighten the expectation by turning the major III into a dominant seventh (D7 or E7). A dramatic example occurs in the verse of 'Innuendo' (E to G#).

The chorus of Abba's 'Dancing Queen' depends on IImaj and IIImaj and the expectation they arouse for its power. The progression in A is:

V	III maj	VI	II maj	IV	I	I
E	C#	F#m	B	D	Bm	A

Notice the delay of chord I to the very end, the fleeting modulation to F#m and the sudden sadness that goes with that chord, the unexpected change from B to D, the second sad change with D to Bm and the final resolution of these emotions on the key chord.

The major versions of II and III are heard in the verse of the Foo Fighters' 'Alone And Easy'.

The minor version of chord IV is an MOR favourite because it lends itself to a romantic emotion. It is found either as the chord change I to IVm or coming after IV in its normal major form and then resolving to I or V. Play these popular changes:

I	II	IV	V	V	IV	I
C	Dm	F	C	G	F	C

Now try:

I	II	IV m	V	V	IV	IV m	I
C	Dm	Fm	C	G	F	Fm	C

You can hear IVm in 'All I've Got To Do' (v Am-E), 'I Believe I Can Fly', 'Do You Want To Know A Secret?' v, 'Hold Me Tight', 'I Call Your Name', 'In My Life' v, 'Riot Act', 'Female Of The Species', 'World Without Love' br, Neil Finn's 'Truth' v, and 'I'll Follow The Sun'. Its deeply tragic potential is heard in Stephen Stills's 'To A Flame'. It can end a minor-key song with an unexpected lift, as in 'And I Love Her', which ends Gm D. 'Nowhere Man' has a bridge of Dm Fm C (II IVm I). You will hear it at the climax of 'She Loves You', in the verse of 'That Means A Lot', in the chorus and verse of 'Bungalow Bill' and in the intro of 'Band On The Run'. Another song with the VI-IVm change is 'The Night Before'. 'The Air That I Breathe' has I III IVm I and I IIImaj IV IVm. Dylan used a IVm for a dramatic first chord in the verses of 'Idiot Wind'. Try a Imaj7-IVm7 for a more sophisticated sound. Rock bands have never been keen on this change, judging it too "soft". Radiohead, however, have incorporated this chord change into their brand of 1990s rock with great effectiveness in songs such as 'Airbag', 'Subterranean Homesick Alien', 'No Surprises' and 'Creep'.

Here are some more unusual possibilities not on the table.

V as a minor

If chord V is turned into a minor it undermines the sense of key. Nevertheless, this can be heard in 'Trash' (ch: C Gm F Ab), 'Lightning Seeds', 'Sense' (ch: Dm C G, where the key is G), 'She's Waiting' (v: I IV Vm IV: G C Dm C), 'Sugar Mountain' (Dm in key of G), 'Heroes' (Am in the key of D on the ch) and 'Behind Blue Eyes' (br: I Vm IV I: E Bm A E).

The chorus of Blur's 'Park Life' features the even rarer bV chord (E Bb B). This is sometimes used as a chromatic approach to chord V - but usually coming from chord IV not chord I.

VI as a major

The major version of chord VI creates the expectation of a key change up a tone. It is much used for quick key changes, as in the verse of 'Good Day Sunshine' and 'Charmless Man'. You'll also find it in the verse of 'It Won't Be Long' (E-C) and on the intro to John Barry's 'Goldfinger' (E-C). The John Barry/Bond association was exploited by Sneaker Pimps' 'Underground', which adds a Bond sample to the change.

Using the Table for Minor Keys

If the song you are writing is in a minor key, you can still use this table on p. 33. Simply locate the minor key in column 6. Your main chords in that minor key will be found in columns 1-7 plus 11. All that would change would be the numbers relative to the chords. Let's say you want to write a song in A minor. If you look down column 6, you find that Am occurs there in the key of C major:

1	2	3	4	5	6	7	8	9	10	11	12
C	Dm	Em	F	G	Am	Bb	Eb	Ab	D	E	Fm

So for A minor, we take chords 1-7 and renumber them:

1	2	3	4	5	6	7
Am	Bb	C	Dm	Em	F	G

Whether you use the major or minor form of chords IV and V in a minor key depends on the harmony you want and the melody of the song. If you're writing a tune in A natural minor (Aeolian mode: A B C D E F G), you will want chords 1, 3-7. If you're writing a tune in A Dorian (A B C D E F# G), you will want chords 1, 3-7 with 4 as D major rather than D minor. [3A] Tunes using the harmonic (A B C D E F G#) or melodic minor scales (A B C D E F# G#) will use the major version of the V chord. [3B] It is perfectly allowable to combine these different minor harmonies in a single song as long as the chord and the melody note are consistent. You can have D and Dm in a song in A minor, but if so an F in the melody must be used over Dm (D F A); a D major chord (D F# A) requires F# in the melody.

A good example of this is The Zombies' classic 'She's Not There'. Both the verse and the chorus repeatedly change from Am to D and then Am to F in adjacent bars. Chord V appears in the chorus both as Em and E.

Key Changing

If there is a change of key in a song you are trying to transcribe, simply locate the new key on the table and work with the chords that belong to that new key.

Now we're ready to look at how songwriters combine chords into songs.

The Two-Chord Song

There are one-chord songs, but they're pretty rare. 'Exodus' by Bob Marley stays on one chord much of the time, as do 'Careful With That Axe, Eugene', 'Within You Without You', 'Tomorrow Never Knows' and Roy Harper's 'Frozen Moment'. There is a tradition in the blues of one-chord songs such as 'I'm A Man', 'Smokestack Lightning' and the original 'Bring It On Home'. Sometimes a single chord will carry a verse, as with Morcheeba's 'Shoulder Holster', or 'The Ballad of John and Yoko' and 'It Takes Two', where IV and V come in with the hook.

The list of two-chord songs includes 'That's The Way (I Like It)' (Cm-Fm), 'Spice Up Your Life', 'Born Slippy', 'Born In The USA', 'Underworld', 'Step It Up', 'Sex Machine', 'Say It Loud – I'm Black and I'm Proud' and, if we allow an instrumental, 'Albatross'. Fleetwood Mac's 'Dreams' is virtually a two-chord song (a third appears briefly under the guitar break).

The challenge of writing a two-chord song is to avoid monotony. Writing a truly arresting song with only two chords is not easy, which is why most writers will include (at least) a third chord.

Two-Chord Changes

It is useful to explore basic changes, so that you get a feel for their varied qualities. To do this we will start from a C major chord and look at all the possible changes. These could form a two-chord song, but the point here is simply to sense the mood these changes evoke so you can incorporate them into songs with any number of chords.

I-II/ C-Dm: a short movement where all the notes change. This is popular in reggae. 'Wait In Vain' ch, 'Something In The Air' v, 'Don't Let Me Down' v and ch. Heard on coda of 'Samba Pa Ti', coda of 'The Carpet Crawlers', 'Alright' (Supergrass) v, 'Like A Virgin' ch, 'Wake Me Up Before You Go-Go' ch, 'ATB 9pm (Till I Come)', and 'Over My Head' v. This is a signature change of Smokey Robinson, who used it in 'Ooh Baby Baby' ch, 'If You Can Want', 'Baby, Baby Don't Cry', 'More Love'.

I-III/ C-Em: an expressive major-to-minor change with two notes in common (C E G, E G B). 'The Universal' i/v, 'Party Girl' v. Its potential is brought out in the chorus of 'A Northern Lad'.

I-IV/ C-F: a lighter, more relaxed feel than I-V. 'My Girl' v, 'Stolen Car', 'Paperback Writer' (G-C), 'It's All Too Much' (C-F), 'Electrolyte' v (G-C), 'Angel Of Harlem', 'All I Want Is You', 'Both Sides Now' v, 'Glad All Over', 'Walk On The Wild Side', 'Tonight's The Night' v, 'Baby I Need Your Loving' v, 'Ways To Be Wicked' v, 'How Sweet It Is To Be Loved By You', 'Souvenir', 'Starless Summer Sky', 'Life Of Riley', 'Hope St.' v. Has dreamy feel as Imaj7-IVmaj7. 'Don't Let The Sun Catch You Crying' v, 'Respect'. I7-IV7 has a harder-edged feel.

I-V/ C-G: a strong sense of major tonality that holds the key firm. Excellent for writing light, novelty, comic or children's songs or where the words and melody are paramount. 'Lily The Pink', 'Memphis Tennessee', 'Baby Come

Back', 'So Far Away' v, 'Respect' ch, 'Give Peace A Chance', 'Yellow Submarine' ch, 'Have I The Right'.

I-VI/ C-Am: significant as one of the strongest changes from major to minor. Only one note changes between these chords (C E G, A C E) yet the mood change is great. 'His Latest Flame', 'Shout', 'Needles And Pins', 'Itchycoo Park' ch, 'What's Going On' ch, 'Rat Trap' i, 'You Really Got A Hold On Me' i, 'Head Over Heels, 'You Do' v.

I-bVII/ C-Bb: often implied in riff-based songs. 'Whole Lotta Love', 'My Generation', 'You Really Got Me', 'We Can Work It Out' v, 'The Rocker' v, 'Somebody' v, 'Hong Kong Garden'.

These are the chords in columns 1-7 of the table. Here are some other, exotic variations. Some are "reverse polarity":

I-Im/ C-Cm: an arresting chord change that unsettles the sense of key. The first change of the verse of 'I'm Not In Love' is from a major to a minor on the same root. Also in 'Those Were The Days' (Am A Dm), 'I Don't Want You To Destroy Me' (A F#m E Em), 'Close To You' (C Bsus4 B Bm). 'Autumn Almanac' has several at the end of one section and start of the next. The verse of 'We Have All The Time In The World' has E to Em in the key of A major.

I-bIImaj/ C-C#: highly unusual – listen to the verse of 'Dancing Days'. In power chords, it's important for the 1980s HM of bands like Metallica.

I-IImaj/ C-D: ambiguous because it sets up the expectation of a key change to G.

I-bIII/ C-Eb: a classic hard-edged blues change. 'Children Of The Revolution' v, 'Can The Can' ch. Can also be exotic, as in the verse of 'Head Over Heels'.

I-IIImaj/ C-E: ambiguous because it sets up the expectation of a key change to A or A minor.

I-IVm/ C-Fm: a staple chord change of ballads and MOR. Expressive to the point of sentimentality.

I-Vm/ C-Gm: ambiguous, because it sets up the expectation of a key change to, or being in, F. This can be heard on the disconcerting intro of Paul Young's version of 'Don't Dream It's Over' and at the start of 'She's Leaving Home'.

I-bVI/ C-Ab: slightly strange-sounding, though the note C is common to both chords. Used by John Barry. Occurs in 'We Close Our Eyes'.

I-VIm/ C-A: ambiguous because it sets up the expectation of a key change to D or D minor. '(Sittin' On) The Dock Of The Bay' ch, 'Road To Nowhere' v.

I-bVIIm/ C-Bbm: very unusual change that will imply a IV-V change in F minor.

Minor Key Two Chord Changes

What happens if we start from a minor chord? These changes work differently in minor keys where, depending on which minor scale or mode is being used, the most common would be:

I-III/ Am-C: heard in 'War'.

I-IV/Am-Dm: 'Shakin' All Over', 'Fool To Cry', 'Miss You', 'Fireworks', 'Dub Be Good To Me'.

I-IVmaj/ Am-D: 'Another Brick In The Wall' v, 'Oye Como Va', 'Miss Sarajevo' v, 'It's A Family Affair', 'Jackie Wilson Said', 'Drive' v, 'It's Too Late' v, 'Kinky Afro'. A powerful change, especially in the major key where it occurs from II to V.

I-V/ Am-E: 'Spice Up Your Life'.

I-Vm/ Am-Em: 'Losing My Religion' v, 'The Model'.

I-VI/ Am-F: 'Eleanor Rigby'. How you 'voice' this makes a big difference. I-VImaj7 (Am-Fmaj7) and I-VI7 (Am-F7) have a very different quality (the latter in 'Glass Onion' v). 'Dreams', 'Rhiannon' v, 'Live Forever' coda.

I-bII/ Am-Bb: Bob & Earl's soul classic 'Harlem Shuffle' makes astonishing use of this – and, to avoid monotony, does a semitone (half-step) key change.

I-VII/ Am G: 'Maps And Legends' ch, 'Horse With No Name' (G as G/B), 'The One I Love' v, 'Matthew And Son' v.

I-#VII/ Am-(G#) Ab: this unusual change can be heard in 'Try Whistling This' and 'O Maria'.

Ways of Writing a Two-Chord Song

Use the "bar-stretching" technique: if the rate of change is one chord to a bar in the chorus, make it two bars to a chord in the verse or vice versa.

- Put the emphasis on the melody and lyric – as in a narrative song.
- Vary the tempo or time signature.
- Change the order of chords in different sections.
- Use first and second inversions of the two chords.
- Change the key and play the same two chords in another key. 'Mull Of Kintyre' starts as a two-chord song in A and changes to D.
- Change the bass note to imply a change of chord. An E under G will imply Em (chord III) even if you're still strumming a G.

The Three-Chord Trick

The three-chord trick is the commonest songwriting device. It means writing a song using chords I, IV and V of any major or minor key. Since these are the three chords that are used in 12-bar blues, a vast number of 1950s rock'n'roll songs by Elvis Presley, Chuck Berry, Carl Perkins, Jerry Lee Lewis, Little Richard, Bill Haley, Buddy Holly, Eddie Cochran, etc, as well as ones by later rock acts who played a lot of 12-bar boogie, such as Status Quo, are three-chord tricks. This is also the formula for many pop songs such as 'Twist and Shout', 'I Fought The Law', 'Should I Stay Or Should I Go?', 'You're Gorgeous' ch, 'Common People', and 'La Bamba'. With care it can be expressive, as in the verse of 'Don't Let The Sun Go Down On Me', which uses just I, IV and V (the first minor chord is not featured until the chorus). The three chords can occur in any order. 'Consider Me Gone' uses two chords to carry the verse and one for the chorus. 'She Bangs The Drums' carries the verse with IV and V before hitting I on the chorus.

I IV V: C F G
'Over You', 'Spanish Stroll'.

I V IV: C G F
'Brimful Of Asha', 'If Not For You', 'Wind Cries Mary' v and
'Maggie May' v (both displaced as V IV I), 'Helpless', 'Sway'.

Variations on the Three-Chord Trick

If we widen the definition to allow any three chords in a key, there are many
other combinations for a song. Let's put a minor chord in with I and V:

I II V: C Dm G
'Boys Are Back In Town' i /ch, 'When You're Gone' (II V I),
'Wendell Gee' v, '(Don't Go Back To) Rockville' ch.

I IImaj V: C D G
'Cigarettes And Alcohol' v.

I V II: C G Dm
'Near Wild Heaven' ch, 'Back On The Chain Gang' v, 'Fade Into
You', 'Knockin' On Heaven's Door' (I V II, I V IV), 'Stay'
(Shakespeare's Sister) ch.

I III V: C Em G

I V III: C G Em

I III VI: C Em Am
'Instant Karma' ch, 'Choice In The Matter' (v in B, ch in E).

I VI V: C Am G
'Still Waters Run Deep'.

I V VI: C G Am
'Jailbreak' v.

Or how about replacing V with IV for a softer, less definite effect:

I II IV: C Dm F
'High And Dry' (displaced as II IV I).

I IV II: C F Dm
'Gonna Give Her All The Love I've Got' ch

I III IV: C Em F
'Queen Of The Slipstream'.

I VI IV: C Am F
'If I Should Fall Behind'.

You can also create a three-chord song by bringing in a "blues" chord from
columns 7-9 of the table and combining it with I and IV, or I and V:

I bIII IV: C Eb F
'Magical Mystery Tour', 'Pride (In The Name Of Love)' br, 'Twenty Five MIles'.

I bIII bVII: C Eb Bb
'The Rocker' ch, 'Nutbush City Limits' v.

I bVII IV: C Bb F
'Desire', 'Won't Get Fooled Again' v (and many other Who songs), 'Crush With Eyeliner' v, 'Addicted To Love', '(This Could Be) The Last Time', 'Alright' (Cast) v, 'Rock and Roll Nigger', 'You Ain't Seen Nothing Yet' (v I, bVII, IV with a three-chord trick ch I, V, IV), 'Praise Him', 'Hand In My Pocket' hk, 'Can't Get Enough' v, 'Don't Stop' v, 'Cigarettes And Alcohol' ch. 'With A Little Help From My Friends (Joe Cocker), 'Gloria' (Them), 'Chasing The Dream' (as bVII-IV-I)

bVI bVII I: Ab Bb C
'Kiss From A Rose', end of 'Wake Up Boo!', 'Lady Madonna' v.

The Three-Chord Turnaround

In blues music "turnaround" means a distinctive phrase played in the last two bars of a 12-bar. In songwriting it is a sequence of chords repeated either as an intro, a verse, part of a verse, a chorus or in a bridge. The turnaround circles its chords, creating an awareness in the listener that it makes a unit within itself. A song can feature one or more turnarounds. When it comes to combining the three-chord trick with the turnaround device, it must be said that three-bar three-chord turnarounds are rare. Writers tend to prefer the symmetry of a four-bar phrase (especially in 4/4 time). A 12-bar verse could divide into four 3-bar phrases:

$$G \quad C \quad D \quad \quad G \quad C \quad D \quad \quad G \quad C \quad D \quad \quad G \quad C \quad D$$

This creates an interesting tension because of the way the three pulls against the expectation of four. Each phrase sounds as though a bar is missing, because we are so accustomed to four-bar phrases.

Three Chord Four Bar Turnarounds in a major key:

It's more common to make a four-bar turnaround out of three chords with a return to the first in bar four. Here are some examples with I, IV and V:

I IV V IV: C F G F
'Wild Thing', 'Wishful Thinking', 'Don't Turn Around' v.

I IV V I: C F G C
'Lay Down Sally' ch.

I IV I V: C F C G
'Peggy Sue' I. 'Teach Your Children' v, 'Brown-Eyed Girl' v.

I V IV I: C G F C
'What Do I Do Now' ch.

I   V   IV   V: C G F G
'What Is Life?', 'Tangerine', 'Avalon' v, 'There She Goes' v, 'The First Cut Is The Deepest', 'Like A Hurricane' ch, 'Stay' (S's Sister) v, 'Ruby Tuesday'.

Here are examples with different combinations of three chords:

I   II   III   II: C Dm Em Dm
'Ask Me Why' v, 'I'm Only Sleeping' ch, 'I Shall Be Released', 'Follow Me, Follow You' ch, 'Ooh Baby Baby' v.

I   II   IV   I: C Dm F C
'Massachusetts' v, 'Don't Worry, Be Happy'.

I   II   bVI   I: C Dm Ab C
'Boys Keep Swinging' v.

I   IImaj   IV   I: C D F C
'Eight Days A Week' i + v.

I   bIII   II   I: C Eb Dm C
'Nobody's Fault But My Own' v.

I   bIII   IV   bIII: C Eb F Eb
'Far Gone And Out' ch.

I   bIII   bVII   bIII: C Eb Bb Eb
'Doll Parts' v

I   III   IV   III: C Em F Em
'I Guess I'll Always Love You' ch.

I   IV   II   I: C F Dm C
'Sense', 'Higher And Higher'.

I   IV   bVII   I: C F Bb C
'Feel'

I   IV   bVII   IV: C F Bb F
'The Size Of A Cow'

I   V   II   V: C G Dm G

I   V   IVm   I: C G Fm C
'Man Of The World'.

I   V   VI   V: C G Am G
'Letter From America' i.

I   Vm   IVm   I: C Gm Fm C
'You Only Live Twice', 'Millennium'.

SECTION 3   43

I VI I V: C Am C G
'Wherever I Lay My Hat' v.

I VI II I: C Am Dm C
'Stoned Love'.

I VI IV I: C Am F C
'One', 'Sailing' v, 'Soul Love' v.

I VImaj VI I: C A Am C
'Heart Of Glass'.

I bVII IV I: C Bb F C
'I Can't Explain', 'Hey Jude' c. 'Blowin'Free' v, 'Just When You're Thinking Things Over' ch.

I bVII IV bVII: C Bb F Bb
'Don't You Forget About Me' v, 'Centerfold'.

Three-Chord Songs in a Minor Key

Analyzing minor-key sequences in popular music is problematic because the natural minor key has chords that are identical to the relative major. In classical music, minor keys tend to be more clearly signaled by the harmonic or melodic minor forms of the scale rather than the natural minor. Keep this in mind when looking at some of these examples. It is not always easy to judge whether a progression is in the natural minor key or its relative major (A minor or C major, for example).

The "default" is therefore assumed to be the natural minor scale and its chords: Am Bdim C Dm Em F G. In this book F is called VI and G VII, not bVI and bVII, because on the natural minor scale the sixth and seventh notes have not been flattened in the way that they can be on the major scale.

I VII VI: Am G F

Minor-chord sequences in pop and rock are dominated by I, VII, VI in either direction. In A minor this is Am G F; in E minor it is Em D C. You will have to check whether this really is in a minor key or is in the relative major, because Am G F could be VI V IV in C and Em D C could be VI V IV in G. Look up these chords on the table to get a clearer sense of this. The same chord sequence can have a different harmonic meaning depending on the key. Fleetwood Mac's 'You Make Loving Fun' has a verse that uses Gm F Eb as a turnaround. This could lead us to think that the song is in G minor, in which case this would be a I-VII-VI in that key. However the chorus starts on a strong Bb and we realize that actually the song is in Bb. The Gm-F-Eb was actually VI V IV in Bb. A similar ambiguity arises in Texas' 'White On Blonde'.

Songs that use I, VII and VI in the minor key include: 'In The Air Tonight', 'Sultans Of Swing', 'Layla', 'Stairway To Heaven' (guitar solo), 'Achilles Last Stand', 'Hello', 'Don't Fear The Reaper', 'Dreams', 'Breathing', 'Slide Away' v, 'Because The Night', 'The Glastonbury Song', 'Wishing Well', 'Don't Believe A Word' coda. It is used ascending in 'Bring On The Night', 'This Time', 'The Beat' v, 'Running Up That Hill', 'Theme From S-Express', 'Weak' and 'Wild Hearted Woman'. In some of these examples, VII may not as strong as in others –

sometimes it is felt only as a passing chord (Am Am7 F).

Played as power chords in A or E, I VII VI is a favourite of 1970s HM bands (Iron Maiden seemed to base their career on it), and you can hear it in 'Paranoid' between some of the verses. Other minor-chord combinations include:

I III VII: Am C G
'Orange Crush' v.

I IV V: Am Dm Em
'Move On Up', 'Dirty Pool'.

I IV Vmaj: Am Dm E
'Elenore' v. 'One Step Beyond'

I IVmaj V: Am D Em
'Sleeping Satellite' ch.

I IV VII: Am Dm G
'Party Girl' (U2).

I V IVmaj: Am Em D

I VI Vmaj: Am F E
'Sweet Dreams Are Made Of This'.

I VII III: Am G C
'Ain't Talkin' 'Bout Love',

I VII IV: Am G Dm
'Cortez The Killer'

I VII IVmaj: Am G D
'In A Room', 'Almost Cut My Hair'

I VII V: Am G Em
'Spirits In The Material World'.

Three Chord Four Bar Turnarounds in a minor key:

I IV V IV: Am Em Dm Em
'Into The Groove' v, 'How Long' ch.

I IVmaj I bVII: Am D Am G
'No More Heroes' hk.

I V I IV: Am Em Am Dm
Displaced as IV I V I in 'The Time Is Now'.

I bVI bVII I: Am F G Am
'Wall Street Shuffle'.

I VI I V: Am F Am Em
'Queen' v.

I VI IV VI: Am F Dm F
'Where Do You Think You're Going'.

I VII I III: Am G Am C
'Sexy Boy' ch.

When you use a four-bar three-chord turnaround, be conscious of the fact that it may begin and end on the same chord. If so you will need to take this into account in terms of lyric and melody at the start of each phrase. This question does not arise with the four-chord turnaround because the last chord is usually different (see below).

The Four-Chord Song

After the three-chord trick, we move up to using four chords. If we have only used I, IV and V, the three major chords of a key, we can now bring in one of the minors II, III, or VI, or even keep it all major with a bII, bVI or bVII as the additional chord. In a song that is economical with chords, the fourth chord could be held back for the chorus or the bridge.

The Four-Chord Turnaround

While many songs have only four chords, some put them in a fixed four-bar or eight-bar phrase that then repeats, either for the verse, chorus or bridge, or some combination, or even goes all the way through the song. The four-chord turnaround is one of the strongest musical hooks going. There is a significant aesthetic relationship between it and pop's favourite time signature, 4/4, which in itself has a tendency to cause melodic and verse/chorus lengths to fall into fours or multiples of four. This is both a blessing and a curse. The turnaround lends itself to lazy songwriting, and this is one reason why the 1980s and 1990s have generated fewer classic songs that other artists want to cover.

The Tyranny of Four

When the different parts of a song are all measurable by four, there is a danger of producing something literally "four-square" and too predictable (although, of course, possibly a hit). Here is an instance in songwriting where artistic and commercial considerations do not see eye to eye. In a nightmare scenario of the "tyranny of four", we end up with a song that has a four-bar intro, leading to a 16-bar verse made up of four four-bar four-chord turnarounds, a chorus of eight bars (twice round a different four-bar turnaround), and an eight-bar middle eight – all in 4/4!

In 1990s UK chart pop, it was not uncommon to hear songs constructed from a single four-bar four-chord turnaround. Verses and choruses were distinguished only by small changes in the arrangement.

Symmetry is pleasing, but too much of it is boring. By analogy, think about architecture. What is more engaging, more mysterious, more human: the unpredictable passages and lanes of a small fishing village where the eye is continually surprised by irregularity and curve, or the wide concrete spaces of a plaza where everything is straight lines, squares, 90-degree angles and can be seen all at once?

One of the most important points of craft a songwriter can develop is a sensitivity to the emotional and artistic possibilities of *asymmetry*, which in its simplest form means working with odd numbers. We will discuss this a little later.

Popular Four-Chord Turnarounds

Turnarounds are so significant in popular songwriting that there are many variations. For convenience, I've sorted them into groups. Remember that the songs mentioned as examples may use the turnaround only for a section, not for the whole song. These sequences not only sound good in themselves but may be incorporated into larger structures. For instance, you might take two turnarounds and join them to make an eight-bar phrase that could then be repeated to make a 16-bar verse.

Group 1

The most popular turnarounds start on chord I and end on chord V, assuring that the sense of key is strong. They are also satisfying because of their positive upward energy. Some of the song illustrations mention "displaced" and "stretched" turnarounds – see section 4 for an explanation of these terms.

The first three examples are satisfying because they move onto a minor but then draw back from the sadness it represents to the reassuring major.

I II IV V: C Dm F G
'Love Is All Around' ch, 'Fall On Me' ch, 'Show Me Heaven', '99 Red Balloons', 'I've Just Got To Get A Message To You' ch, 'Poetry In Motion', 'A Northern Lad' v, 'Somebody', 'Away From The Numbers', 'They Are All In Love' v, 'Vincent' v, 'Eton Rifles' v stretched form: I II (x4) IV V, 'Somebody To Love' ch displaced as IV I II V, 'If It Makes You Happy' ch displaced as II IV V I.

I III IV V: C Em F G
'Down In The Tube Station At Midnight', 'Going Underground', 'Waiting For An Alibi' ch, 'Have I Told You Lately', 'Let's Get It On', 'Bright Side Of The Road' v (notice the difference if you make F here F7), 'The More You Ignore Me, The Closer I Get' v.

I VI IV V: C Am F G
This is the Big Daddy of all pop turnarounds. During the doo-wop era of 1958-63, many hits were written with this sequence. It seemingly took The Beatles to break its stranglehold on the charts, though even they used a displaced version for 'I Wanna Hold Your Hand' ch (IV V I VI). Later Lennon ironically evoked its 1950s associations in 'Happiness Is A Warm Gun' and its innocence worked in 'Octopus' Garden'. It has been used in countless songs. Here are a very few!
'I Can't Explain' b, 'Concrete And Clay' ch, 'Strange Town' v, 'Teenage Dream' v, 'Runaround Sue' v, 'A Teenager In Love' v, 'Stand By Me', 'Every Breath You Take' v, 'All I Have To Do Is Dream' ch, 'Please Mr Postman', 'Dance Away', 'Duke Of Earl', 'Crocodile Rock', 'Let's Twist Again', 'D'yer Mak'er', 'Lonely This Christmas', 'True Blue' ch, 'Unchained Melody' v, 'When You're Young And In Love', 'It's In His Kiss' hk, 'I Will Always Love You', 'Brass In Pocket' v. 'Wonderful World' v. 'Angel Interceptor' I, 'Say My Name', 'I Guess I'll Always Love You' v.

Marc Bolan of T.Rex was fond of combining a 12-bar I IV V progression in one part of a song with I VI IV V in another. This turnaround is now difficult to use in a "straight" way because it sounds corny and over-familiar. It probably works better in a displaced form, IV V I VI: 'I Can't Let Maggie Go' ch, 'Eton Rifles' ch, 'Independent Love Song', 'Sad Eyes' ch, 'Don't Dream It's Over' ch, 'Dead Ringer For Love' ch. 'Heart Of Gold' v displaces it to VI IV V I. 'Ashes To Ashes' has it on the verse and displaced on the chorus.

I VI V IV: C Am G F

This switches the last two chords of the previous sequence in order to make a descending progression.
'Come Back To What You Know' ch, 'Two Princes', 'Purple Rain' v, 'Dancing In The Moonlight' v. In 'Chance' v, 'Ways To Be Wicked' ch, 'Sweet Soul Music' hk, 'Give Me Just A Little More Time' ch, 'Love The One You're With' ch, 'Cast No Shadow' pch, the sequence is displaced to VI V IV I.

I IV VI V: C F Am G

'More Than A Feeling' ch, 'Talking About A Revolution', 'Never Forget', 'Dig Me', 'Room For The Life'.

Here are some related sequences in which the middle chords have changed place:

I II VI V: C Dm Am G

I VI II V: C Am Dm G

'Tell Me Why' v , 'Diana' v, 'How Do You Do It' ch, 'Lipstick On Your Collar', 'All My Loving' displaced as II V I VI, 'Metal Guru' v in stretched form, 'Hungry Heart', 'You Don't Have To Say You Love Me', 'Return To Sender', 'The Wonder Of You' v, 'I Will' v, 'This Boy' v, 'You're Gonna Lose That Girl' ch, 'Without You' ch, 'All I Have To Do Is Dream', 'Oblivious' ch. This turnaround is closely related to I VI IV V and can be used as a substitute for it.

I III VI V: C Em Am G

'I Think We're Alone Now', 'Waiting For An Alibi' v displaced as VI I III V.

II III IV V: Dm Em F G

This creates a sense of suspension because I is delayed until another part of the song. 'Come And Get These Memories' v, 'This Old Heart Of Mine' v, 'Do Anything You Wanna Do' v. It is powerful as the approach to a chorus, as in 'Heatwave', 'Wake Me Up

Before You Go-Go', 'I Guess I'll Always Love You' and 'Everybody Wants To Rule The World'. It is the main hook of 'Olympian'.

Group 2

This is variation on group 1 – change IV to its relative minor II or switch their positions.

I III II V: C Em Dm G
'Where Do You Go To My Lovely?', 'Goodnight' v, 'Kiss Me' as displaced II V I III, 'Ferry Cross The Mersey' ch.

I IV II V: C F Dm G
'The Sidewinder Sleeps Tonight' ch (displaced), 'Loco In Acapulco' ch, 'More Than This' v, 'Don't Turn Around' ch.

I IV II bVII: C F Dm Bb
'Great Things' ch, 'What's The Frequency, Kenneth?' v.

I IV III V: C F Em G
The gut-wrenching drop from F to Em is "saved" by the reassuring climb back to V. 'A Little Bit Me, A Little Bit You'.

I VI III V: C Am Em G
'She Loves You' v, 'That's Just What You Are' v.

I VI V III: C Am G Em
'Baby I Need Your Loving' ch; easily confused with IV II I VI in G major.

Group 3

A variation on Group 1. When V goes to the second place and IV is last, it has a softer, less sure effect.

I V II IV: C G Dm F
'Driftwood', 'Halo' ch. The popularity of this progression is indicated by the number of variations on it: 'Try Not To Breathe' v. displaced to V II IV I, 'On A Day Like Today' ch. displaced to II IV I V, 'Walking On The Moon' ch displaced as IV I V II.

I V III IV: C G Em F

I V IV II: C G F Dm
'The Day We Caught The Train' ch. 'September Girl' v.

I V IV III: C G F Em
'Stand And Deliver' ch.

I V VI II: C G Am Dm
'Half A World Away'.

I V VI IV: C G Am F

The most popular of these. 'Since You've Been Gone' ch, 'Torn' ch, 'With Or Without You', 'So Lonely', 'No Woman No Cry', 'Beast Of Burden' v, 'Inside Out' (Adams), 'Crash And Burn' v, 'Possession' ch, 'Actually It's Darkness'.

Chord V is often played as a first inversion so the bassline will move down in step (in C major, C G/B A): 'Bold As Love' v, 'Down Under' ch, 'Still' (Macy Gray), 'Sketches Of China', 'Motorcycle Emptiness'.

Group 4

Another variation on Group 1: change V into its relative minor, III.

I II IV III: C Dm F Em

I VI IV III: C Am F Em
'True' i.

I VI III IV: C Am Em F
'Holes'.

Group 5

I IV III II: C F Em Dm

This has a mournful quality because of the descending minors. 'Presence Of The Lord' i = IV III II I, 'Long Long Long' v, 'Day After Day' hk, 'Lovin' You', 'So It Goes' (Nick Lowe). You get a different effect by changing these into all majors or fifth chords, as in 'Holidays In The Sun' i, 'God Save The Queen' c. Another variation is IV III II V, as in 'This Old Heart Of Mine'.

I II III IV: C Dm Em F
'Here There And Everywhere'.

Group 6

I II VI III: C Dm Am Em
'Daysleeper' ch.

I III IV II: C Em F Dm
'I Am The Mob', 'At My Most Beautiful'.

I III VI IV: C Em Am F
'A Day In The Life' v, 'Sonnet' ch.

I III VI V: C Em Am G*
'Please Forgive Me' (David Gray) v

I VI II IV: C Am Dm F
'New York City Serenade'.

I VI IV II: C Am F Dm
'Toledo'.

Group 7

This group takes Group 1 and replaces the minor chords with majors (reverse polarity), or uses IVm. Some of these turnarounds arouse an expectation of a key change that does not happen.

I IImaj IV V: C D F G
This has a 1960s pop effect. 'As Time Goes By', 'Silver Machine' v.

I IV IImaj V: C F D G
This sounds as though you have changed the key to G. 'Shop Around' i and v. To nullify this effect, make the G a G7. 'Goodbye Yellow Brick Road' opening of v displaced to II V I IV. 'Hold Me Tight' v has these all as dominant sevenths.

I IImaj III IV: C D Em F
'Modern Love' ch.

I IIImaj II V: C E Dm G
'You're Gonna Lose That Girl' v.

I IIImaj IV IImaj: C E F D
'(Sittin' On) The Dock Of The Bay' v – plenty of surprise in this sequence.

I IIImaj IV IVm: C E F Fm
'Creep'.

I IIImaj IV V: C E F G
'Waiting For An Alibi' ch, 'Imagine' br. displaced as IV V I IIImaj.

I IIImaj VI IV: C E Am F
'She's Electric' v.

I IV IIImaj V: C F E G
This has quite an unpredictable sound.

I IV IIImaj VI: C F E Am
'Caught By The Fuzz' v. This gives the sense of having changed key to A minor.

I IV IVm V: C F Fm G
A combination of romantic and unpredictable.

I IV VImaj V: C F Am G

I IV VI IImaj: C F Am D
'Green Grow The Rushes'.

I VImaj IV V: C A F G

I VI IV IIImaj: C Am F E
'Don't Dream It's Over' v.

I VI IImaj IV: C Am D F
'Five Years' v.

Group 8

These turnarounds are mostly major.

I bIII IV V: C Eb F G
A tougher-sounding ascending sequence than I III IV V.

I bIII bVII IV: C Eb Bb F
'Step Inside Love' ch.; displaced as bIII bVII IV I in 'Daisies Of The Galaxy' along with bIII bVII II I

I bIII V bVII: C Eb G Bb
Played once only in 'Going For The One' as a link to the last verse. As a turnaround it has a powerful ascending energy.

I IV V bIII: C F G Eb
'Israelites'.

I IV bVI bVII: C F Ab Bb
'Desperate People' v.

I IV bVII V: C F Bb G
'Street Life', 'Can't Get There From Here' ch displaced as IV bVII V I.

I V bIII bVII: C G Eb Bb
'Single Girl'

I V bVI bVII: C G Ab Bb
'Only Happy When It Rains' (Garbage) ch.

I V bVII IV: C G Bb F
'Turning Japanese' ch, 'Give Me Just A Little More Time' v, 'You Make Me Feel Like A Natural Woman' v, 'Ball Park Incident' v. 'Sexy Boy' v.

I bVI bVII IV: C Ab Bb F
'Violet' ch

I bVII bIII IV: C Bb Eb F
'Pinball Wizard' ch, 'Crush With Eyeliner' ch. 'I'll Stick Around'.

I bVII IV V: C Bb F G

This is a popular sequence with a strong circularity. 'Champagne Supernova' ch (with IV as iIV). As I bVII V IV (C Bb G F) 'Asking For It' v.

I bVII IV VI: C Bb F Am

'Crazy On The Weekend' displaced to VI I bVII IV

I bVII IV bIII: C Bb F Eb

'Middle Of The Road', 'The Wake-Up Bomb' v.

I bVII VI V: C Bb Am G

'My Weakness Is None Of Your Business' v (with a variation in which bVII becomes bVIIm - C Bbm Am G)

Group 9

Here are some typical minor-key turnarounds. Remember that the "default" minor harmony is one based on the natural minor scale. In A minor this means I = Am, III = C, IV = Dm, V = Em, VI = F, VII = G.

I III IV V: Am C Dm Em

I III IV Vmaj: Am C Dm E

I III IV VI: Am C Dm F

'A House Is Not A Motel' v.

I III VI Vmaj: Am C F E

'I Want You'

I III bVII IVmaj: Am C G D

'Wonderwall' v, 'Run To You' ch.

I III IV VII: Am C Dm G

'Swan Swan H' v.

I III VI IV: Am C F Dm

'The Night They Drove Old Dixie Down' v.

I III VI VII: Am C F G

A strong rising progression. 'Harbour Coat' v. 'Breathing' ch.

I IV VII Vmaj: Am Dm G E

'Talk Of The Town' v, 'Fame' ch.

I Vmaj IVmaj VI: Am E D F

'Sale Of The Century' (Sleeper) v.

I V VII IVmaj: Am Em G D

'You've Got My Number', 'Fireball' ch displaced as VII IVmaj I Vmaj (G D Am E)

I VI III VII: Am F C G
'The Passenger', alternates with I VI III Vmaj (Am F C E).

I VI IV VII: Am F Dm G
'Expresso Love' v.

I VI IVmaj VII: Am F D G
'Queen' ch.

I VI VII IV: Am F G Dm
'Message In A Bottle' v, 'December Will Be Magic Again' i.

I VI VII Vmaj: Am F G E
'Overground'.

I #VIm III VII: Am F#m C G
'Israel' v.

I VII IV V: Am G Dm Em
'You Do Something To Me' v displaced as VII IV V I

I VII VI IV: Am G F Dm
'Animal Nitrate' v. 'Paradise' v.

I VII VI V: Am G F Em
This is a common minor sequence. 'Like A Hurricane',
'Trimartolod'

I VII VI Vmaj: Am G F E
Popular version of the above with V as a major. 'Sultans Of Swing'
v, 'In The Year 2525', 'Good Vibrations', 'Runaway' v, 'Standing In
The Shadows Of Love' ch, 'Love Child' ch, 'Roads' v, 'On Her
Majesty's Secret Service' (with a transposition onto Bbm).

Group 10

Here are some exotic turnarounds which you will not come across very often.
Add one of these to spice up a song!

I Im Vm IV: C Cm Gm F
'La Femme D'Argent' i

I III bVII II: C Em Bb Dm
'Lay Lady Lay', 'No More Mr. Nice Guy' v.

I IV bIII bVI: C F Eb Ab
'Smells Like Teen Spirit' – an ambiguous, harmonically dislocated sequence. It could also be described as V-I in F followed by V-I in Ab – a turnaround half in one key and half in another. Compare this with I IV IImaj V (C F D G), which also implies two keys but is more symmetrical. It is the asymmetrical nature of Cobain's riff (the original started on F) that makes it so great.

I IV bVI Vm: C F Ab Gm
'Not So Manic Now' (Dubstar I).

I bV IImaj bVI: C Gb D Ab
'Credit In The Straight World' v

I bVI V IIImaj: C Ab G E
'Wuthering Heights' v.

I bVII VI V: C Bb Am G
'The Bitterest Pill'. 'China Girl' br.

I bVII bVI Vm: C Bb Ab Gm
'The Sensual World' v.

This is not an exhaustive list - and there are always new combinations to be created. But all the popular sequences are here and we have already covered a huge amount of potential song material. You can use the above ten groups in any number of ways by using one turnaround in a chorus and then having a non-turnaround verse and bridge, or by linking them with each other. You can also mix any of the sequences in these ten groups with any earlier in the section. It all comes down to what sounds good to your ears and what chords you can pitch a good melody over. A turnaround might be deployed in each section of a song - one for the verse, one for the chorus, and one for the bridge - but I would advise against this. You will find that the energy and feel of these sections will seem too similar.

As your ears get familiar with their sound you will be astonished at how common turnarounds are in recent popular music. This is partly because the element of repetition and the fact that they are short makes them easy to remember. But don't get trapped by the tyranny of four'. Turnarounds are seductive and they can make you a very lazy and predictable writer. To inject more interest into their use there are various techniques for messing about with turnarounds. These form the subject of our next section.

Developing Turnarounds

As I said in the previous section, turnarounds definitely represent the laziest form of songwriting. It's important to try and do more with them – different turnarounds could be used for different parts of a song, verse, chorus, bridge, etc.

> **I   VI   IV   V (v) + I   VI   II   V (ch): C Am F G + C Am Dm G**
> 'Beechwood 4-5789'.

Two different turnarounds can be linked together to make a longer phrase. Two four-bar turnarounds linked would make an eight-bar phrase; repeated, that would be a 16-bar verse, but each of the turnarounds would have been played only twice.

> **I   IV   II   V + I   IV   bVII   V: C F Dm G + C F Bb G**
> 'Yes It Is' v.

The important factors that determine the effect of a turnaround are:

● Direction – is it going harmonically up or down?
● Tonality – the mix of major, minor and flattened chords
● Expectation – the inclusion of a chord that suggests a key-change that doesn't actually happen, or is momentary
● Where it starts and finishes (especially the position of I or V)
● Displacement
● Stretching
● Use of inversions
● Frequency of chord change
● Repetition
● The type of chord, i.e. whether II in a sequence is a minor 7, 6, 9, etc.

Displacement

The classic turnaround starts on I and often ends on V. This strongly emphasises the key. A *displaced* turnaround is one in which chord I has been moved off the "pole position" and no longer leads the sequence. Displacement is one way to make turnarounds more interesting and less predictable. Consider the

way the chorus of 'Knowing Me Knowing You' starts on V and no sooner lands on I ("do") than it moves off to IV and then V. 'My Love' comes in on IV, uses a VImaj and doesn't land on chord I until bar eight, at a slow tempo. Displacement is stronger if I moves into the middle of the sequence. 'Wuthering Heights' has a chorus with an excellent example of displacement: IV II V I IV V I IV.

Chord I is made to feel like a place where you cannot rest. The music keeps moving off it and onto IV. The ultimate displacement is to miss out I altogether. 'When You're Young And In Love' has a chorus of VI II IV V. 'There Must Be An Angel (Playing With My Heart)' creates anticipation by delaying chord I to the end of each phrase: II V VI IV IV V bIII I.

Notice the unusual resolution from bIII to I, instead of the more predictable IV-I or V-I.

Substitution

In order to create a more interesting musical effect, it is possible to substitute turnarounds for each other in such a way that minor chords turn into their relative majors (and vice versa) but retain the same position in the sequence. For example:

Main turnaround
I VI IV V: C Am F G

Substitutes
I VI II V: C Am Dm G

I VI IV V: C Am F Em

This kind of substitution can be powerful for illustrating something in the lyric. Imagine a love song with the turnaround C Am F G.

Verse:

C   Am   F   G
The world is suddenly strange, I feel a fear.
C   Am   F   G
My steps falter, can't find my way, the path is unclear.
C   Am   F   G
I seem to stumble around in the dark in the middle of the day
C   Am   Dm   G
Right is wrong since you've gone far away

The switch from F to Dm in the last line puts extra weight on the word "gone" – which is, after all, the reason the speaker is complaining. Instead of merely repeating a single turnaround, a little bit of variety is introduced.

Another type of substitution is to retain the root-note sequence but use techniques such as "reverse polarity" (major to minor, minor to major).

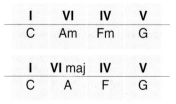

I	VI	IV	V
C	Am	Fm	G

I	VI maj	IV	V
C	A	F	G

The Stretched Turnaround

There are two basic methods for "stretching" a turnaround. First, simply stay on a

chord for several more beats or an extra bar. Second, repeat a change within the turnaround several times before you proceed to the next one.

'Tracks Of My Tears' exquisitely stretches its three chords like this:

I	IV	IV	V
C	F	F	G

'Heat Treatment' is based on I VI IV V but repeats the I-VI change before IV and V:

I	VI	I	VI	I	VI	IV	V
C	Am	C	Am	C	Am	F	G

'When You're Young And In Love' plays about with the latter chords:

I	VI	IV	V	IV	V
C	Am	F	G	F	G

You can displace and stretch at the same time – and the turnaround no longer sounds as four-square. Take 'My Sweet Lord', where a I VI II V has metamorphosed into this:

II	V (x4)	I	VI	I	VI
Dm	G	C	Am	C	Am

If we assume 'Step Into My World' to be in F# minor, we get a I VII VI IV stretched to this:

I	VII	I	VII	VI	IV	VI	IV
F#m	E	F#m	E	D	Bm	D	Bm

'Cum On Feel The Noize' takes I VI II V and uses the same repeat approach:

I	VI	I	VI	II	V	II	V
G	Em	G	Em	Am	D	Am	D

Stretching by Harmonic Variation

You can also stretch by harmonic variation. This means lengthening a sequence by changing the form of a chord from straight major or minor to seventh, sixth, etc. The most common harmonic variation is probably when a major chord moves through its major and dominant seventh chord forms: I Imaj7 I7. This is satisfying to the ear because the root note can be heard falling (on a C chord) from C to B to Bb. After that, it can either return to C or fall to A and be harmonized by an F, A, Am or Dm chord (or something more exotic). This happens in 'Something' v, 'Bell Bottom Blues' ch, 'Pyjamarama' and 'Everybody's Talkin'. In 'Jesamine' and 'Up The Ladder To The Roof', the intro progression is I I7 IV IVm I. In 'I'm Living In Shame', it's I Imaj7 I7 IV IVm.

The equivalent on a minor chord, which is Em Em/maj7 Em7, can be heard in 'Cry Baby Cry' (where it keeps going to Em6 and then C), 'Got To Get You Into My Life', and 'Michelle'. Augmented chords can create similar effects: D D+ D6 D7 (where the ear hears a rise from A to A#, B and C).

Stretching by Division

Another way of putting turnarounds to different use is to split them in half and assign the first two chords to a verse and the last two to a chorus. R.E.M did this in 'Everybody Hurts', where the verse is a repeated I-IV change and the chorus is II-V.

Disguising Turnarounds

Turnarounds are less obvious if they are slow, displaced (not centered on I) or arranged in a less conventional manner. If no instrument is playing the whole chord but several instruments are contributing to the overall sound of a chord, then it will seem less solid and the turnaround less obvious. Two great examples are the harpsichord parts on 'Caught A Lite Sneeze' and the strings on 'Cloudbusting'.

This is also heard in one of U2's contributions to popular music, typified by a number such as 'With Or Without You'. It's a simple four-chord sequence (I V VI IV: D A Bm G). Most bands would have had the guitar chugging out those chords. U2's arrangement has the bass *imply* those changes whilst The Edge gets on with other ideas around the chord of D. To try this technique, let the bass play the root notes but don't follow the chord sequence on guitar.

The Five-Chord Turnaround

It is possible to have a turnaround of five or even more chords. Consider the chord sequence bVI bIII bVII IV I: C G D A E – which is 'Hey Joe' (and in the middle eight of 'A Day In The Life'). These chords cover only four bars, which then repeat throughout the song. Another example would be 'Hard Day's Night', which is I IV I bVII I – only three different chords but used in a fixed pattern of five.

A turnaround stops being a turnaround once the the rate of chord change is no longer fast enough for the ear to hear it as a single unit of music repeated. 'Hey Joe' crams five chords into four bars, so we are aware of the fact that it is a single unit. If those chords were spread out across eight bars at the same tempo, it is unlikely we would hear it as a turnaround. The effect of the turnaround depends partly on tempo and number of bars. Quicker tempos emphasise it.

Here are some other examples of five-chord patterns (not necessarily five different chords):

I II V bIII II	C Dm G Eb Dm	'A Design For Life'
I II III V I	C Dm Em G C	'I Shall Be Released'
I bIII IV bVI bIII	C Eb F Ab Eb	'Stardust' v.
I III IV I V	C Em F C G	'Hymn To Her' ch.
I III IV II V	C Em F Dm G	'Trash'
I III VI IV V	C Em Am F G	'Till Death Us Do Part' ch.

I IV bIII bVII bVI	C F Eb Bb Ab	'Free Man In Paris'
I IV III IV V I	C F Em F G	'The Drugs Don't Work'
I IV V II III II	C F G Em Dm	'Je T'Aime'
I IV bVII IV I	C F Bb F C	'Fine Time'

I V II IV IIImaj	C G Dm F E	'Country House'
I V II IV V	C G Dm F G	'Live Forever' v (with VI V II IV V as a variation), 'I Try'
I V II V IV	C G Dm G F	'Where Did Our Love Go?'
I V VI V IV	C G Am G F	'Might Be Stars'

I VI III II V	C Am Em Dm G	'Across The Universe'
I VI III IV V	C Am Em F G	'Going For The One' c
I VI IV I V	C Am F C G	'Some Might Say' v.
I VI IV V I	C Am F G C	'He's On The Phone' v.

Five chord turnarounds can be subject to stretching in the same way as the four-chord types. The Vapors' 'Turning Japanese' has a verse where a I VI II IV V sequence is extended by a repetition of the first chord change. The chorus of 'Can't Stop This Thing We Started' (IV V VI IV I) and Adams' 'It's Only Love' (VI V III IV I) both use displacement.

Beyond Turnarounds

As popular as turnarounds are, songwriters (fortunately) often construct longer chord progressions, sometimes non-repeating and increasingly sophisticated. It is possible to compose a 16-bar verse which is a single chord progression. A turnaround might then be used for the chorus and sound all the more effective by contrast. Let's have a look at one of these longer structures.

Sequences usually combine major and minor chords, but there are songs that stay on minor chords for dramatic effect. 'Blackberry Way' is extraordinary for the stream of minor chords in its verse: Em F# Am, then Em Bm Bbm Am Cm Em. 'December Will Be Magic Again' has Cm Gm Dm Am Em Bm in its first verse and the second time adds Fm Cm at the end.

Exclusively major chords in a song have been used for a psychedelic effect. 'I Am The Walrus' has no minor chords, and songs such as 'Silver Machine' and 'Arnold Layne' are dominated by major chords. The psychedelic effect is heightened if you spend a long time on a dominant seven chord, or if you use chromatic half-step shifts as in Hendrix's '1983'.

You can, of course, construct verses, choruses and bridges without reference to a turnaround at all. Consider 'Like A Rolling Stone', where the verse is I II III IV V (twice) + IV V (twice) + IV III II I (twice) + II IV V, or 'Do Anything You Wanna Do', where the verse is V I IV + V I + II III IV V IV III II I.

Peter & Gordon's hit 'World Without Love' (written by Lennon / McCartney) shows what can be done with two reverse polarity chords and a flat chord:

I	III maj	VI	I	IV m	I	II	V	I
Eb	G	Cm	Eb	Abm	Eb	Fm	Bb	Eb

Notice how this progression pulls off chord I onto different chords and then returns, in a sense giving different views of it. After the vocal line finishes, there is a bVI V (Cb Bb) link. Dubstar's 'Just A Girl She Said' is worth studying for the number of progressions, including this one heard on the intro:

I	II	IV	V	III	VI	IV	V
A	Bm	D	E	C#m	F#m	D	E

The expectation of a turnaround generated by the first four chords is quickly dispelled by III.

Rate of Harmonic Change

When composing a song, pay close attention to the duration of chords and when they change. It is easy to fall into the trap of having every chord occupy a bar and every change happen on the first beat of a bar. Inject variation so the chords change at differing rates. Change halfway through a bar or after one-and-a-half bars, or write a sequence where you're changing every two beats, or include a bar where there is a different chord on each beat.

If you use several turnarounds in an uptempo song, you run the risk of creating a feeling of bewilderment. You will need to have a small stretch where the chords are not changing so frequently to allow the listener to grasp what's going on. Think of the I-V changes in 'I Should Have Known Better' and the chord-change rate of one every two beats in the chorus of 'Some Might Say'. 'Days' has rapid chord movement in its chorus. In a song with a lot of rapid changes, there may be a need to cool out for a bit and hang on a single chord, as in 'I'm A Believer' and 'A Little Bit Me, A Little Bit You'.

Unusual Chord Changes

In the January 1995 issue of *Mojo*, Noel Gallagher was quoted as saying, "There's 12 notes in a scale and there's 36 chords and that's the end of it. All the configurations have been done before." That's a revealing comment when you consider Oasis's "borrowings" from various bands. Of course, there aren't just 36 chords. This is a view that does not encourage innovation. And if you think all the "configurations" have been done before, you aren't likely to go looking for new ones. It's a recipe for laziness.

Perhaps that's one of the reasons why Oasis have not yet come up with a song like Radiohead's 'Just', which has several innovative touches. The intro is I bIII IImaj IV (all majors, C Eb D F), and the verse is Am Ab Eb F /Am Ab Eb Bb /Am Ab G F# F. The chord changes are unusual, and the melodic phrases fall into three bars each. The chorus adds a C F# F to the C Eb D F change from the intro. 'Just' was probably the first song on a commercially successful album to have these particular unusual chord movements.

One of the challenges is to find less common chord changes and make them work. Common chord changes are popular because they sound pleasant and are self-reinforcing – that is to say, familiar. They have been heard so many times they feel comfortable and seem to express familiar emotions. They are recognized faster (an important point for commercial songwriting) on first listen. Unusual chord changes are by their nature disconcerting because they have not been heard very often. They are not immediately recognized and make the emotion of the song seem less familiar, too. They do, however, offer the songwriter a tantalising hope.

Rodgers & Hammerstein's Law: If you can make an unusual chord change accessible in a song, you have immediately distinguished your song from thousands of others, past and present, that use common changes.

There have been thousands of hit records based on I IV V. But there is only one I know of that bases its verse on the haunting change of two minor chords three semitones (half-steps) apart. That is 'Light My Fire' by The Doors, in which the verse moves Am to F#m and back again. This change is so rare that it conjures up only that one song. Anyone else trying to use it has an immediate problem, whereas anybody can write a I IV V song and not have it confused with anything else.

Consider what I call the "Songwriter's General Theory of Relativity": *the weirdness of the change is relative to the strength of the sense of key.* Too many weird chords and you lose the sense of the original key, or the listener's ear will decide you've changed key anyway – in which case it will orient the chords around a new key center and the original "oddness" you were aiming at will disappear.

What qualifies as an "unusual" chord change? In simple terms, we're talking about chords that don't belong together in the same key. The technical name for this is "non-diatonic" or "chromatic". In C major, this could mean changing from C to:

bIImaj/min	C#/Db major or minor
bIIImin	D#/Eb minor
bVmaj/min	F#/Gb major or minor
bVImin	G#/Ab minor
VImaj	A major
bVIImin	A#/Bb minor
VIImaj/min	B major or minor

The verse of 'Light My Fire' is haunting because of its harmonic ambiguity. We think at first the key must be A minor, but the F#m immediately confuses the ear. Because F#m is not in A minor, we decide F# minor is the "true" key. The return to Am is equally confusing because you can't have Am in F# minor either. The ear gives up trying to fix the key and accepts this strange movement. The same change occurs in 'Edge Of Darkness' (Em-Gm) without going back to Em, and under the guitar solo in Queen's 'Tenement Funster' (G#m-Bm); there's a Gm-Bm change in 'Stone Cold Crazy'.

Contexts for unusual chord changes

Some themes demand strange changes. Songs about madness often use peculiar progressions to mimic the mental displacement of the subject. Bowie's 'The Bewlay Brothers' has a coda that juxtaposes Bm with F. This is another change that cannot be reconciled with either chord being the key chord. (In F you would have Bb; in Bm you would have F#.) Bowie used unrelated chords for a similar reason on the coda of 'Ashes To Ashes'. In 'I Want You' Costello communicates the deranged jealousy of the speaker not only through the lyric but through the D#m chord which keeps interrupting the Em G C B turnaround. D#m is completely unrelated to E minor. The coda of 'I Want You (She's So Heavy)' is worth careful examination not only for the unusual chord changes (a five-chord turnaround) and 6/8 time but also for its asymmetry.

Strange chord changes sometimes suit comic songs. UK singles outfit Madness scored a string of hits in the 1980s with a wacky mix of ska, new-wave, and pop. The slightly bittersweet flavour of their songs partly arises from the music's frequent use of minor chords and keys, and unusual changes. 'Night Boat To Cairo' features a C-Bbm change and a sequence that moves from Fm-G#m-Fm-Db (twice) before Eb and C. 'The chorus of 'Baggy Trousers' uses repeated changes from a major chord to a minor on the same note (IV IVm I Im). Few bands have created such a distinctive musical world through such specific harmonic means.

Non-diatonic chords

Other ways of using odd chords include putting an unrelated chord between two diatonic ones: C F# Am; G C# D. In the verse of 'Do You Want To Know A Secret?', we get III bIIIm II. If you extend this as IIIm7 bIIIm7 IIm7 V7 I, you get a popular sequence from the 1920s. In 'Pump It Up', the chords are B Bb A for the main verse; the Bb is a passing chord. The movement of major chords a semitone (half-step) apart is a classic rock'n'roll trick that goes back to 1950s rockers like Eddie Cochran and was revived in both glam and punk rock. Semitone shifts also occur in 'I'm So Tired' and 'Sexy Sadie', where Lennon moves from I to VII7 before landing on IV or III. In G this would be G F#7 C or G F#7 Bm.

Altered harmony

The correct sequence of sevenths for a major key is Imaj7 IIm7 IIIm7 IVmaj7 V7 and VIm7 (in C major: Cmaj7 Dm7 Em7 Fmaj7 G7 Am7). Using different types of sevenths changes the effect. Take, for example, a I bIII IV sequence. If this were in G major, it would be G Bb C and given the presence of the bIII might suggest a G7 Bb7 C7 blues harmony. In the Dylan-Harrison song 'I'd Have You Anytime', the effect of these chords is considerably altered by the harmony, which is Gmaj7 Bbmaj7 Cm7, an unusual but beautiful progression for a verse. The first three chords of the verse of 'Absolute Beginners' are D Bm Amaj7. For D major chord V should be A7. The Amaj7 is startling.

Similarly 'Protection' (Massive Attack with Tracy Thorn) uses a three chord change where the first chord is initially Bmaj7 but then turns into Bm7.

If a song has some unsettling changes, it makes good artistic sense to juxtapose them with conventional ones. 'The Ballad Of Tom Jones' starts in fine John Barry-esque style with Em G Fm Bb, a sequence that cannot sit in any one key. It is followed by a Dm-G change, repeated four times, that turns out to be II-V in C and then a chorus of Cmaj7 Fm G (I IVm V) – exotic but not weird. As for Barry himself, the verse of 'Thunderball' is based on I IV Vmaj in Bb minor, but in bar 10 a wonderfully unexpected Dm chord appears as Barry neatly works in part of the 007 theme. The middle eight has a key change to Ebm that leads to some colourful changes.

Linking Unrelated Chords

Odd chord juxtapositions can be made less so if the chords have a note in common. Consider 'Avalon': the verse is a stately I V IV V in F (F C Bb C). The chorus / hook (where Ferry sings 'Avalon') goes to a chilly bVII VI V (Eb Dm C). These three chords would normally have no note in common to all of them, with the addition of an F (right hand box) makes all the difference:

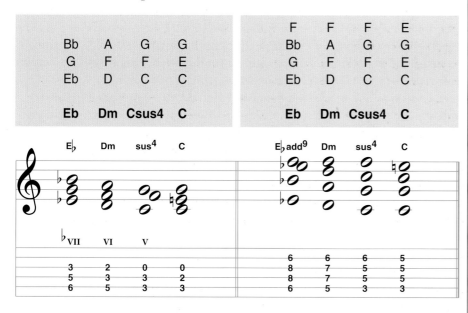

Now the chords are linked by the note F. Notice how whilst its pitch remains constant its harmonic function alters. In the first chord (Eb) F is a ninth; in the second (Dm) it is a third; and in C it is the suspended fourth which finally resolves to E. This is a technique which can apply to a host of musical situations.

Having looked at many different harmony and chord ideas in this chapter, it is now time to think about song structure and how these chord progression ideas can slot into place in verses and choruses.

SECTION 5 **SONG STRUCTURES**

ABBREVIATIONS

Roman numerals I VII
indicate chord
relationships within a key.
m *minor*
maj *major*
Song sections:
br *bridge*
c *coda*
ch *chorus*
hk *hook*
i *intro*
pch *pre-chorus*
v *verse*
Most of the chord-sequence examples
are standardized for comparison
into C *or* A minor.
Famous songs referred to in C *major*
or A *minor are not necessarily in*
the key of the original recordings.

The classic popular song structure has three primary sections:

verse + chorus + bridge/middle eight

These are sometimes referred to by the letters A, B and C – which is where Genesis got the title for 'ABACAB'. Cream's 'Badge' was named after one of the writers misread the word 'bridge' on a piece of paper.

Secondary sections include an intro, an outro (or coda, literally meaning "tail") and any instrumental solos, links or riffs that are used to get from one primary section to another. Let's look at these one at a time.

The Intro

The intro has several functions. It establishes tempo, key, style and mood. It is strongly affected by the question of who your audience is. If you are writing a song intended to be a single, your intro has to be shaped to fit certain commercial considerations. It will have to be brief – perhaps only a few seconds – and it will have to grab the listener's attention. If the song is not intended as a single, then you can take more time – but this is one area where commercial considerations and aesthetic values need not conflict. An intro can be very short ('A Design For Life' takes five seconds to get to its verse) or extended (the intro of 'Some Might Say' is 36 seconds owing to an initial guitar solo, and 'Do You Know What I Mean' takes as long to get to its first chorus as many 1960s rock singles required to get to their codas). 'Ten Storey Love Song' has a 50-second atmospheric intro. Many amateur songs are spoiled because there has not been ruthless enough cutting of the length of various sections. Guitarists in particular need to be aware of this. A riff may be fun to play but do you really need to do it 36 times before the verse starts?

It is perfectly legitimate to have no intro at all. You could start straight away with a few words in a pickup bar followed by the instruments entering on the first beat of the first whole bar. This might be a verse or a chorus. Think about the dynamics of your intro. Ballads can start quietly to set a mood. A dance song needs to be loud. Sudden beginnings will certainly make people sit up and pay attention. Some songs, such as '2000 Miles' or 'Eight Days A Week', fade in – but this is not so effective on the radio as at home.

One common trick is to use part of A, B or C as the intro and simply not have a vocal on it. It could be an instrumental version of the chorus or a section of the verse. You might have some kind of instrumental theme or motif, possibly part of the chorus melody. This means that the listener will have heard the chorus tune already when the first chorus is reached.

Guitar intros

Since the guitar has been a central instrument in popular music, there are many different types of guitar intros. The instrumental motif could be a rhythm guitar ('Whole Lotta Love', 'If It Makes You Happy', 'In A Room', 'In The City'), a burst of lead guitar (Chuck Berry's signature), or the low-string melody that starts 'Radar Love' in such a threatening way (and at a different tempo to boot). It could be a single chord, as with 'The Kids Are Alright' (*bbrraaanggg*! "I don't mi-i-ind ...") or 'Hard Day's Night' (G7sus4 on a 12-string, apparently), or Keef's chopped open tuning chords for 'Brown Sugar'. Dissonance will sure as hell get people's attention. Think of Hendrix's grinding flattened fifth to kick-start 'Purple Haze' or the Aleister Crowley-meets-the Arabian-Nights snakebite of Page's bent flattened fifth (C# against G) for 'Dancing Days'. There's also a flattened fifth in the riff of R.E.M's 'Feeling Gravity's Pull' where it is not as expected as it might be in a heavy rock number such as 'Enter Sandman'. A song like Robert Plant's 'Big Log' starts with an instrumental guitar passage because the song is half guitar instrumental anyway.

Other instruments

The intro instrument could be a horn, like the one that starts 'God Only Knows', or a keyboard, as on 'Superstition'. A trumpet has the intro on many a Bacharach tune ('We've Got All The Time In The World'). It's a saxophone on 'Baker Street', and there's what critic Dave Marsh aptly called the "rattlesnake" tambourine on the intro of 'I Heard It Through The Grapevine'. It might be the lush orchestral intro of 'Dazzle' or the solo bassline of 'My Girl', 'Erotica' or 'Cuyahoga'. Think of the repeated bass motif that starts 'Under Pressure'. What about an unusual instrument, like the Coral electric sitar heard on 'No Matter What Sign You Are' and 'Signed, Sealed, Delivered' – guaranteed to make people wonder what the hell is that? People who are recognised stars on their instruments get to start songs with short solos, like the guitar break that opens 'Brothers In Arms'. Some songs start with other people's tunes. Dire Straits put an extract of 'The Carousel Waltz' at the head of 'Tunnel Of Love' because it conjured up a fairground. The copyright will cost you, of course.

Drum intros have strong impact, especially in music for dancing. John Bonham's drum intros for 'Rock And Roll', 'When The Levee Breaks' (sampled on, among others, 'Army Of Me') and 'The Crunge' (sampled on Mansun's 'Stripper Vicar') are exemplary. Other notable drum intros include the ones on 'Lipstick Vogue', 'Sat In Your Lap' and 'I Don't Live Today'. On hits such as 'Can The Can', Suzi Quatro made the drum intro a trademark.

Vocal intros

Think of the way 'Hound Dog' comes straight in – "You ain't nothin' but a ..." - on an unaccompanied vocal. You could whistle, or use a spoken phrase like "Is she really going out with him?" on 'Leader Of The Pack', which The Damned appropriated for 'New Rose'. There's Ian Hunter's cheery "Allo!" on 'Once Bitten Twice Shy', or even a laugh, as Kate Bush did on the single of 'The Man With The Child In His Eyes'. A heartfelt spoken intro, such as the one Smokey Robinson put on 'Baby, Baby Don't Cry', would probably be thought kitsch now. Remember the heavily echoed "Hey! Don't watch dat, watch dis!" of 'One Step Beyond' and the party chatter that starts 'What's Going On' and 'I Can't Get

Next To You'? How about Little Richard's immortal rock 'n' roll war-cry 'Awopbopaloobopalopbamboom!' at the start of 'Tutti Frutti', or the Beatlesque dominant 7 crescendo that kicks off 'Let's Dance'? Intros require drama, involvement, expectation. A crescendo or an ascending or descending figure gets our attention immediately because we know it's moving *towards* something, and we are curious to hear what it will be. Anticipation can be aroused by suggesting that you are about to land on chord I but delaying it to the verse (or later). 'Can't Ignore The Train' does this.

Sampling voices from films can produce excellent results - witness Kate Bush's use of a fevered male voice exclaiming, "It's in the trees! It's coming!" ('Hounds Of Love'), or The Banshees' "Did you know that more murders are committed at 92 degrees Fahrenheit than any other temperature? I read an article once ... at lower temperatures people are easy going, over 92 it's too hot to move, but just 92 people get irritable!" ('92 Degrees'). 'One Of Us' has a field recording of on-the-porch singing before the song proper starts.

You might use a sound effect of some sort. This could illustrate the theme of the song, as with 'Apeman' (car horns) and 'Exhuming McCarthy' (typewriter). It could be trains ('5.15', 'Down In The Tube Station At Midnight'), rain and storm ('Riders On The Storm', and all over The Who's *Quadrophenia*), the waterfront ('Champagne Supernova') or seagulls ('I Wish It Would Rain'). How about a sax imitating a ship's foghorn ('Night Boat To Cairo')? Pink Floyd started 'Money', appropriately, with cash-tills. Kate Bush used whale song to start 'Moving'. You could also use pure sound effects generated on a synth, as the acoustic guitar fed through synth that spits out the intro to 'Relay'. Samplers have been used to put the sound of crackling vinyl at the start of songs, for that extra touch of analogue warmth.

The "False Intro"

We assume that an intro leads to what follows. But an interesting effect is an intro that does not dovetail with the rest of the song – this is a "false intro". False intros work by arousing a sense of involvement and then giving us a mild shock. They manipulate involve either tempo or harmony, or both. You could start in one style and then proceed in another, although that's a fairly way-out trick. R.E.M. put a few seconds of goofing around pretending to be James Brown before the country rock of '(Don't Go Back To) Rockville'.

Tempo variations often work well. 'Man Out Of Time' starts in double-time with a manic punk thrash that suddenly subsides into a stately piano-driven song. Intros can be in free time, such as in 'Here There and Everywhere' and 'American Pie', where the time is controlled by the singer's phrasing. 'My Love' has a clever false intro in which a horn plays the note A. It would be logical to assume A is therefore the key note – but the first chord that fades in is a Bb (Bb D F), so the A note makes a Bbmaj7 chord (Bb D F A).

Some intros are long enough almost to be termed "pre-verses". This is where you realize that the boundaries between sections of a song are not always rigid and easily identified. Take The Beatles' 'If I Fell': it opens with a descending chord sequence in C#major, which then changes key to D major for the first chorus. An intro could be in a different tempo and a different key from the song proper. Led Zeppelin's 'Tea For One' starts medium-tempo in F before subsiding into a 12/8 slow blues in C minor. R.E.M.'s 'I Believe' commences with a banjo in G, but the band enter in F at a faster tempo, almost as if they have cut across the banjo.

Intros offer an opportunity to play around with the listener's sense of key. Smokey Robinson did this on 'More Love' and the Isley Brothers' 'Put Yourself In My Place'. starts with a bewildering progression of E A C Bb G/B before settling in C major at the commencement of the verse.

The Verse

The verse is lyrically where you lay out the situation and establish the song's style. Verses are anything from about eight bars up to 24 or more in length, usually in a figure divisible by four. Verses of any length can have their own internal structure. Two lines of lyric could be set to a four-bar four-chord turnaround repeated, or four lines to four times round:

C Am G F (x4)

It would be more interesting to use the turnaround only three times and then change to something else:

C Am G F (x3) G F G F

This type of 3 + 1 formula is very common, as is the making of a verse by constructing an eight-bar sequence and repeating it:

C G F G F Em Am G (x2)

Notice how this stays off the key chord, C, until the start of the next eight bars. 'Hotel California' is a famous 8-bar progression:

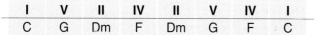

I	Vmaj	VII	IVmaj	VI	III	IV	Vmaj
Bm	F#	A	E	G	D	Em	F#

Sam Cooke's 'Cupid' does this with just four chords:

I	VI	I	IV	I	V	I	V
C	Am	C	F	C	G	C	G

Notice how it never loses touch with chord I. The changes are like short steps away from the key centre, not a long journey. Compare it with 'Hotel California' where once the music has left the key chord of B minor it does not reach it again until the start of the next phrase. Manfred Mann's 'Fox On The Run' has a lovely chorus progression:

I	V	II	IV	II	V	IV	I
C	G	Dm	F	Dm	G	F	C

Notice how the second Dm is poignant because somewhat unexpected and the approach to the last C via F is softer than it would have been via G.

A common trick is to repeat an eight bar phrase with a change of the last chord second time around. Big Star's 'The Ballad Of El Goodo' does this:

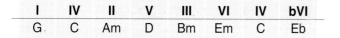

I	IV	II	V	III	VI	IV	bVI
G.	C	Am	D	Bm	Em	C	Eb

The second time through Eb is replaced by F.

Verse Asymmetry

A verse could have an odd number of bars tacked on the end, sometimes to allow a few extra words to be added. These assymetrical verse extensions can be great touches because they break the "tyranny of four". The chorus might appear a couple of bars early or late, either of which can be exciting. Another nice technique is to take out a bar to make a second phrase arrive earlier than you would expect. 'It Won't Be Long' cuts a bar from its verse after the first phrase so the second has more impact. (Try singing the song with the "cut" bar restored and notice how much less interesting it is.) In 'Do You Know The Way To San Jose', there is a good example of asymmetry: the chord sequence I IV I V is five bars long, with the V covering two bars.

The Through-Composed Verse

A verse can also be "through-composed". I use this term for a verse that has no repeated chord-change unit, such as a turnaround, but is a single structure without internal repeats that is maybe 12 or 16 bars (or even longer). This type of song is less common because it is more demanding to write. It is also less favoured in a commercial context because the listener has to wait until the end of the verse to grasp the whole. The lack of chord repetition can be offset by repeating lyric phrases or having melodic motifs in the instruments that repeat regardless of the changing harmony. Although unusual, the through-composed verse does offer marvellous opportunities to develop the melodic line. 'Alone Again (Naturally)' and 'For All We Know' would be examples.

If a verse is short, the distinction between verse and chorus can be blurred. There is one song structure that has two sections, A and B, and A is a verse that climaxes with a hook – in other words a "mini-chorus" is incorporated into it. In 'Love Grows (Where My Rosemary Goes)', there are only two lyric lines sung in four bars before the song arrives at the hook. The whole section is wrapped up in about eight bars. Badfinger's 'No Matter What' is another example with an eight-bar A section. Both songs have a bridge that modulates away from the home key. The Beatles' early albums contain quite a few examples of this AB structure.

Verses can be constructed by using 8-, 12- and 16-bar blues-derived forms.

8-bar three-chord verse

I	I	IV	I	I	V	V	I

'Act Naturally'

I	I	IV	I	I	V	IV	I

'Barbara Ann'

I	I	IV	bVdim	I	VI	II	V	I	IV	I	V

'Need Your Love So Bad'
Typical 12-bar

I	I (or IV)	I	I	IV	IV	I	I	V	IV	I	V

12-bar in Dm

I	I	V	V	I	I	IV	IV	I	V	I	I

'Black Magic Woman'
Songs can have verses with different sequences and structures, all leading to the same chorus.

The Pre-Chorus

One further refinement of the verse is the "pre-chorus", a section that sounds a step beyond the first part of the verse. It may be a musical or a lyrical phrase that gives this feeling of moving forward. For example, if the verse has used only the key chord, a pre-chorus could bring in IV or V or both. A classic pre-chorus chord change is to move from IV to V repeatedly, creating the musical expectation that you are about to land on chord I at the chorus, as in 'Karma Chameleon'. It might even feature an ascending sequence like II III IV V, which progresses firmly toward the chorus.

The rate of chord change can increase, as in 'Got To Get You Into My Life'. The pre-chorus definitely has its eyes and ears fixed in the direction of the upcoming chorus. It can also be a way to bring another hook into the song. The pre-chorus usually retains the same lyrics from one verse to another, even if the verse changes. In a song that goes verse, chorus, verse, chorus, middle eight, a prechorus can be used to get to the last set of choruses if it is felt that putting in a third verse would delay things too much.

The Chorus

Sigh ... the chorus. Okay, can I confess now? I'm in love. A great chorus is pure magic. The chorus is the passionate, declamatory, joyous, tearful, wistful heart of the popular song. You know what I mean – it has you walking two feet off the carpet. Put another nickel in that machine.

Musically, it's where we find the hook, the notes that lodge in your mind (and millions of other minds – you're in good company, you know); the notes that make you want to hear the song again; the notes that drive you to your local record shop. A hook is a catchy melodic and harmonic phrase, possibly reinforced by backing vocal, instrumental counter-melodies, a riff, or rhythm. This is where we reach the center of the lyric's meaning. It could be a resolution ('I'm Gonna Make You Love Me', 'I'll Pick A Rose For My Rose'), a revelation ('She Loves You','You're All I Need To Get By'), a realization ('It Must Be Love'), a question ('Do You Wanna Dance?'), a metaphor ('Blinded By The Light') or a statement ('I Want To Know What Love Is'). Lyrically, the chorus sums up the central issue and/or expresses the over-riding emotion.

Choruses often involve repetition of words and/or the accompanying harmony. The music intensifies and focuses, and this can be achieved in a variety of ways. You could delay chord I until the chorus, or quicken the rate of harmonic change (chords changing twice a bar instead of once a bar). Listen to the way the chorus in Aretha Franklin's 'I Say A Little Prayer' gains urgency as the chords change every two beats instead of every four beats as in the verse. The same trick happens in Madonna's 'Cherish', where the chords change on the beat. You can lift the melody to higher notes, bring in other instruments, change the key, quicken the tempo, alter the predominant rhythm, or strengthen the beat. Great choruses really need an inspiration – this is where you pray to the Muse when composing.

The Link

After the chorus, you have to find a way to get back to the verse. You can have no link and go straight to the verse. Whether this will work depends on the what the melody does at the end of a chorus. Is there enough time between the finish of that phrase and the start of the verse lyric? Does it sound rushed and breathless? Does the listener need a break? Does the singer need a break?

The faster the tempo, the more likely it is you will need a link. A couple of bars will probably do the trick. In a hard rock song, the guitar riff will often return at this point

SECTION 5

for an outbreak of head-banging. You could reprise the intro, perhaps in a shortened form. It is often good to have a change of dynamics and texture at this point.

The Middle Eight/Bridge

Or as James Brown famously exclaimed, "Shall I take it to the bridge?", and Robert Plant answered, "Where's that confounded bridge?"

The middle eight usually comes after the second chorus, though it might be inserted after the second verse as a way of delaying the next chorus. If it is short enough, it can even be inserted more than once.

The term "middle eight" reminds us that the commonest length is eight bars, though the term is now used regardless of its length. The term "bridge" reminds us of its function, which is to link different parts of the song. After the second chorus, songs often "need" to go somewhere else for a bit. New lyrical and musical material is introduced. The easiest thing to do is introduce a solo of some sort – a rock song would probably have a guitar solo, an MOR ballad might prefer soft, breathy sax. (That way you don't have to write more lyrics). This tactic is not as common as it was.

Harmonically, a middle eight might have a key change, or work towards one. The traditional key change is to the dominant (eg, from C to G) from whence it is easy to return to the home key:

F G Am F C F D7 G

This song is in C major, with a middle eight that changes key to the dominant G major. But since G major is also chord V of C, you can easily go to a C chord at the start of the next verse and be back in C. Simply turn G into G7. 'That'll be The Day' does this.

'I Saw Her Standing There' and 'Into The Groove' are examples of a IV-V change – two major chords a tone (full step) apart – used for a bridge phrase.

Harmonically, the middle eight may have some chords that have not been played elsewhere in the song. The Beatles had a wonderful trick of combining 12-bar verses that were all tough dominant seventh chords (I7 IV7 V7: C7 F7 G7) with a bridge that sweetened the emotion with minor chords II, III or VI (Dm, Em or Am). Listen to 'Can't Buy Me Love', 'I Feel Fine', and 'Hard Day's Night'. 'You Can't Do That' has a brilliant bridge in which the sharp-talking bluesy swagger of the verse lapses momentarily into vulnerability:

III maj	VI	II	III	I	III maj	VI	II	III	V
B7	Em	Am	Bm	G7	B7	Em	Am	Bm	D

The fleeting modulation to a wounded Em is cancelled out by the surly G7 (Em needs F# and G7 has an F on top).

Lyrically, the middle eight might give a new or different slant to the theme – perhaps leading to a realisation that will be settled in the last verse. A middle eight might be full of questions that are answered in the song's conclusion.

Last Chorus

Since the chorus is the beating heart of the pop song, songs often end with several of them back to back. Assuming that there is a coda and not just a fade-out on the chorus itself, last choruses often have a little extra something to spice them up. You can do this through the arrangement itself, adding more instruments, maybe changing a word or two in the lyric, adding more voices, etc. The cheapest trick in the book is to ratchet up the excitement by changing key up a semi-tone (half-step) or tone (full step). This is discussed in section 10.

Reharmonizing is a delightful way of adding interest to a final chorus. This means the melody stays the same (or nearly the same) but the underlying chords are changed. This can be very expressive. In 'Don't Dream It's Over', the first two choruses use a IV V I VI sequence (F G C Am), but the third chorus is II III I VI (Dm Em C Am). The first two major chords, F and G, have turned into their relative minors. This adds a sudden, tragic note that heightens the emotional effect. (Wisely, they do it only once.) In the consciously Beatlesque 'This Year's Model', we have the line "All this but no surprises for this year's girl" that is harmonized IV V I (F G C). In the last choruses, it is reharmonized IV V I VI (F G C Am), IV V III VI (F G Em Am) and finally IV V I again. The appearance of the minor chords adds an exquisite emotional flourish that suggests the speaker has more sympathy with the beleaguered model than the song has let on.

The Outro or Coda

All good things, even great 45s, have an ending. Sad but true.

After the last chorus, you have to find a way to finish. The time-honoured pop tradition is to fade out on repetitions of the chorus. This is effective, especially if you want to leave an impression of the music going on forever – a profound metaphysical idea, that. Perhaps the chorus of 'God Only Knows' eternally echoes in the mind of God (along with everything else, of course!). Using a fade does mean, however, that if you perform the song live you'll have to think of an ending later.

Occasionally songs fade out and then come back. 'In Every Dream Home A Heartache' fades out on a solo and then, after a few seconds of silence, returns in a blizzard of phasing. This was obviously not designed for radio, as it is liable to catch the DJ in the middle of the next announcement. One of my favourite endings is the "tape-cut". Love's 'A House Is Not A Motel' has a coda consisting of two duelling electric guitars playing solos that are unrelated to each other. The song abruptly ceases as if the tape had vanished. (Whoever faded this out on the CD pressing deserves to be shot).

Some codas merely reprise the chorus instrumentally, with vocal ad libs or another solo, or have another refrain over the music for the chorus, or use the intro sequence. Many songs have a refrain so you can join in. Extended instrumental codas can create an engaging mood of their own, as with 'More Than This', 'Step Into My World', 'Hotel California', 'Freebird', 'Tunnel Of Love' and 'Thunder Road'.

The Smiths' 'Panic' reaches its coda at a mere 1:42, with a satirical use of kids' voices – satirical because kids are so often used on ghastly pop records. In 'Panic' the kids get their revenge with the gleeful refrain of "Hang the DJ." Alice Cooper's 'Department of Youth' ends with an amusing call-and-response routine in which he asks, "Who's got the power?" and they answer, "We do!" Eventually he adds, "And who gave it to you?" to which they reply, "Donny Osmond." "Whaaat!" screams the appalled and betrayed Alice.

A few hit records have had codas longer than the main part of the song. In 'Hey Jude', the "la la" coda goes on for several minutes. Another No. 1 single with a long coda was T.Rex's 'Hot Love', where the verse was used for another "la la" coda. The full-length version of 'Layla' has a long instrumental coda that introduces new melodic ideas; it was edited out from the single.

If a coda does not fade, the last chord is usually the key chord: major for a happy ending, minor for a sad one. The precise form of the last chord I will contribute to the effect – the dom7 is hard, the maj7 soft, the sus2 empty, the sus4 tense, the maj6 slightly jazzy. The dominant chord is a viable alternative that gives a pleasing feeling of suspension, of stopping somewhere new but not unrelated. 'When You're Gone' is in C but ends on an F, chord IV, leaving you with the feeling that it has changed key.

Approaching chord I via the minor form of IV is fine for slushy, romantic finishes. You can hear this in the weeping melodrama at the end of 'The Kick Inside', where Kate Bush implies the singer's suicide by ending with IV to IVm. It is also at the end of 'I Got The Blues' by the Stones. Use Fm7 to Cmaj7 voicings for more slush than a New York winter. There is a centuries-old tradition of ending a minor-key song on the tonic major for a redemptive gesture, technically known as a tierce de picardie. The opposite – ending a major song on a minor chord – is disconcerting. 'From Me To You' is in C but ends on Am. Does the lyric justify the minor chord? The penultimate chord of 'The One I Love' (E Bb D# G B E, which can be called Em/maj7/addb5) is certainly notable before the final Em.

In 1990s UK chart music, it became fashionable to end with a solo vocal. 'A Design For Life' had the unusual ending of drums only.

STRUCTURES

Having looked at the individual bits of songs, it is time to consider different ways of piecing them together.

The Groove Song

Dance music has given us the groove song. It does not even have a chord sequence, because for long stretches it stays on one chord. James Brown tracks such as 'Sex Machine' are a good example, as are some of John Lee Hooker's blues tunes. This approach can also be used just for the verse, as in 'Erotica'.

The Loop

The simplest song structures are no more than four- or eight-bar loops that simply repeat. Boredom is regulated to acceptable (ie, non-psychotic hi-fi/radio smashing) levels by the manipulation of the arrangement to make it sound as though the sections are different. 'I Will Survive' is an eight-bar sequence of eight chords (I IV bVII IIImaj7 bVImaj7 IIm7b5 Vsus4 V) that spins round memorably until Ms Gaynor disappears down the hole in the middle. 'With Or Without You' is a I V VI IV turnaround that gradually gathers in intensity thanks to a highly dynamic arrangement. 'Justify My Love' is essentially a four-bar loop with breaks created by pulling out everything except voice and drums.

Rarely, a lyric will justify this type of structure. 'I Was Made To Love Her' is little more than a four-bar five-chord turnaround, with only a brief four-bar break to interrupt the flow. The simplicity of structure expresses the theme of unchanging truth. He's loved this girl from childhood and nothing will change their love. Any risk of tedium is avoided through the sheer quality of the musicianship, whether it be Stevie Wonder's exhilarated vocal, the lovely guitar fills or James Jamerson's astonishing bassline.

Standard Structures

1 Verse Verse Verse Verse
Strophic form common in old ballads, blues and folk music. The hook may be a short refrain tacked on at the end of each verse. The intro might be no more than a few bars on the key chord. 'Simple Twist Of Fate' is a good modern example.

2 Intro Verse Verse Bridge Verse Bridge Verse
This form was favoured by The Beatles in the early years of their career. Again, the hook is part of the verse itself. One of the bridges or Verse 3 could be

instrumental rather than vocal. The last verse is likely to have the hook repeated. There is an old formula for a 32-bar song that goes: Verse 1, eight bars; Verse 2, eight bars; Bridge, eight bars; Verse 3, eight bars.

3 Intro Verse Chorus Verse Chorus Verse Chorus Coda or fade

4 Intro Verse Chorus Verse   Chorus Bridge Chorus Coda or fade

5 Intro Verse Chorus Verse Chorus Bridge Verse Chorus Coda or fade

6 Intro Verse Chorus Bridge Verse Chorus Coda or fade
This is the structure of the single version of 'More Than A Feeling'. This edited version is much snappier than the album track, offering a good example of how radio edits are often aesthetically right, too.

7 Intro Chorus Verse Chorus Bridge Verse Chorus Coda or fade
This is a radio-friendly format because it starts with the chorus.

8 Intro Verse Verse Verse Solo/Bridge Verse Extended Coda

9 Intro riff Chorus Verse Verse Chorus Coda on intro riff
Used by The Byrds for their adaptation of Dylan's 'Mr. Tambourine Man'.

10 Intro Verse 1 Verse 2 Verse 3 Verse 4 Solo Verse 2 Verse 3 Verse 4
This is the structure of Smokey Robinson's 'The Hunter Gets Captured by the Game'. What's interesting is that it never returns to Verse 1 (in D major); the rest of the song is in B minor. Each verse is short, and in the Marvelettes' version the whole thing comes in under three minutes.

Remember that it is perfectly possible to either cut a first chorus in half, or to cut a second or third verse in half, in order to tighten up a song's structure.

Other Types of Structure

When thinking about structure, it is important to keep sight of the overall "shape" of a song. A song may have a dynamic curve that over-rides its verse/chorus sections, as in the case of 'With Or Without You', 'You'll Never Walk Alone' and 'It's Over', songs that build to a climax and then ebb away or stop. It's important to realize that songs can be made to seem almost seamless – 'This Used To Be My Playground' is a good example. In too much recent songwriting, the "joins" between sections are all too obvious.

Some of Springsteen's longer early songs, such as 'Rosalita' and 'Jungleland', have complex structures with many dynamic moments of crescendo and ebb. These were written with live performance in mind and partly influenced by the "soul revue" approach. Meatloaf is a performer who has, against the odds, made a career out of batty (pun intended) long numbers that are like mini-operas. In rock, there are such unconventionally structured songs as 'Paranoid Android', 'Bohemian Rhapsody' (and its lesser-known precursor, 'March Of The Black Queen'), 'Happiness Is A Warm Gun', 'Stairway To Heaven' and 'Band On The Run'. Be warned, however – that way, the rock opera and concept album lie!

If you have never written a song, it can seem daunting to listen to a piece three or four minutes long and think, How am I going to invent all that? It is much easier to reflect on how long each section is. Let's say we need an intro, a verse, a chorus and a bridge: 4 + 8 (twice) + 4 (twice or four times) + 8. That's a total of only 24 bars of music for the whole song. Cut down to size songwriting need not seem so difficult.

Rhythm is a vital aspect of popular music. In fact, it is one of the things that makes popular music popular. Rhythm is fundamental to human consciousness. In the womb, we grow to the beat of our mother's heart. Everyday activities have rhythm – walking, or tapping our fingers on a table. Rhythm can be intoxicating, and it can carry people out of themselves. Armies march to the sound of drums, and some religious rituals have used drums to assist with the inducing of trance and altered states of consciousness. The overtly rhythmic nature of rock music itself was characterised by some critics in the 1950s as primitive, a reversion to the jungle.

In classical music, the beat is implicit. A conductor signals the beats with waves of a baton, but rarely do classical pieces have a percussion instrument marking every beat. Percussion is deployed at specific moments in order to accent a theme or a dynamic change. By employing the drum kit (and, more recently, the drum machine), popular music has insisted on making the beat explicit. This is part of its long-established connection with dance. In any music intended for dancing, which much popular music always has been, rhythm is obviously important. But a catchy rhythm can do more than just set your feet tapping; it can be an important part of what makes a song memorable.

Songs Driven by Rhythm

In Section 1 we looked at this formula:

a song = lyric + melody + harmony + rhythm

Occasionally, we hear a hit song where the rhythm seems more important than anything else. This might be because of an unusual drum pattern or percussion instrument, or because of a stark arrangement that exposes the drums. Much dance music – from 1960s R&B, Stax, James Brown, Motown and funk to 1970s Philly and disco to 1990s dance tracks – centers on rhythm. The drum track is usually loud in the mix, and the harmonic and melodic elements are secondary. The impulse to reduce the melodic and harmonic elements of popular music as much as possible has created genres like drum'n'bass.

The Chemical Brothers' 'Loops Of Fury' offers a good example of this reductionism. The instrumental lasts 4:38 and its harmonic content is nothing more than a riff with a couple of variations based on a I-bVII change in B. The various sections are largely differentiated by the presence or absence of the drum track. A breakdown of the structure looks like this:

A: Intro: riff 1, one bar, no drums (x4)
A: riff 1, drums in (x8)
B: riff 2, one bar (x16)
C: synth figure (x16)
D: drum break, four bars
C: (x8)
E: drum break, vocal sample (x2)
C: (x8)
F: [E] drum break (x8)
C: (x8)
E: (x2)
C: (x8)
G: synth figure 2 (x7) + one bar drums
F: (x4)
C: with EQ effects (x16)
B: riff 2 (x16)

The rigidity is typical of 1990s dance music. Notice how the "tyranny of four" is in full operation, with section lengths based on multiples of four, with the added reductive factor of individual sections usually consisting of a single bar repeated. The tempo is unvarying and the drums simply enter and exit at the mixing stage, without any warning fills.

Fat Boy Slim's 'Praise Him' is similar. It consists of two riffs: the first is bVII IV I in G over two bars; the second is I IV bVII in D for one bar. The first riff is repeated something like 43 times and the second 32 times. Almost all the sections repeat four times, occasionally eight. Only the abrupt addition or subtraction of percussion, or bass, or a guitar phrase, varies the arrangement. The musical basis of the song is little more than three bars. Dreadzone's 'Little Britain' takes a two-bar two chord phrase and repeats it over 70 times.

The singles charts have from time to time featured records that push percussion to the front of the mix. This includes tracks such as 'Message Of Love', 'Waterfront', 'Sat In Your Lap' and the claps and foot-stomping of 'Baby Love' and 'Cecilia'. There have been chants like 'Neanderthal Man' (1970), recorded by members of the as-yet unformed 10cc. In 1971, 'Burundi Black' brought the sound of African drumming to the UK chart, later used on Joni Mitchell's *The Hissing Of Summer Lawns* and Adam Ant's 'Kings Of The Wild Frontier'. That same year also saw two hit singles by the South African John Kongos, 'Tokoloshe Man' and 'He's Gonna Step On You Again' (covered as 'Step On' by the Happy Mondays), both with an African rhythmic influence. Glam rock picked up on the "tribal" vibe, as heard on records such as 'Rock And Roll', 'Devilgate Drive', 'We Will Rock You', 'New York Groove' (in a Bo Diddley style) and 'Dance With The Devil'. Alan Stivell's electric folk on *From Celtic Roots* drew on unusual rhythms. Further on in the 1970s there was 'Tusk'. Peter Gabriel and Phil Collins both pursued a different drum approach, temporarily banning cymbals from their recordings. On *Ju-Ju*, Siouxsie & The Banshees imitated non-Western drumming patterns. The influence of world music in the 1990s has increased the variety of rhythms heard in popular music, and even heavy rockers like Page and Plant used Moroccan drum loops for the *No Quarter* project.

The Elements of Rhythm: Time Signature

Music is written in a time signature. Just as the key signature tells you which notes to sharpen or flat in a given key, so the time signature tells you how many beats there are in a bar. This is the pulse of the music. Here is a diagram of basic note values and rests.

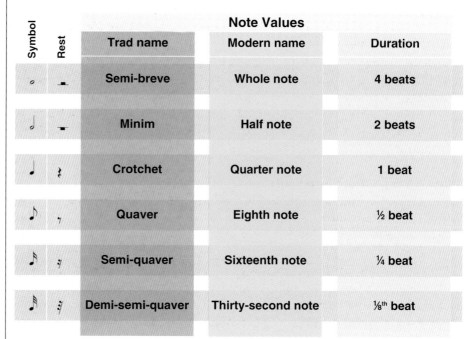

Symbol	Rest	Note Values		
		Trad name	**Modern name**	**Duration**
𝅝	▬	Semi-breve	Whole note	4 beats
𝅗𝅥	▬	Minim	Half note	2 beats
𝅘𝅥	𝄽	Crotchet	Quarter note	1 beat
𝅘𝅥𝅮	𝄾	Quaver	Eighth note	½ beat
𝅘𝅥𝅯	𝄿	Semi-quaver	Sixteenth note	¼ beat
𝅘𝅥𝅰	𝅀	Demi-semi-quaver	Thirty-second note	⅛th beat

Simple Time

The most common time signature in popular song is 4/4, a form of what is known as "simple time" where the beats are marked by quarter-notes/crotchets. Other simple times include 3/4, typified by the waltz dance form, and 2/4. Well-known songs in 3/4 include 'Amazing Grace', 'Mull Of Kintyre', 'America', 'Annie's Song' and 'Only Love Can Break Your Heart'. 'It's All In The Game' was originally in 3/4 but the Four Tops turned it into 4/4. Even a hard rock song in 6/4 tends to have a languid feel – witness Soundgarden's 'Fell On Black Days'. The difference between a bar of 6/4 and adjoining bars of 4/4 and 2/4 is one of emphasis. The first beat of any bar has more stress than the remaining beats in that bar, so the 4/4 + 2/4 combination is *one* two three four *one* two and the 6/4 bar is *one* two three four five six.

A 6/4 bar is useful if you want to heighten expectation for the start of a section by making the listener wait another two beats:

| I | . | VI | . | V | . | IV | . | . | . |

It is difficult to write a song in an odd-numbered time signature such as 5/4 or 7/4. It can be done, though, and hit singles in 5/4 include 'Living In The Past' and the Dave Brubeck Quartet's instrumental 'Take Five'. (Note that these two came from the jazz and progressive rock fields.) The 1960s TV theme for *Mission Impossible* is also in 5/4 time – but when it was re-recorded for the 1990s film version, it was changed to 4/4, losing the asymmetry of the original. Pink Floyd used 7/4 for 'Money'. Led Zeppelin's 'Four Sticks' is a memorable example of a hard rock tune in 5/4 and 'The Ocean' has bars of 7/8 (4/4 minus an 8th note). Although they did feature the occasional odd time signature, some of Zep's weirder timings were made in 4/4 by shifting the accent. This can be heard in 'Black Dog' and in the link from the guitar solo back to the guitar riff in 'Over The Hills And Far Away'.

Compound Time

In compound time a dotted note marks the beat, allowing it to be subdivided into three instead of two. This creates an immediately recognisable "swing" feel. Like 4/4, 12/8 has four beats in a bar, but each one is a dotted quarter-note/crotchet. This is the most popular compound time signature, especially in blues and blues-influenced songs. After this, 6/8 is sometimes used, and others are possible. Notable songs in 12/8 include 'You Don't Have To Say You Love Me', 'I Got You Babe', 'Just Like A Woman', '2000 Miles', 'I Go To Sleep', 'Yes It Is' and 'This Boy'.

At slower tempos, it's often difficult to distinguish 6/8 from 3/4. In 6/8, there should be a feeling of two beats to a bar with each divided into three. Whether 6/8 or 3/4, the "three pulse" is felt in songs such as 'House Of The Rising Sun', 'Nights In White Satin', 'Delilah' and 'Anyone Who Had A Heart'. Hendrix gave us 'Manic Depression' in churning 9/8. Time signatures like 5/8 and 7/8 are rarely heard.

Contrasting Time Signatures

Just as changing the key can inject new dimensions into a song, so can contrasting time signatures. This is not popular in dance-oriented music because it tends to embarrass the dancers, who may lose the beat. It was delightfully mischievous of R.E.M. not only to start 'Shiny Happy People' in 6/8 and then go to 4/4, but to drop back into 6/8 for an instrumental bridge halfway through.

Changing time has never been common in popular music, and the advent of the drum machine has made it even less so. There is one time-change effect that you can use relatively easily with a drum machine, and that's "half-time" or "double time", where instead of treating the quarter-note as the beat you take the quaver (eighth-note) or the minim (half-note) as the beat. Note that the tempo does not change, only the rhythmic emphasis and the interpretation of the pattern the drum machine plays. This is even more effective if 4/4 becomes 12/8. The machine maintains tempo, but each quarter-note beat is divided into three. Therefore you have "slowed" the tempo by playing against it.

'Shout' and 'Suspicious Minds' mix 4/4 with 12/8. 'Dedicated To The One I Love' mixes 6/8 and 4/4. 'White Room' has an intro and bridge in 5/4 while its verses are in 4/4. 'Kiss From A Rose' mixed 6/8 and 9/8. 'Those Were The Days' has a verse in 4/4 and a chorus in 2/4.

Other Rhythmic Options

Rhythm can be altered without a change of time signature. In simple time, beats can be temporarily divided into triplets or 16th-note triplets (grouped in six). Quarter-notes can be played three in the time of two, allowing six to be played in a 4/4 bar. This is a common effect in Latin American music, and Madonna used it in 'La Isla Bonita'. Springsteen has one of these on the word "edge" in the chorus of 'Darkness On The Edge Of Town'. Conversely, you can force compound into simple time by having four eighths (a quadruplet) on a beat – think of the chorus of 'Dedicated To The One I Love' after "baby" and before "whisper". Either of these can be melodically arresting or at least hold up the relentless march of 4/4 for a bit.

Tempo

It is important to distinguish between tempo and time signature. A time signature does not specify the speed – the fact that a song is in 4/4 doesn't tell you whether it is slow or fast. Only the tempo does that. Tempo is measured in beats per minute. This is indicated on sheet music by the sign of [crotchet/quarter-note] = 120bpm. Anything under roughly 90bpm can be thought of as on the slow side;

90-130 is medium tempo; anything above 130 is fast.

Decide on a tempo early in the songwriting process. Often a musical idea will come to you with an implicit tempo. Make a note of this, either by using a drum machine or a metronome. Once you have planned your song, count the number of bars in each section and add the total. Establish the tempo and if the song is in 4/4 divide that number by 4. You will have the number of bars per minute. Here's an example:

> SONG: i (4) + v (16) + ch (8) + v2 (16) + ch (8) + b (8) + v3 (8) + ch (8) + ch (8) = 84 bars

At a tempo of 100bpm it takes a minute to play 25 bars, so this song will take just under three minutes. This is a handy check if you want the song to be a certain length. It is also a helpful "early warning system" if you tend to write songs that are too long (a common fault in amateur songwriting). Shortening songs is good discipline. Always ask yourself if you (your listener, EMI or the world) really need that fourth verse or fifth chorus. "Leave 'em wanting more" is a sound adage. One of the best comments people can make about a song is, "It's great but it's too short."

Here's another tip: After you've finished writing a song and are ready to record the first tracks of drums and rhythm guitar, always try playing it faster. Increase the tempo slowly and see how far you can go before the tempo is incompatible with the mood of the song. You will be surprised how often a song will benefit from being played slightly faster than the speed at which it first came to you. Bands often discover this when they play a new song live. This is often true of ballads, where slow tempos increase the risk of boredom.

Tempo Performance Variation

Tempo performance variation or "TPV" – meaning, slowing down or speeding up – is the kind of sarcastic numbskull term that might have been dreamed up by the sort of misguided producer who believes everyone should record to a click track.

Before the advent of click tracks in studios, it was perfectly normal for band performances to speed up slightly, especially through excitement. Rock music is supposed to be exciting, after all. This effect can be approximated when recording with a drum machine by increased the tempo setting by 1bpm at the start of a given section. Don't increase by too much or it will be noticeable. When you record instrumental tracks against this, you must listen carefully for this point and adjust your playing in response to the machine.

The Mechanization of Rhythm

It is true that drum machines are wonderful for home recording. You may be lucky enough to know a drummer with the invention of Stewart Copeland, the power of John Bonham or the explosive force of Keith Moon. Unfortunately, though, if you stick this drummer in your home studio/front room/flat, the neighbours are not going to be very happy.

That said, click tracks and drum machines are two of the worst things ever to happen to popular music. First, drum machines – like all machines – are expressionless in the true sense. No human being is behind the sound at the moment that sound is made. Of course, the technology is a human artefact, and the programming carries human intention that may contain aesthetic expression. But it is the machine that executes the actual music. The essential link in the moment of performance between the soul and sound waves is not there. The music is literally "soul-less". It is a huge irony that "beatboxes" came to dominate a type of music that once termed itself "soul".

Second, both click tracks and drum machines force an inhuman straitjacket onto music-making. Much of the prejudice against popular music that exists in the field of so-called "serious music" is based on a mixture of ignorance, cultural brainwashing and an inadequate critical vocabulary with which to describe how popular music achieves its greatest effects. But with regard to tempo, for once, the reaction of the classical musician is right on the money. If you suggested to an orchestra that they could improve their performance of a Beethoven symphony or a Rachmaninov piano concerto with a click track, so they would all be perfectly in time, they would fall off their stools laughing. When they recovered, they would insist that your click track idea would, at one digital stroke, remove all the expression from the music. In order for music to "breathe", performers must be free to pause slightly before a chord or modulation or phrase. Classical scores are full of terms such as *accelerando, ritenuto, rallentando, a tempo* – all of which indicate departures from strict time. In other words, "TPV" is an essential element of music performance. Why should popular music be any different?

Since the mid-1980s, popular music has become increasingly mechanized. It has lost the beautiful rhythmic effects achieved in a song such as 'Wouldn't It Be Nice'. If you want an example of the potential beauty of this, listen to 'I Close My Eyes And Count To Ten'. It starts at approximately 106bpm, quickens to 111bpm and then, at 0:53 and again at 2:06, all the instruments pull up sharply. Notice the emotional "weight" this gives the music, much like the mild G-force you feel while standing up on a train as it brakes into a station.

One effective rhythm technique is to have an opening section in a kind of "free time" where the performer dictates the length of phrases, as with 'American Pie'. Some records speed up deliberately, as with 'Goody Two-Shoes'. Dylan's 'Tangled Up In Blue' starts at about 93bpm but ends at 100bpm. Siouxsie & The Banshees' 'Sin In My Heart' starts at 120bpm, reaches 144bpm just before the vocals enter, moves up to 150bpm in the verse and by the end is hurtling along at 162bpm. 'Stay With Me' starts at a fast tempo of approximately 164bpm, drops to 89bpm for its verses and choruses and then goes back to the faster tempo for the coda. There are tempo changes in 'Fire', 'Here Comes The Night', 'Question' and 'For Your Love'.

The Principle of Rhythmic Asymmetry

Inserting 3/4, 5/6 or 6/4 bars into a song can be an effective way of resisting the "tyranny of four", which in rhythmic terms usually means the predictable symmetry of 4/4. As mentioned above, such inserted bars can be used to support the development of the lyric, the melody or the harmonic progression, and to arouse or deflate expectation. A bar of 3/4 on the end of a verse will make a 4/4 chorus arrive one beat earlier than you expected.

Here are some examples of songs with "insert bars": 'All The Young Dudes' has a chorus that ends with a bar of 3/4; this was copied by Oasis for 'Stand By Me'. 'I Love Rock'n'Roll' has a 3/4 bar in its chorus, and 'Strawberry Fields Forever' has a 3/4 bar in its verse. 'Lily The Pink' includes a bar of 6/4 to illustrate a stammer. 'Ha! Ha! Said The Clown' drops a beat in the verse. There are 2/4 bars in 'See Emily Play', 'Farewell, Farewell' and 'Ain't Nothing Like The Real Thing'. Two bars of what Ian MacDonald vividly dubbed "hard-braking" 3/8 end 'I Wanna Hold Your Hand'. 'Blackbird' has 2/4 and 3/4 bars in a 4/4 meter. 'If You Leave Me Now' and 'Pretty Woman' have 2/4 bars. The choruses of 'Knowing Me, Knowing You', 'Jealous Guy' and 'Tragedy' have bars of 2/4 . The Indian influences on 'Within You Without You' show up in its mix of 2/4, 3/4,

↓ strum down
↑ strum up

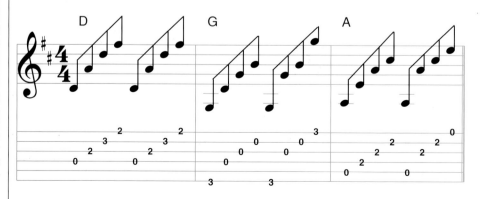

(↓) = percussive hit of dampened strings

Simple upward pick

4/4 and 5/4 bars. Hendrix's 'All Along The Watchtower' has been notated with a bar of 9/8 as the first complete bar where there is lead guitar because of an anomaly in the rhythm. Whether this was deliberate or an accident is a moot point – but try counting 4/4 through this section and you will find it does not work.

In folk music and some blues there is a recognized practice of making the gaps between phrases an irregular length. This would create chaos in an ensemble because the other musicians wouldn't know what you were going to do. For solo performers, though, it's an option. It can be heard in performances by singers such as John Lee Hooker and the early Bob Dylan. You sing a line, wait however many beats you feel like and then sing the next line.

Rhythm on the Guitar: Strumming

Most guitarists learn to strum without thinking about what they're actually doing. A strummed guitar fulfills two functions: one is rhythmic, the other harmonic. The harmonic function is to supply a "wash" of sound relating to a chord, the equivalent of holding a chord on a keyboard. But because the guitar does not have much sustain, the notes will die unless they are struck again. Repeated striking sustains the presence of the chord. The relationship between strumming technique and sustain can be vividly heard on the mandolin, where rapid strumming is required to keep the notes "present". Violinists solve this problem when they draw a bow across the string, continually exciting it to vibrate.

The rhythmic function has two components: the rhythm with which the chords are produced and the percussive attack (usually produced by a pick) on the guitar strings. Both aspects are important for solo performers accompanying themselves on the guitar. Guitarists working with a rhythm section or recording with a variety of instruments need to realize, though, that they no longer have to carry the whole of the rhythm with their strumming.

Good strumming patterns balance tempo against sustain. At a slow tempo, you hit the strings more frequently because the chords die away. At faster tempos, you might not need to hit them so often, unless like Jimmy Nolan or Nile Rodgers your guitar part is at least as significant for its percussive effect as for its harmonic effect.

To experiment with strumming, try first strumming eighths down and up, as in Example 1, and then start to subtract some of the strums to produce different effects.

Fingerpicking

Fingerpicking is a technique popular in less rhythmic arrangements and styles. It is vulnerable to being drowned out by a loud mix. It is typically used in light arrangements where the notes will be audible, often in ballads. It is well suited to solo performance, since it offers the chance for a single guitarist to play a bassline, a harmony and even a melody, all at once.

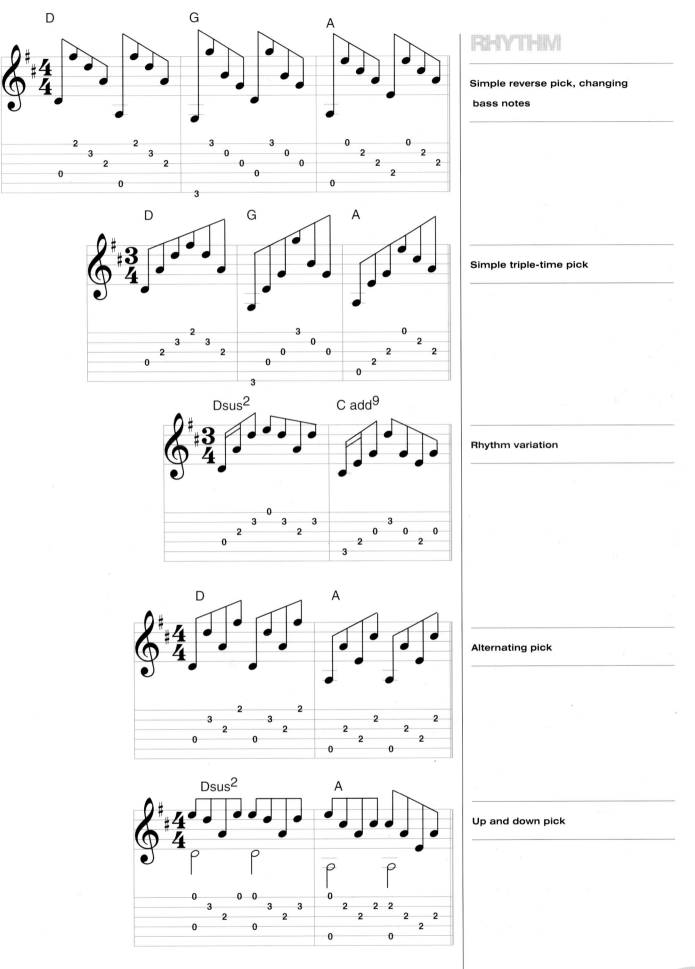

RHYTHM

Simple reverse pick, changing bass notes

Simple triple-time pick

Rhythm variation

Alternating pick

Up and down pick

RHYTHM

Thickening, ascending

Thickening, descending

Rhythm variation

Syncopated, alternating thumb

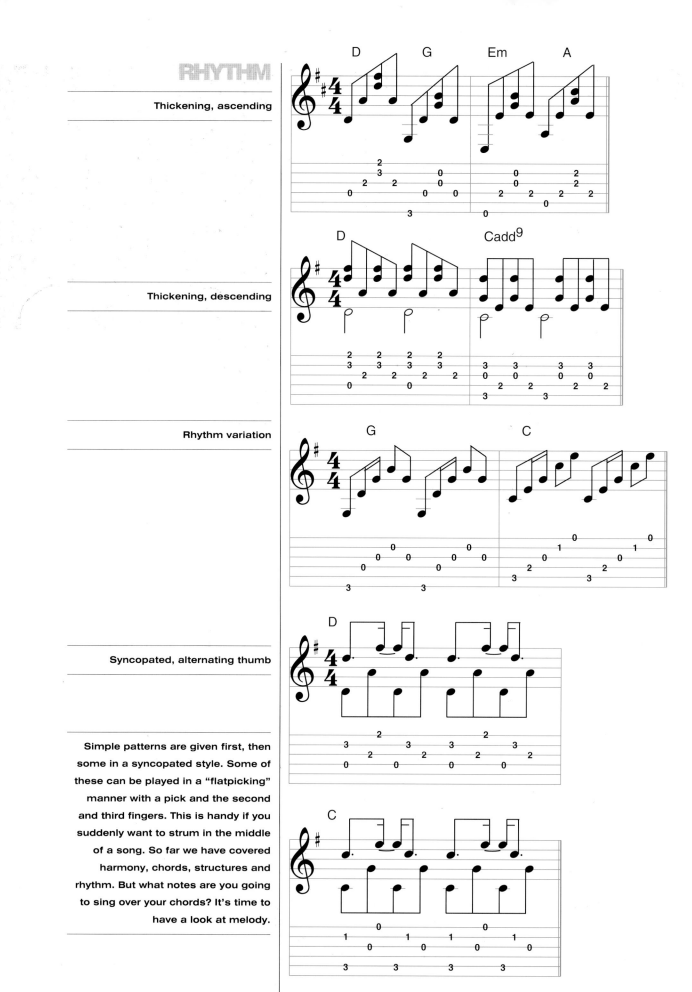

Simple patterns are given first, then some in a syncopated style. Some of these can be played in a "flatpicking" manner with a pick and the second and third fingers. This is handy if you suddenly want to strum in the middle of a song. So far we have covered harmony, chords, structures and rhythm. But what notes are you going to sing over your chords? It's time to have a look at melody.

More than anything else, melody impresses a song into the minds of its listeners. You hear people singing a popular song in the street, taking pleasure in recalling the tune. So what makes a good melody?

Great melodies have a certain magic about them. They sound and feel right. They fit with the lyric in such a way that it seems inevitable that those notes had to go with those words. Perhaps more than any other aspect of songwriting, writing a great melody is a matter of inspiration. Even so, an appreciation of the shape of melodies, their rhythm and their relationship to the chords that harmonize them will help you to write better ones, and to improve those you have already composed.

How do you know which notes will fit with which chords? Many good songwriters have an "ear" for this, sometimes backed up with no theoretical knowledge at all. For the rest of us, an understand· of a few fundamental principles for harmonizing a tune can help.

HARMONIZING NOTES

Melody notes have three basic relationships with their accompanying chords. We can describe these as "sits inside", "sits outside" and "sits against".

1 **"Sits Inside"** is where a given melody note is the 1, 3 or 5 of a chord. This means that if you strum a C chord, your melody note will be C, E or G. If the chord is A minor, the melody note would be A, C or E. A melody note that sits inside blends perfectly because it is part of the chord. If the chord has more than three notes, you could sing the additional note of the harmony. For example, if you sing B against a Cmaj7 chord – C E G B – the note still sits inside, though not so perfectly as 1, 3 or 5. The more complex the chord, the weaker the effect.

2 **"Sits Outside"** is where you use one of the notes of the scale apart from 1, 3 and 5. If you are in the key of C major and singing over a C major chord, you would sing D, F, A or B. Each of these has a slightly different quality in relation to the chord, but they all sound more or less tense. You will feel that they want to move to one of the notes of the chord and sit inside the harmony. This tension can be very expressive. If you listen to the end of 'Good Year For The Roses', you can hear Costello come down to the key note (1) and then move off it onto 2 for a more expressive finish.

The strength of the tension will also depend on how long you remain on that note. Melodies consist of a mixture of notes that belong to a chord and those that don't. The notes that sit outside often occur as brief passing notes lasting only a beat or less. Their tension is momentary. If you stay on such a note for more than a beat over a chord that does not change, then the tension is much stronger.

If a melody were written using only the notes of the major and minor triads in the harmony, it would run the risk of sounding bland and too comfortable. Music needs tension to give it drama and make it capable of fully expressing the range and complexity of human feelings. Tension, asymmetry and dissonance are essential to this. That's why the notes of many good melodies move constantly from "inside" to "outside".

3 "**Sits Against**" is where you choose a note that is not even part of the scale. In C major, this would mean Db, Eb, F#, Ab and Bb. These are very dissonant (try singing F# against a C chord), but the flattened third and flattened seventh notes (Eb and Bb) are common in popular music. These are the so-called "blue notes". Singing them against C major is permitted if the music has a blues influence. The harmonic discrepancy between them and the scale creates an effect that our ears understand as "blues". This can be over-used in an all-too-predictable attempt at being "soulful", in which case it is merely the exploitation of a formula. Properly used, these notes can be evocative. 'Army Of Me' implies the key of C minor (C D Eb F G Ab Bb), but the main melodic phrase has a recurring Db that fits the threatening mood of the song.

Here's a summary of the three types of note related to a C chord (I = sits inside; O = sits outside; A = sits against):

1	b2	2	b3	3	4	#4	5	#5	6	b7	7
C	Db	D	Eb	E	F	F#	G	G#	A	Bb	B
I	A	O	A	I	O	A	I	A	O	A	O

You may well be thinking at this point, Does this mean that composers think about all this stuff when they write a tune? Did Lennon and McCartney have exchanges when they were writing 'Ticket To Ride' in which Lennon said (imagine the Liverpool accent), "Yer can't sing that note, Paul. It's a 'sits inside' note – it's too dull. Yer want a note that 'sits outside.'"? Of course not. Most melodies are written instinctively, following words or chords or both, or by just humming something the writer "hears" internally. But the ability to focus on a couple of notes or a phrase and then apply some of these concepts is good craft. It can add a touch of polish to the finished song.

Knowledge of other melodic tricks and approaches can also be helpful for starting a tune. It is possible to write a two-bar melodic fragment and then develop the rest of the melody from that initial idea. Much of this you will do intuitively. But, sometimes, awareness can be brought to bear on a melody to get a better result.

OTHER MELODIC FEATURES
Contour

It is important to cultivate an aesthetic sensitivity to melody. Try listening to melodies that really please you. What is it about them that does this? Listen for the rise and fall of a melody, the use of intervals, step-wise movements, rhythm, repetition, arpeggio figures (moving up and down the notes of a chord) and so on.

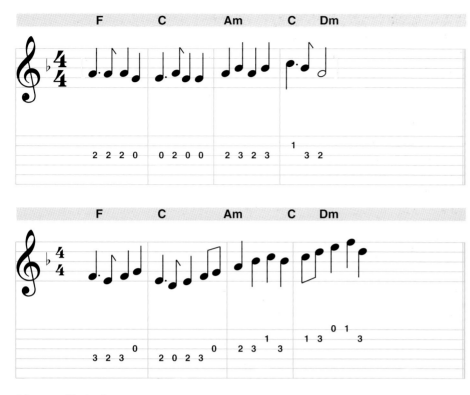

Linear

Stepwise, rising

Linear Melody

Some melodies lie within a narrow range. Imagine writing a song in C major in which you used only the notes C, D, E and the B below C. The entire melody would be spanned by no more than two-and-a-half tones (full steps). This might work, but it runs the risk of not sustaining our interest. Narrow-range melodies are sometimes the result of vocal limitations. Partly for this reason they are more common in male singer-songwriter material. As mentioned in section one, Bob Dylan, Jackson Browne and Bruce Springsteen have written many songs that exhibit linear, narrow-range melody. In Springsteen's case, it comes as a shock when he does a non-linear melody, as on 'Sad Eyes', where the chorus has what is for him an unexpected and beautiful melodic leap. It might be argued that The Verve's 'History' and 'This Time' are both flawed by melodies which spend too long on a single note.

For a different perspective, listen to the chorus of 'I Want You Back', where "Won't you please help me" is sung on the note C. This works because each note is harmonized with a different chord:

Note:	C	C	C	C	C
Chord:	Fm	Cm	Db	Ab	Bbm
Chord in Ab:	VI	III	IV	I	II
Chord note:	5	1	7	3	2
Sits:	I	I	O	I	O

The harmonic value of the note C changes with each chord.

SECTION 7

Linear melodies that remain on one note for a long time can sound "trippy" with the right backing; 'Tomorrow Never Knows' and 'I Am The Walrus' are good examples. 'Helter Skelter' and 'Sgt Pepper' both stay for quite a while on a single note within each chord change. Songs such as 'Give Peace A Chance', 'The Sensual World', 'Subterranean Homesick Blues' and 'It's The End Of The World As We Know It' use linear melody to put greater emphasis on their lyrics. 'Pump It Up' features a verse sung almost entirely on one note for a punchy effect. The T.Rex hits 'Ride A White Swan', 'Get It On' and 'Telegram Sam' use a narrow range of notes like the Chuck Berry songs on which they were modelled.

Vertical Melody

Vertical

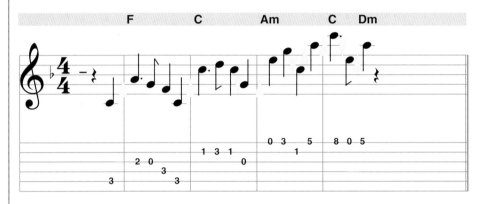

Vertical melodies are those in which large interval leaps occur quite frequently and the notes span more than an octave. These are often written by female singer-songwriters such as Joni Mitchell, Kate Bush and Tori Amos, who usually have more range to exploit than their male counterparts (though there are notable exceptions, such as Sting, Smokey Robinson, Leo Sayer and Colin Blunstone). 'Penny Lane', 'In My Life', 'There She Goes', 'Jesamine' and 'Alfie' are songs with strong vertical melodies.

Melodies built on the notes of a chord (arpeggios) will tend to be vertical. Burt Bacharach's melodies often develop chordal melodic ideas. Think of the opening of 'Close To You', with its leap of E G D against a C chord. The first two notes sit inside, but the last one sits outside and creates an expressive tension.

Chordal

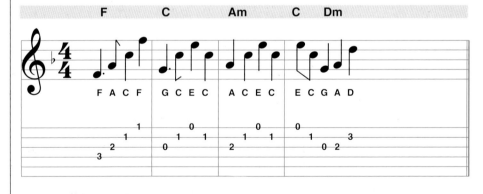

One effective way to start a melody is with an interval leap – anything bigger than a fourth. The most dramatic is the octave, as in the Rodgers and Hammerstein tune 'Bali Hai' from the musical South Pacific and Led Zeppelin's 'Immigrant Song', where Robert Plant turns the octave figure into a Viking war cry by going up an octave, down a semitone (half-step) and back to the octave.

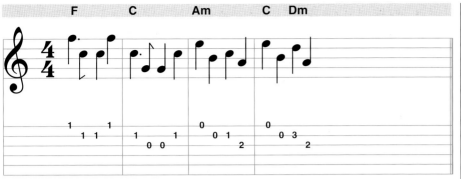

Table of intervals

Number	Degree	Interval	Distance	Name
1	Tonic	C to C	0	Unison
♭2		C to D♭	1	Minor second
2	Supertonic	C to D	2	Major second
♭3		C to E♭	3	Minor third
3	Mediant	C to E	4	Major third
4	Sub-dominant	C to F	5	Perfect fourth
+4		C to F♯	6	Augmented fourth
-5		C to G♭	6	Diminished fifth
5	Dominant	C to G	7	Perfect fifth
+5		C to G♯	8	Augmented fifth
-6		C to A♭	8	Minor sixth
6	Sub-mediant	C to A	9	Major sixth
-7	Sub-mediant	C to B♭♭	9	Diminished seventh
♭7		C to B♭	10	Minor seventh
7	Leading note	C to B	11	Major seventh
8 (1)	Tonic	C to C	12	Perfect Octave

Using Chromatic Notes

Chromatic

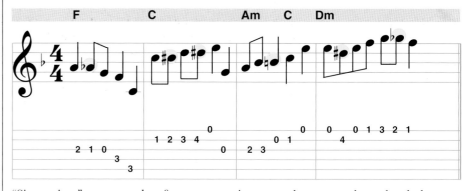

"Sits against" notes used as frequent passing notes between others that belong to the scale can create some intriguing effects. This spices up a melody and can sound jazzy and sophisticated. If you linger on a chromatic note, you may need to support it in the harmony with an unusual chord of some sort. Listen to 'Can't Get Used To Losing You' and many of Costello's later songs for chromatic notes and other unexpected twists.

Rhythm and Timing

Remember that a melody also has rhythm, and this rhythm needs to be appropriate for the words and the overall rhythm of the song. Listen for how long or short a melodic phrase is, and which notes are emphasised by the rhythm. Many Michael Jackson hits have melodies in which the rhythm of the melody is more noticeable than the harmonic value of the notes. Consider the rhythm of a melody such as 'This Guy's In Love With You', 'All Of The Day And All Of The Night', Marshall Crenshaw's exquisite 'Laughter' or Kate Bush's 'Suspended In Gaffa. Be aware of the beat you use to start a phrase. Watch out that you don't put unimportant words such as prepositions in prominent places – like having "the" on the first beat of a bar.

Smooth rhythm

Staccato rhythmic

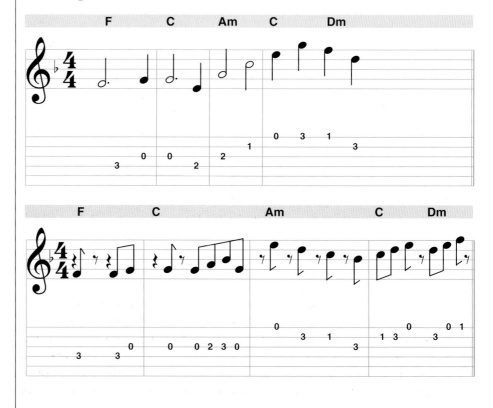

SECTION 7

Maximising a Melodic Phrase

A melodic phrase can be transposed by the same interval with which a chord sequence is moved up. In other words, when you change chords, simply sing the same tune but higher by the same distance. This way of developing melodic material is called "sequential repetition". You can hear this in the climbing bit of the verse in 'Now I'm Here', in 'Good Vibrations' and in the chorus of 'California Girls'.

Reharmonizing

The same melodic line will sound different if you use different chords underneath it. In the verse of 'Yes It Is', the same melody is used for two lines of lyric. The first time it is harmonized I IV II V, the second time I IV bVII V. The third chord, F#m in the original key of E, is replaced by a chord that is major, D. The switch from minor to major makes the melody sound different, even though its notes are the same. (The vocal harmony changes in keeping with the substituted chord.) In the first and second verses of 'If You're Going To San Francisco', the first four bars are:

VI	IV	I	V
Em	C	G	D

In the last verse, this is reharmonized as:

VI	II	IV	I	III	V
Em	Am	C	G	Bm	D

The additional minor chords add a poignant twist. Other examples include the choruses of 'Paradise By The Dashboard Light' and Bryan Adams' 'Cloud No.9' where the chorus contains a substitution of VI for chord I (Bm for D).

Counter-melody

One of the most powerful devices for making a song commercial is the counter-melody. A counter-melody is sung by a second voice (or backing vocalists), sometimes using different words. A good counter-melody can not only liven up the repetition of a verse but introduce devastating strength to the chorus by effectively multiplying the number of hooks. This can be heard on 'Jesamine', 'You've Got Your Troubles, I've Got Mine', 'Help', 'Near Wild Heaven', 'Fall On Me', 'It's The End Of The World As We Know It' ch, 'I Get Around', 'If Paradise Is Half As Nice', 'My Name Is Jack', 'Fox On The Run' (last ch) and 'Hello Goodbye'. The early R.E.M. albums have many inventive shared vocal parts.

One individual can happily sing the tune of a hit song. But not so with a hit that has a counter-melody – a single voice cannot sing both parts at once. Therefore, the only way of satisfying the need to hear the song is to play the record again.

Personal Style in Melody

Singers and songwriters often develop, sometimes unconsciously, certain melodic, harmonic and rhythmic habits, which lend their compositions a certain "fingerprint". It could be a favourite tempo or chord sequence or key change, or a habit of building the tune around certain notes. If you've been writing songs for a while, can you identify any things you tend to repeat? Do these fingerprints create a strong musical identity? Or do they make all your songs sound the same? If so, awareness will enable you to change whatever needs to be changed. For example, check to see if you are always starting a melody on the same note of the chord.

When Morrissey came to fame as vocalist of The Smiths, it was not uncommon to hear people say they thought the band's songs sounded alike. One major reason was Morrissey's use of certain step-wise movements in his melodies, regardless of what the chord sequences were doing. He was fond of starting tunes on the fifth note of the scale and moving step-wise down: 5, 4, 3 and then to 1. He also excluded any blue notes and blues-influenced phrasing. This gave The Smiths a more English sound. Around the time of the albums *Green* and *Out Of Time*, Michael Stipe of R.E.M. repeatedly moved from 1 to 4 and 3, exploiting the tension of the 4, as on 'Nightswimming'. Joni Mitchell often ends phrases on the blue b7 note and then rises to the 1. Her melodies are full of unpredictable leaps and descents. Paul Rodgers of Free established an immediately recognisable style with heavy use of blue notes, especially the b3 and b7. Many classic Beach Boys tunes have phrases that end with a decorative 5-4-3 flourish, a trick copied by 1990s bands like Supergrass in 'Alright' (bridge) and Foo Fighters in 'This Is A Call'. Natalie Merchant's melodies with 10,000 Maniacs are often quite similar. During the mid-1960s Dylan often created tension in his melodies by singing the fourth note of his underlying chord (in effect like a suspended fourth)

Singers

A melody can be given a certain amount of spontaneous decoration. This is called "melisma" and is frequently heard in blues, gospel and soul and their derivatives. Soul singers such as Aretha Franklin, Sam Cooke, Otis Redding, Wilson Pickett and their white counterparts and admirers – Dusty Springfield, Janis Joplin, Joe Cocker, Rod Stewart – decorate melodies by slightly extending notes in various ways at the end of phrases. In the 1990s, this was taken to hideous extremes by Whitney Houston, following the example of Michael Jackson and Stevie Wonder, who often seems to use a melody to show off her vocal technique with rapid downward and upward scales at the end of a word. This can be as witless and redundant as a heavy metal guitar solo. Don't over-decorate a melody – let it speak for itself.

It's not unusual (to quote Tom Jones) to meet songwriters who find the hardest part of songwriting is not the music but the words. Sometimes this difficulty arises from having too high expectations, with the consequence that everything you write seems terrible. Another problem is trying to write words that have impact even without the music. But listen to a few contemporary Top 40 hits and you will realise that the current standard of lyric writing is pretty poor. The sheer banality of many hit singles (especially in dance music) is appalling. From this you can take heart. Maybe your words are not so bad after all – maybe they will still do the job, commercially, even if they wouldn't cause Bob Dylan to lose sleep.

Like melody and harmony, lyric writing is a subject that deserves a book in its own right. That said, I will present a few tips and points of craft. If you have never written or completed a lyric, the next few pages should give you some ideas. If you have already written some song lyrics but are frustrated because you seem to write the same thing over and over, or feel you lack inspiration, then here's food for thought.

Are Lyrics Poetry?

This confusion of two quite distinct crafts often leads to a good deal of trouble for people in the early stages of writing songs. The answer is simple, though: do not confuse poetry and song lyrics.

It is true that some lyrics read quite well away from their music, and some lyrics have a 'poetic' quality in terms of their imagery or phrasing. But that alone does not turn a song lyric into a poem. The language of poetry is often too complex to be set to music. Poetry is intended to convey its meaning and emotion purely through words. True poetry has much less tolerance of cliché than lyrics. There are images you can get away with in a song lyric that you could never use in poetry.

Lyrics are words whose effect depends upon, and is symbiotic with, music. The music can supply whatever profundity is not there in the words. A banal phrase delivered by a great singer like Levi Stubbs or Aretha Franklin can sound fresh and full of meaning. In the same way, great music can excuse or even temporarily revive clichéd words and images.

Music is such a powerful modifier of meaning that a lyric that is essentially saying "I hate you' could end up leaving the listener with the impression that although the singer says he hates her (or she hates him), really and truly he still loves her. Take 10cc's 'I'm Not In Love'. In this song, the speaker is at pains to

ABBREVIATIONS

Roman numerals I VII
indicate chord
relationships within a key.
m *minor*
maj *major*
Song sections:
br *bridge*
c *coda*
ch *chorus*
hk *hook*
i *intro*
pch *pre-chorus*
v *verse*
Most of the chord-sequence examples
are standardized for comparison
into C *or* A *minor.*
Famous songs referred to in C *major*
or A *minor are not necessarily in*
the key of the original recordings.

insist that he does not love the addressee, yet the poignant music is undermining all his denials and turning them into excuses. In the end, though, the speaker never comes clean and admits it. He is saying that he's not in love to the very end. In Dylan's 'Just Like A Woman' the music seems to be almost rebelling against the acid disdain of the lyric. Other songs with a marked tension between lyric and music include The Police's 'Every Breath You Take', Blue Oyster Cult's 'Don't Fear The Reaper' and Elvis Costello's 'Oliver's Army'. The respective themes of possessiveness, suicide and imperialism are deliberately presented in musical disguise, the bitter pill sugar-coated. And all three were big hits.

Theme: What Shall I Write About?

The most common subject in popular song is, of course, romantic love. Adapting the title of the famous psychological book I'm OK, You're OK, we can group love-song lyrics in accordance with which of these existential positions they express.

Existential Positions in the Love Song

Our starting point is simple and straightforward:

I love you, you love me (the bliss song)

Happy songs are not so easy to write as unhappy ones, as most songwriters know. Happy songs that celebrate fulfilled love are apt to rub listeners the wrong way – because they're sentimental, banal, over-simplified, liable to arouse envy or seem unrealistic.

Happy love lyrics benefit, therefore, from an element of drama. This could be adversity or a problem – some kind of "but" that clouds the picture. So let's introduce some complications. How about qualifying the happiness with a time factor:

I love you, you love me ... tonight (but maybe not tomorrow)
I love you, you love me ... forever (so let's get married as soon as ...)
I love you, you love me ... but I'm so much older/younger than you

Love can be complicated by external factors such as geography and the demands of life and work:

I love you, you love me ... but I'm/you're leaving for a while
I love you, you love me ... but we're far apart

Or by constrictions closer to home:

I love you, you love me ... but my/your/our parents don't agree

Or by moral conflicts owing to a run-in with The Law:

I love you, you love me ... but I've/you've just killed a man (cue 'Bohemian Rhapsody')

Or by the sufferings of mortality:

I love you, you loved me ... but you're dead (have a cry in the chapel)

Or by the mysteries of fate:

I love you ... I've always loved you (the star-fated-lovers-meeting song)

I love you ... wherever you are (the one-day-I'll-find-you song)

Lyrics thrive on trouble of some kind. Songwriters are more often inspired by turbulence and conflict than bliss, peace, serenity and happiness. Imagine 'Satisfaction' with Mick Jagger singing "Ah've gat lats erf ... sah-tiz-fak-shern!' Not quite the same, is it? So here are existential positions for the love lyric where things are not going smoothly:

I love you, you don't love me yet ... but you will (the heroic determination song)

I love you, hey! your luck's in! (the how-can-you-resist me? song)

I love you, you don't love me, and I'm going to die (the unrequited love torture song)

I love you but I'm not going to admit it (the exquisite self-denial song)

I don't love you, you love me (the isn't-life-ironic regret song)

I love you, you don't love me anymore, and I give up (or I don't give up)

I love you, you don't love me anymore, but I'll always be here for you (the Diana Ross Big Orchestra Self-Immolation Special)

I don't love you, you don't love me ... anymore (the shall-we-be-noble-about-this? song)

I don't love you, but I used to (the free-at-last, move-on-up, I will survive song)

I love you, you say you love me, but maybe you love him (the jealous-guy song)

These situations are capable of an infinite variety of lyrical and musical treatments. As the clichè says, the whole of human life is there.

Triangular Existential Positions in Love Songs

If you want to be mischievous, you can generate much more trouble by playing a three-card version – namely, the introduction of The Other Person.

I love you, you love me, and he/she can only watch and regret

I love you, you love me ... tonight (while he/she is away)

I love you, you love me ... forever (so let's get our divorces)

I love you, you love me ... but he's/she's taking me away for a while

I love you, you love me ... even though I'm with her/him right now

I love you ... I've always loved you, but why couldn't you have appeared 10 years ago?

I love you, you don't love me yet ... but you will because I'll treat you right

I love you, so does he, but I'm the better bet

I love you, you don't love me because you love him ... but he doesn't love you either

I love you but I'm not going to admit it because you belong to my best friend

I don't love you, you love me, but we don't have a future

I love you, you don't love me anymore because you've gone back to her/him

He loves you, but I love you more
He doesn't love you so why don't you forget him/come on over to me

Sexual Encounters

Needless to say, many times what appears to be a love song is, consciously or unconsciously, really about sex. There are a huge number of songs about sex and sexual encounters, comprising all shades of innocence and explicitness. Songwriters have tried all kinds of ingenious procedures to disguise what their songs are really about in this field. Think of 'Maggie May' (the schoolboy and the hooker), 'More Than Words' (the persuasion song), 'Young Girl' (illicit love), 'Does Your Mother Know', 'Me and Mrs. Jones', 'Some Of Your Lovin'', 'Help Me Make It Through The Night', the unparalleled vulgarity of 'Tonight's The Night', 'Let's Get It On', 'Sexual Healing' (badgering), 'Norwegian Wood', 'Orgasm Addict', 'Relax', 'Feel Like Makin' Love', 'Let's Spend The Night Together', 'Hi Hi Hi', 'Midnight At The Oasis', 'Je t'aime (Moi Non Plus)', 'Wet Dream', 'This Is Hardcore', 'Melt' and, of course, vast tracts of Prince's back catalogue.

Given the relationship between pop music, teenagers and confusion over sexual identity, it's not surprising this should also be an issue in songs such as 'I'm A Boy', 'Girls And Boys', 'A Boy Named Sue', 'Lola', 'Walk On The Wild Side', 'Sexuality', 'House Of Fun', 'Teenage Kicks' and 'Pictures Of Lily' – all of which deal with teenage sexuality. 'Will You Still Love Me Tomorrow?' looks at this issue from a distinctly female perspective, as do 'Papa Don't Preach' and 'Like A Virgin'.

Subjects Other Than Love

There are hundreds of possible categories of themes that have been (and will be) the subject of song lyrics. Here are a few categories to get your imagination working. Some songs fit more than one category.

Geography

Write a song about a place, travelling into the unknown, living in a city or in the country, or wanting to live somewhere else. This involves more than mere description of a place. It encompasses such profound questions as: Where are you? Where have you been? Where do you want to be?

Geography has been highly significant in American song lyrics. There are so many songs named after American places you could construct an atlas out of them. The U.S. is so varied in terrain and culture the notion that a better life waits for you at the end of a long highway can seem plausible. This is a big theme in the blues music of the migrating workers from the South in the early 20th century, and the idea of travelling to the Promised Land is important in the music of Bruce Springsteen. Here are a few famous songs with American place names in their titles: 'Do You Know The Way To San Jose?', 'Anchorage', 'Wichita Lineman', 'Boulders To Birmingham', 'Sweet Home Alabama', 'Stuck Inside of Mobile With The Memphis Blues Again', 'If You're Going To San Francisco', 'New York, New York', 'No Sleep Till Brooklyn', 'LA Woman', 'Pasadena', 'Viva Las Vegas', 'What Made Milwaukee Famous', 'Yellow Rose Of Texas', 'Don't Go Back To Rockville', 'Witch Queen Of New Orleans', 'Lights Of Cincinnati', 'The Bus From Amarillo', 'California Dreamin'', 'California Uber Alles', 'Mississippi Queen', 'Toledo', 'Baltimore', 'Atlantic City', 'Philadelphia Freedom', 'Please Come To Boston', 'The Night Chicago Died', 'Blue Moon Of Kentucky', 'Night Train To Georgia', 'Kansas City', 'Kokomo', 'Union City Blue',

'By The Time I Get To Phoenix', 'San Bernadino', 'Love Field', 'Nantucket Sleighride', 'Texarkana' and 'Massachusetts'.

Even if the place is not in the title, it can be in the lyric. Chuck Berry listed place names in 'Sweet Little Sixteen' and The Beach Boys did likewise in 'Surfin' USA' and 'California Girls'.

British songwriters aren't as free to use geography because the U.K. is smaller. There are plenty of place names in the traditional folk songs of the British Isles (think of 'Scarborough Fair'), but they date from an age when lack of transport made the country seem much bigger. A British songwriter invites ridicule if he or she tries to suggest in the manner of Springsteen that spiritual salvation or a new life lies at the end of a motorway. A British songwriter who starts a song (apologies to Jimmy Webb) with a line like "By the time I get to Plymouth, she'll be waiting ...' is liable to get a laugh. Billy Bragg's wonderful takeoff of 'Route 66', 'The A13 Trunk Rd to the Sea', has UK audiences creased with laughter as it name-checks the singularly unromantic Basildon, Wapping, Dagenham and Southend. This didn't stop Kula Shaker from celebrating the 'A303', which is, in fact, a delightful road – but UK audiences are prejudiced against this idea. (Talking of Wiltshire does anyone remember 'Warminster Woman' by Bronco?) The English can't see their country as heroic and epic in the way that the Scots and the Welsh do. Maybe it's the lack of mountains.

Popular songs do, however, often mention London and its environs: 'Streets Of London', 'Waterloo Sunset', 'London Calling', 'London, Can You Wait?', 'London Traffic', 'A-Bomb In Wardour Street', 'London', 'Londinium', 'Finchley Central', 'Baker Street', 'West End Girls', 'Portobello Road', 'Wild West End', 'I Don't Want To Go To Chelsea', 'Last Night In Soho', 'White Man In The Hammersmith Palais'. Mind you, the nearest we get to Berry's roll-call of place names in 'Sweet Little Sixteen' is The Smiths' 'Panic', which mentions London, Birmingham, Dublin, Dundee, Humberside, Grassmere, Leeds and Carlisle. There's also 'Winchester Cathedral', 'Fog On The Tyne', 'Solsbury Hill', 'Penny Lane', 'England Swings', 'England Rocks', 'Oh England My Lionheart' and 'Strawberry Fields Forever'. The Isle Of Wight gets a mention in 'Happy Jack' and 'When I'm Sixty Four', and Salisbury in 'Sat In Your Lap'.

Telephones and Letters

Places often evoke distances, and distances evoke separated people, who need either letters and telephones, or transport. Lyrics based on phone calls include 'Memphis, Tennessee', R.E.M.'s 'South Central Rain', 'Rikki Don't Lose That Number', 'Beechwood 4-5789', 'Telephone Line', 'Telefone (Long Distance Love Affair)', 'Girl On The Phone', 'Baby Don't Forget My Number', 'Just Seven Numbers (Can Straighten Out My Life)', 'I Just Called To Say I Love You' and Blondie's 'Hanging On The Telephone'. 'Sylvia's Mother' had a protagonist who kept getting asked for another 40 cents by the operator. The post features in 'The Letter', 'Please Mr Postman', 'Return To Sender', 'Dear John' (John R. Sullivan, 1985), 'Paperback Writer' and 'P.S. I Love You'.

Mobile phones and email will probably feature soon in pop hits of the 21st Century.

Cars

Ever since Chuck Berry and the birth of rock'n'roll at a time when teenagers were obsessed with getting their hands on the wheel, pop lyrics have often revolved around cars: 'Pink Cadillac', 'Little Red Corvette', 'Mustang Sally', 'Drive My Car', 'Day Tripper', 'Cars', 'A Car That Sped', 'Big Yellow Taxi', 'Little Deuce Coupe', 'Mercedes Benz', 'Car Wash', 'Get Out Of My Dream, Get Into

My Car', 'No Money Down', 'Baby Driver', 'Racing In The Streets', 'No Particular Place To Go', '2-4-6-8 Motorway', 'Don't Worry Baby', 'Tell Laura I Love Her' and 'Pink Thunderbird'. Driving a car often becomes an image for a certain other popular activity, as in 'Radar Love'. 'Convoy' took care of long-distance lorries and immortalized the expression 'rubber duck'.

Trains

Train songs include '5:15', 'Last Train To Clarksville' (which also features a telephone call), 'The Day We Caught The Train', 'Rock Island Line', 'Leaving On A Jet Plane', 'It Takes A Lot To Laugh, It Takes A Train To Cry' and 'Morning Train (9 to 5)'.

Crime and Punishment

In songs such as 'Hey Joe' and 'Killing Floor', the singer hopes to escape the Long Arm Of The Law by going down (usually) to Mexico. If the singer is also In Love at this point, we have plenty of drama. 'Indiana Wants Me', 'I've Just Got To Get A Message To You', 'The Green, Green Grass Of Home', 'Last Night In Soho' and 'Gotta See Jane' are further instances. If there isn't an execution and the prisoner is released, you get 'Tie A Yellow Ribbon 'Round The Old Oak Tree'. (On second thoughts, throw that switch, y'all ...)

Names

Since so many popular songs have been about love, it's not surprising there are so many songs whose titles include, or are, a woman's name. How many names in this list can you match to the correct artist?

Alison, Amanda, Amelia, Angie, Annie, Barbara Ann, Bernadette, Beth, Betty, Billie Jean, Brandy, Bridget, Candida, Candy, Carol, Caroline, Carrie Ann, Cathy, Cecilia, Cindy, Clair, Claudette, Debora, Delilah, Diana, Dolly, Donna, Eileen, Elaine, Eleanor, Elise, Eloise, Emma, Emily, Gaye, Jackie, Jane, Jean, Jesamine, Jennifer, Jessie, Johanna, Jolene, Judy, Julia, Julie, Juliette, Kayleigh, Lana, Layla, Lily, Linda, Lucille, Lucy, Maggie, Mandy, Maria, Marie, Martha, Mary, Mary Lou, Maybelline, Michelle, Nikita, Nikki, Pamela, Patricia, Paula, Peggy Sue, Polly, Prudence, Rhonda, Rita, Rosalita, Roseanna, Rosetta, Rosie, Roxanne, Sadie, Sally, Samantha, Sara, Sharona, Sheila, Sherry, Shirley, Stephanie, Sue, Suzanne, Suzie, Sylvia, Tammy, Tracy, Virginia, Wendy. (Phew!)

The Urban Landscape

Many popular songs evoke aspects of city and town life without necessarily referring to specific places: 'Bus Stop', 'Heartbreak Hotel', '59th Street Bridge Song', 'Twenty Flight Rock' (about a girl who lived on the 20th floor), 'No Milk Today', 'Another Day', 'Don't Sleep In The Subway', 'Down In The Tube Station At Midnight', 'Strange Town', 'Ghost Town', 'Babylon's Burning', 'Downtown', 'Disco 2000', 'Want Ads', 'Rent', 'Expresso Love', 'Money For Nothing', 'Walk Of Life', 'Pinball Wizard', 'YMCA', 'Semi-detached Suburban Mr Jones' and 'Fire Brigade'. There are also songs about leaving the city for the country: 'Take Me Home, Country Roads' and 'I'm Gonna Be A Country Girl Again'.

Answer Songs and Parodies

If you're stuck for lyric ideas, why not write an 'answer' song? The Silhouettes' 'Get A Job' was answered by the Miracles' 'Got A Job'. The titles of 'Heartbreak Hotel' and 'Hotel Happiness' are obviously linked. Would 'Miss Judy's Farm' have existed without 'Maggie's Farm'?

You can do this with your own songs, and in commercial songwriting there has often been pressure on writers to come up with a sequel in the same mould. One label that practised this was Motown. The title of 'Baby I Need Your Loving', the Four Tops' first hit, started the lyric of the follow-up 'Without The One You Love'. Holland-Dozier-Holland drew attention to this technique with breathtaking honesty in 'It's The Same Old Song'. The Supremes' 'Love Child' was succeeded by another social-conscience theme, 'Livin' In Shame', and Edwin Starr was reportedly not thrilled when the company wanted to emulate the success of 'War' with 'Stop The War Now'. In each case, the follow-ups were not as successful, either commercially or artistically.

Try starting a verse with the first line of another song and put a twist on the original's theme. Echoing Cliff Richard's innocent "We're all going on a summer holiday", Elvis Costello sang the line over an arch I VI IV V progression, only to continue with the distinctly un-Cliff "Vigilante's coming out to follow me" in 'The Beat', a song about teenage lust. In 'Possession', he echoed the lines "If there's anything that you want/If there's anything that you need' that feature as the hook in The Beatles' 'From Me To You'.

Parody

Parody is a special category that usually involves rewriting the lyric but keeping the music the same. 'I've Got A Brand New Combine Harvester' parodied Melanie's 'Brand New Key', and Billy Connolly parodied Tammy Wynette's 'D-I-V-O-R-C-E' with a tale of a "wee scabby dog". The legal wrangle over 'My Sweet Lord' and its alleged resemblance to 'He's So Fine' was lent additional colour by The Chiffons recording 'He's So Fine' in the style of Harrison, while Jonathan King, ever the opportunist, did 'My Sweet Lord' in the arrangement style of 'He's So Fine' (doo lang doo lang doo lang, indeed).

Time

The past, present and future, and our relationship to these, is an abiding source of song lyric ideas. Time itself has inspired 'Time After Time' (Cyndi Lauper, Chris Montez and R.E.M.), 'Time Is On My Side', 'Time Is Tight' and 'Time Of The Season'.

Time encompasses a huge theme like memory ('Fields Of Gold', 'All Those Years Ago', 'In My Life', 'Those Were The Days') as well as being young ('Sweet Little Sixteen', 'At Seventeen', 'This Used To Be My Playground', 'Summer Holiday', 'In My Room', 'School's Out', 'Almost Grown'), leaving home ('She's Leaving Home', 'The Dean And I'), and broader songs of exile such as 'No Woman No Cry'. There are family relationships – with mothers ('Mother', 'Promise To Try'), fathers ('Winter'), siblings and other relatives ('It's A Family Affair', 'Alone Again (Naturally)', 'My Perfect Cousin') and also wayward friends ('My Brother Jake'). Songs about growing old tend to be jokey ('When I'm Sixty Four', 'Your Mother Should Know'), but 'Silver Threads Among The Gold' is a touching lyric.

Some songs have been inspired by the time of day: 'Midnight Hour', 'Stay With Me Till Dawn', 'Quarter To Three', 'Angel Of The Morning', 'All Night Long', 'Afternoon Delight', 'Rock Around The Clock', 'Reelin' And Rockin'', 'School Days (Ring! Ring! Goes The Bell)'. There are songs about days of the week: 'Lazy Sunday', 'That Sunday That Summer', 'Pleasant Valley Sunday', 'Rainy Days And Mondays', 'Monday Monday', 'Tuesday Afternoon', 'Ruby Tuesday', 'Everything's Tuesday', 'Wednesday Morning 3 am', 'It's Friday I'm In Love', 'Friday On My Mind' and 'Saturday Night's Alright For Fighting'. Songwriters seem to have less time for Thursday.

Quite a few songs mention months or seasons: 'January', 'January February',

'April Love', 'April Come She Will', 'First Of May', '4th of July Asbury Park', 'In The Summertime', 'It's Summer', 'It Might As Well Rain Until September', 'Autumn Almanac', 'November Rain', 'December Will Be Magic Again', 'Hazy Shade Of Winter'. Some years have been memorialized: Mott The Hoople's 'Late In '58', 'December, 1963', The Stooges' '1969', 'Summer of '69', Ash's '1977', Smashing Pumpkins' '1979', Hendrix's '1983' and Prince's '1999'. And there is, of course, a whole genre of songs about Christmas.

Or you can write a song about a historical event. 'The Night They Drove Old Dixie Down' is an evocation of the American Civil War. 'Born In The USA' and 'Pull Out The Pin' recall the Vietnam war. 'Cities In Dust' refers to the eruption of Mt. Vesuvius that buried Pompeii. Often such songs have a protest element in them – like Neil Young's 'Ohio' or 'Alabama'. Other historical examples include Joni Mitchell's 'Woodstock', 'Enola Gay', 'The Wreck Of The Edmund Fitzgerald' and 'Amelia'. History can itself be a source of metaphors, as with Abba's 'Waterloo'.

People

Many songs focus on famous people and celebrate (or criticize) their lives and deeds. Don McLean's two most famous songs celebrated the lives and art of Buddy Holly ('American Pie', re-recorded by Madonna) and Vincent Van Gogh ('Vincent'). Other artists (of various types) who are the subjects of songs include Mozart, Beethoven, Delius, Woody Guthrie, Elvis Presley, Gene Vincent, Levi Stubbs, Smokey Robinson, Scarlet O'Hara, Bette Davis, Marilyn Monroe, John Wayne, Robert de Niro, Michael Caine, Andy Warhol and Andy Kaufman. Madonna name-checked many Hollywood celebrities in 'Vogue', and Ian Dury wrote about Noel Coward, Van Gogh, Einstein and Segovia in 'There Ain't 'Alf Been Some Clever Bastards'. It seems to be hip to drop the name of the British group T.Rex, judging by citations in 'All The Young Dudes', 'You Better You Bet' and 'Wake-Up Bomb' (where Michael Stipe promises to "practise my T.Rex moves'). 'The Seeker' mentioned many 1960s counter-culture figures.

Such historical figures as Davy Crockett, Lady Godiva, Robin Hood, Christopher Columbus, Gary Gilmore, Al Capone, St.Augustine, General Custer, Richard III, Henry VIII, Houdini, Nostradamus and Jack the Ripper have had songs written about them. Political figures who have made it into songs include Steve Biko, Nelson Mandela and Joseph McCarthy. Eva Peron got a whole musical. 'Abraham, Martin and John' paid homage to three assassinated icons: John F. Kennedy, Robert Kennedy and Martin Luther King Jr. Dr King was also eulogized in U2's 'MLK', and John F. Kennedy was memorialized in The Byrds' 'He Was A Friend Of Mine'. JFK is mentioned in an alliterative pairing with Khruschev in 'Killer Queen' and appears again in Living Colour's 'Cult Of Personality', which, like 'No More Heroes' (Shakespeare, Lenin, Trotsky), is an anti-hero song. If writing about a political or historical figure, always take into account your audience. Elvis Costello knew that his song about the 1930s British fascist Oswald Moseley, 'Less Than Zero', would not translate to the U.S., so there it became a song about another Oswald – Lee Harvey Oswald, alleged assassin of President Kennedy. Many songs, like Dylan's 'Hurricane' (about the boxer Hurricane Carter), have been written about individuals who were the victims of injustice.

Songs have also celebrated fictional characters such as Charlie Brown, Snoopy and the Red Baron, Tarzan, Jane and King Kong, Romeo and Juliet, Captain James T. Kirk, and Mulder and Scully. Popular music has its own roll-call of fictional characters, and in some cases these characters seem as real as any from a film or novel. Think of Desmond and Molly, Terry and Julie, Arnold Layne, Emily and Eugene, Lola, Rita the meter maid, Polythene Pam, Mr Mustard, Mr Kite, Bungalow Bill, Rhiannon, Shorty, Dan and Miss Lucy, Dora the female explorer, Aqualung, the fashion-conscious Carnabetian of 'Dedicated Follower Of Fashion', Dizzy Miss Lizzy, Mr Bojangles, David Watts, Billericay Dickie and Jumpin' Jack Flash. Incidentally, what rank was 'Fernando', was he deaf and was that why she kept asking him if he could hear the drums?

Books and Films

You can also base a song on a book or film, and in the lyric try to condense the story or at least capture its atmosphere. 'Watching The Detectives' conjured up the whole world of pulp crime fiction. 'White Rabbit' was a counter-culture tribute to *Alice In Wonderland*. Kate Bush wrote about *Wuthering Heights* and 'The Sensual World' was inspired by the closing 30 pages of James Joyce's *Ulysses*. Led Zeppelin's 'Ramble On' and 'The Battle Of Evermore' were both shaped by J.R.R. Tolkein's *Lord Of The Rings*.

Put-Down Songs

You will find plenty of these in the punk rock repertoire, such as The Sex Pistols' 'Satellite', 'Liar', 'No Feelings' and 'New York'. Elvis Costello had plenty among his early songs, including 'I'm Not Angry' – a title that contrasts ironically with the content. After he went electric, Dylan had a phase of what he called "finger-pointing' songs. Probably the most elegant put-down song is Carly Simon's 'You're So Vain', with its booby-trapped chorus: "You're so vain, you probably think this song is about you'.

What's on the Radio?

Another option is to write a song about what's on the radio – or what's not on the radio. Since rock has always had a thing against disco, it's not surprising that Bryan Adams ('Kids Wanna Rock'), The Smiths ('Panic'), Elvis Costello ('Radio Radio') and R.E.M. ('Radio Song') wrote songs to criticise what they were hearing over the airwaves. 'Oh Yeah', 'Radio Free Europe', 'Yesterday Once More' and '29 Palms' are four of many songs that mention the effect of hearing music on the radio. You could extend this by going to television, as in Springsteen's '57 Channels'. It won't be long before someone has a hit with a song that mentions the World-Wide Web.

Articles of Apparel

Sometimes it's clothing that sparks a story or a mood: 'Blue Suede Shoes', 'Blue Jean Bop', 'Wherever I Lay My Hat', 'Famous Blue Raincoat', 'Homburg', 'Hole In My Shoe', 'These Boots Are Made For Walkin'', 'Venus In Furs', 'Raspberry Beret', 'A White Sport Coat (And A Pink Carnation)', 'Hi Heel Sneakers', 'Red Shoes', 'Lady In Red', 'Bell Bottom Blues', 'Chantilly Lace', 'Dedicated Follower Of Fashion' – and from the opposite view, 'It's Still Rock and Roll To Me', where Billy Joel decided that fashion didn't matter.

Dances

Some lyrics offer instructions for how to do a dance: 'Resurrection Shuffle', 'Let's Twist Again', 'Hey Let's Twist', 'Monster Mash', 'Hippy Hippy Shake', 'Agadoo', 'Do You Want To Dance', 'Mickey's Monkey', 'Dance To The Music', 'Land Of A Thousand Dances', 'Harlem Shuffle', 'Do The Funky Chicken'. Thousands of other songs, like 'Peppermint Twist', 'Boogie Fever', 'You Should Be Dancing', '(Shake Shake Shake) Shake Your Booty' and 'Dancing Queen' just mention dancing. 'Slowdive' sounded like dance instructions but was actually auto-erotic.

Fantasy

In fantasy lyrics, you can let your imagination run riot – though whether your listener will be inspired or confused is something to be considered. The words may obliquely refer to the "real world", as in 'Whiter Shade Of Pale', or not. John Lennon wrote a number of outstanding fantasy songs, including 'Lucy In The Sky With Diamonds', 'Come Together' and 'I Am The Walrus', and he parodied the genre with 'Glass Onion'. 'Being For The Benefit Of Mr Kite' was a fantasy inspired by an old poster.

You will find loads of such writing in Hendrix ('Spanish Castle Magic') and early 1970s progressive rock, where David Bowie, Marc Bolan (T.Rex), Genesis, Hawkwind and Yes all featured fantasy. Gothic horror was mined by Alice Cooper and later Michael Jackson, on 'Thriller'. There have been plenty of sci-fi lyrics involving aliens and UFOs, such as 'After The Gold Rush', and end-of-the-world scenarios like '99 Red Balloons' and 'Five Years'. Within fantasy writing lies the realisation that words can make sense even when they don't, as with the famous line "The movement you need is on your shoulder" from 'Hey Jude', which Lennon rightly told McCartney not to change.

A special sub-section of fantasy might involve songs based around the mind-expanding properties of certain drugs. Psychedelia helped to create lyrics such as 'I Can Hear The Grass Grow', 'Cloud Nine' and 'I Can See For Miles'. More general drug songs run the gamut from 'I'm Waiting For The Man' and 'Green Manalishi' to 'The Needle And The Damage Done' and 'Caught By The Fuzz'.

Songs about Writing Songs

When all else fails, songwriters write about what they do. The self-referential song-about-writing-a-song has a higher percentage of turkeys than any other category. Love-obsessed singer-songwriters tongue-tied in the presence of their beloved are notorious for perpetrating these. Nothing is guaranteed to make you sound more like a self-obsessed egomaniac who ought to get a life than starting a lyric with "I'm sitting here writing a song, I'm waiting for chords to come along. . . ."

This rogues' gallery includes 'Pop Muzik', 'I Write The Songs' (... and we hate 'em), 'Gonna Write A Classic' (... I don't think so), 'Thank You For The Music' (... but we prefer 'Dancing Queen'), 'I'd Like To Teach The World To Sing' (... in atonal harmony), 'Silly Love Songs' (... but we've not had enough of 'Maybe I'm Amazed') and the pompous 'Music' (music is our first love, too, so shut up!). Odd references to songwriting within a song, if the song is about something else, are acceptable, as in 'Romeo and Juliet', 'Sunflower' and 'Your Song', but not in the case of 'True', where the question "Why do I find it hard to write the next line?" invites a whole series of colourful replies. 'Killing Me Softly With His Song' provides an interesting perspective from the recipient's point of view.

Sarcasm and humour are welcome here, as with George Harrison's sarcastic 'Only A Northern Song', Noddy Holder singing "So you think my singing's out of time/Well, it makes me money" ('Cum On Feel The Noize') and in 'Halleluja', where Jeff Buckley spells out the chord sequence.

There is a whole genre of songs that deal with the music business and corrupt managers ('Death On Two Legs', 'So You Wanna Be A Rock'n'Roll Star'), touring ('Homeward Bound', 'All The Way From Memphis') and groupies ('Sick Again'). BoyzIIMen made a hit title out of their two favourite record labels: 'Motownphilly'. And there are, of course, zillions of songs with "rock" or "rock and roll" in the title – but you don't want to add to them, do you? You do? Oh, all right then ... but make it snappy!

The two coolest couplets ever written about rock'n'roll are, of course, 'The drummer relaxes and waits between shows / For the cinnamon girl' ('Cinnamon Girl') and 'What's that guy moving 'cross the stage? / It looks like the one used by Jimmy Page' ('Rock Show').

Politics, Religion and Protest

With these themes, the song lyric turns outward to much bigger issues. This raises the question of whether a popular song is the best place to do this. Each area has its own problems.

Outside of gospel ('Oh Happy Day'), hymns, carols and the songbooks of fundamentalists, religious songs are difficult – especially in rock ("the devil's music"). If artistically done, religious rock numbers can be highly effective because rock's earthy energy keeps religious expressions from becoming sentimental and wooly. Think of Townshend songs about Meher Baba such as 'Bargain', some of U2's tunes and, in reggae, Bob Marley. Biblical themes inspired 'Turn, Turn, Turn', 'Sire Of Sorrow', '40', 'Rivers Of Babylon', 'Song Of Solomon' and 'Heaven Help Us All'. 'The Glastonbury Song' is impressive because, despite the broad-ranging imagery of the lyric, the poignancy of the music suggests the human cost and struggle that faith entails.

Political songs sometimes merely sloganize or preach to the converted. They become more interesting as they move beyond a black-and-white situation. 'Shipbuilding' is a wonderful political song that examines the human realities of the relationship between war, economics and employment. 'Sunday Bloody Sunday' is another notable peace-sentiment song. 'Orange Crush' is about defoliants in Vietnam. There's always room for humour here, as in 'Fixin' To Die', the anti-Vietnam War song by Country Joe & The Fish.

Other notable songs with political and social themes include 'Invisible Sun', 'Give Ireland Back To The Irish', 'Night Rally', 'Pills And Soap', 'Stand Down Margaret', 'Love Child', 'War', 'Bring The Boys Back Home', 'Young, Gifted And Black', 'Indian Reservation', 'Woman Is The Nigger Of The World', 'Power To The People', 'Ebony And Ivory', 'Candy Man' and 'A Thousand Trees'. The Mission's 'Amelia' is about child abuse. Charity songs such as 'Do They Know Its Christmas?', 'Bangla Desh' and 'We Are The World' are a specialized form of this genre. Dystopian warnings about the future can be heard in songs such as 'Eve Of Destruction' and 'In The Year 2525'.

Ecology has always been a safe bet: 'Big Yellow Taxi', 'Silvery Rain', 'Crazy Horses', 'Cuyahoga', 'Breathing', 'Mercy Mercy Me (The Ecology)'.

How You Write

Having considered some theme categories, let's look at techniques. First, if you are writing lyrics get yourself three books: a thesaurus, a book of proverbs and famous quotes, and a rhyming dictionary.

Point of View

Consider the question of point of view. When you write your lyric, through whose eyes are you looking? How does this affect what you describe?

First Person

Song lyrics tend to use "I", the first person, as the main point of view. This is popular because a writer may be writing from experience, and it is certainly popular with singers as it allows them to identify with the speaker (and for their audience to make this identification). You can also write in the voice of someone else, such as an invented character. Suzanne Vega's 'Luka' is sung from the point of view of an abused child. In 'Wuthering Heights', Kate Bush voiced the feelings of Cathy Earnshaw from Emily Bronte's 1848 novel. In 'The Intruder' Peter Gabriel impersonated a psychotic, and 'The Boxer' features a down-and-out character.

Second Person

This is where the lyric speaks of "you". To disguise the personal nature of a lyric, sing it in the second person. This can make it seem as though you are talking about someone else, when in fact it might be yourself. This is used in 'You Should Hear How She Talks About You' and 'Tell Her About It'.

Third Person

To grasp how significant point of view is, think of some famous songs and imagine them sung from a different one. 'My Way' sung from the third person would be absurd – it wouldn't be anywhere near as dramatic. Imagine the climax as Sinatra sings "And he did it ... his way!" The audience would wonder why the singer is so worked up over someone else's trials and tribulations.

But the third person can offer an excellent way to distance yourself from material that may be too personal, or to tell a story from more than one person's perspective. Many of The Beatles' mop-top period hits were in the first person, but with 'She Loves You' they tried something different. The lyric tells how the speaker tries to reconcile the two lovers who have quarrelled. The song not only celebrates the reunion of the lovers but, implicitly, the generosity of the person who did the patching-up.

Combined Points of View

Consider the lyric of David Bowie's 'Space Oddity'. Passages of first-person reflection by Major Tom in space are combined with the voice of a technician at Mission Control doing the countdown and last checks, and another earth-bound voice telling the astronaut of his new-found celebrity. Compare it with 'Rocket Man'.

Duets

Differing points of view can be made explicit with the duet, where two voices are heard. 'Don't Go Breaking My Heart' and 'Don't Give Up' are variants on the love duet, with the female voice reassuring the male. In most pop love duets, the two voices are in blissful agreement, as in 'It Takes Two', 'Ain't Nothing Like The Real Thing' and 'You're All I Need To Get By'. Bryan Adams, Rod Stewart and Sting came on like three romantic musketeers with 'All For Love'. 'Fairytale Of New York' is a song where the two singers insult each other.

Narrative

A song can be cast as a story, whether true or invented. The folk ballad is a good historical precedent. Stories can be told from a variety of perspectives. 'Leader Of The Pack' and 'Tell Laura I Love Her' were early 1960s teen hits that played on a morbid fascination with death in an automobile accident. 'Don't Stand So Close To Me' is about the relationship between a schoolteacher and a student; 'Down In The Tube Station At Midnight' tells of violence in a subway; 'She's Leaving Home' relates the story of a daughter breaking away from her parents with commentary from both sides. 'In The Ghetto' is a marvellous compressed narrative of a young man who grows up in poverty, takes to crime and gets shot by the police. 'Someone Saved My Life Tonight' is a revealing narrative about a relationship that engenders suicidal feelings. 'Chestnut Mare' is a story of seduction dressed up as a man pursuing a horse. 'Cut Across Shorty' is the tale of a young woman who helps the man she loves to cheat and win the race against a rival for her affections. 'Meeting Across The River', a story of two small-town crooks, is one of many Springsteen songs with a novel-like quality. For an imaginary tale of maritime mystery check out Procul Harum's 'A Salty Dog'.

Aspects of Language

Rhyme

Lyrics don't have to rhyme but often they do. In contrast to poetry, where rhyme schemes can be complex, song lyrics are often in couplets or alternating rhyme. Couplets are punchier. Rhymes don't have to be exact, because the last syllable of a word often gets lost in the pronunciation. Pop lyrics tend to use the same obvious rhyme sounds. To make the whole business of rhyming easier and less predictable, use a good rhyming dictionary.

Poor rhyming makes the rhyme itself predictable, forces you into a nonsense line to complete it or makes you distort the syntax (word order) of a statement. Therefore, avoid ending a line with a word for which there is no easy rhyme. Two common examples are "world' and "love'. If a line ends with "world', then something is likely to be "unfurled'; if with "love', then something is coming down from "above' or is like a "dove' (a punk song might give it a "shove"). Don't allow a rhyme to trap you into an archaism: "I give my love for free, I give it all to thee." Modern people do not address each other as "thee". Or how about Edwyn Collins's rhyming of "before" with "days of yore". Yore? Even the great are sometimes guilty of this. Dylan, in 'Don't Think Twice, It's All Right', uses "know'd" instead of "knew" for the sake of a rhyme. Neil Diamond in 'Play Me' gives us, 'Songs she sang to me, songs she brang to me'. Brang?? What happened to 'brought'? Ah, but it doesn't rhyme with 'sang'.

Polysyllabic abstractions generate plentiful rhymes but need to be used sparingly, unless you plan to make the lyric revolve around them, as with 'Give Peace A Chance' and 'The Logical Song'.

As an exercise, find a few interesting rhymes and write a lyric to fit them.

Type of Statement

What type of statement do you use in your lyrics? Are the lines declarations, questions, replies, descriptions or action?

Imagery

Primary imagery consists of descriptive elements that denote actual things. In 'I Get Around', the "Strip" is the place where the speaker is getting bored racing his car. If a song lyric said that something was "like a road", you have secondary imagery, which is conveyed by similes and metaphors. The problem with most similes and metaphors in pop lyrics is that they are too predictable. I mean, complete the following: "beats like a ...", "cuts like a ...", "sweeter than ...". (Isn't hard to guess, is it?) Sometimes a great vocal can overcome a cliché. Images can work as titles, as with 'Love Is Like A Battlefield' and '(Love Is) Thicker Than Water'. 10cc deliberately poked fun at pretentious metaphors with 'Life Is A Minestrone' (which started "Life is a minestrone served up with parmesan cheese").

The truly poetic moments in pop lyrics occur when a writer disregards cliché and finds something fresh. The line "Like a cat in a bag waiting to drown" ('The Drugs Don't Work') is inspired in this respect, as is "The face that she keeps in a jar by the door" ('Eleanor Rigby'). Effective language is not always about an image. In the line "I hear him before I go to sleep, and focus on the day that's been', ('Man With The Child In His Eyes') the word "focus" is crucial for evoking the reality of what is described. With "I know I'll often stop and think about them' ('In My Life') the crucial word is the verb "stop": it is not only that he will think about the past – he will stop and think.

The most common imagery in popular song is meteorological: the weather. Think of clichès like "winds of change", "my tears fell down like rain", "swept away by a flood", "like a raging sea", "life is a desert without you", etc. And a great many songs have weather in their titles: 'The Sun Ain't Gonna Shine Anymore', 'Heatwave','Good Day Sunshine', 'You Are The Sunshine Of My Life', 'Blues Skies Are Around The Corner', 'I Wish It Would Rain', 'Blame It On The Rain', 'I Love A Rainy Night', 'Raindrops Keep Falling On My Head', 'Here Comes The Rain Again', , 'I Wish It Would Rain Down', 'Rain', 'Just Walking In The Rain', 'It Never Rains In Southern California', 'Only Happy When It Rains', 'Laughter In The Rain'. As a universal experience, the weather is something to which everyone can relate. Amateur songs tend to be dominated by weather images. If this is true of your lyrics, try banning them for a while. If you must use weather images, then find a new angle or twist.

The other common group of images is drawn from nature: sun, moon, stars, seas, rivers, oceans, lakes, deserts, woods, forests, rocks, sand, stone, jewels, fields, fire, etc. 'Annie's Song' somehow gets just about all of them in. You will find this kind of imagery in numbers such as 'I Still Haven't Found What I'm Looking For', 'Ain't No Mountain High Enough', 'In A Big Country' and 'Fields Of Fire'. Such images tend to go with generalized and often exaggerated emotions – we're talking MOR ballads and stadium rock. If the music and/or the performer is not suitably larger-than-life, then it can be unconsciously funny. The skeptic's response to the dramatically titled 'Where Were You When The Storm Broke?' is the facetious "phoning a plumber instead of hiding under the table'.

In terms of their overall style, lyrics such as 'Both Sides Now', 'MacArthur Park', 'If You Could Read My Mind', 'Windmills Of Your Mind' and 'Unchained Melody' either aspire to be poetry or use words and imagery in quite an extravagant way. At the opposite extreme are songs whose imagery is drawn from the mucky detail and nitty-gritty of everyday life. Lyricists like Jarvis Cocker (Pulp), Morrissey (The Smiths), and Paul Weller (with The Jam) consciously seek out the everyday and find poetry in the unheroic. The image "looking like something that the cat brought in" ('Invisible Sun') is effective because it is drawn from colloquial speech. In songs such as 'That's Entertainment', 'Suzanne', 'Kayleigh' and Dylan's 'Sara', images can be specific yet somehow, paradoxically, attain universality.

Try applying a set of images to a theme that would not normally be thought of in those terms – this can be especially effective in a love song, where less obvious "cooler" imagery can imply a depth of passion beneath.

Mini-Dictionary of Pop Clichès

These words and phrases are threadbare and should be used with caution, humour or irony:

Little girl, little miss, blue jeans, forever, body, fantasy, reality, hearts that beat like a drum, sorrow that cuts like a knife, winds of change, love deep as the ocean, all night long, angel, baby, fire/desire, no matter what (they say), set me free, swallow my pride, right from the start, out on the streets, standing in the rain, end of time, shines like the sun, walk the line, going round my head, just about to go insane, it's all in my mind, heaven above, deep inside, hanging on the wire, I was lost and now I'm found, I give it to thee, turn to stone, cold as ice, by your side, sweeter than/taste like wine, get me through, get on down, heart like a stone, catch me/you if I/you fall.

In pop lyrics, prediction is an easy business: mountains tend to crumble into the sea, rivers always flow to the sea and stars fall from the sky. Try not to use filler words – *well, baby, just, really.* These add nothing to the sense and only occupy space in a line.

Redeeming Clichès

One way to redeem a clichè is to exploit its latent meaning. This requires looking at it with a fresh eye to see how it might be developed in an unexpected direction. In 'Clubland' Elvis Costello came up with "The long arm of the law slides up the outskirts of town", and in 'Possession' he wrote "You lack lust – you're so lackluster". Robert Plant's 'Heaven Knows' has the wordplay "You were pumping iron as I was pumping irony", and 'Substitute' has a memorable line that was created by replacing "silver" with "plastic" in "I was born with a plastic spoon in my mouth".

First Lines

A good opening line is valuable. Not only does it set you, the writer, up for the rest of the lyric, but it grabs the listener's attention. Here are a few fine opening statements that show different approaches:

"When I met you at the station you were standing with a bootleg in your hand' (character)
  –'Hi Hi Hi'
"Punctured bicycle on a hillside desolate' (imagery)
  –'This Charming Man'
"I may not always love you' (the unexpected)
  –'God Only Knows'
"He always runs where others walk' (enigmatic)
  -'Thunderball'
"Stopped into a church I passed along the way' (dramatic)
  –'California Dreaming'
"Why do birds suddenly appear' (question)
  –'Close To You'
"A long, long time ago' (story)
  –'American Pie'
"This is the modern world' (title and declaration)
  –'This Is The Modern World'
"The screen door slams; Mary's dress waves' (cinematic)
  –'Thunder Road'
"There must be some kind of way out of here' (problem)
  –'All Along The Watchtower'
"I am an anti-Christ' (defiance, blasphemy)
  –'Anarchy In The UK'
"I blame you for the moonlit sky' (apparently illogical accusation)
  –'Sleeping Satellite'

Word-Play and Titles

Titles themselves can be inspiring. Sometimes they fix a mood long enough for you to get to grips with it. It is satisfying to come up with a title that no one else has used – so be aware that some of the most popular first words in a title are: can't, dance, don't, give, good, I, I love, I want, I'll, I'm, just, let, little, love, more, my, never, one, only, rock, she, some, take, that's, too, walk.

Some titles are memorable because they feature wordplay: 'Maid In Heaven', 'If I Said You Had A Beautiful Body Would You Hold It Against Me?', 'Aladdin Sane', 'Animal Nitrate', 'High Fidelity', 'Money, Money, Money, I do, I do, I do, I do, I do', 'The Only Thing That Looks Good On Me Is You', 'Mellow Yellow', 'Yester-me, Yester-you, Yesterday', 'Eight Days A Week', 'Function At The Junction', 'Bummer In The Summer', 'Seven Deadly Finns'.

You can also take common phrases and twist them: 'Don't Get Mad Get Even', 'Fifty Ways To Leave Your Lover', 'When The Going Gets Tough, The Tough Get Going', 'Shoplifters Of The World Unite'. This can include proverbs and other well-known sayings: 'Needle In A Haystack', 'Beauty Is Only Skin Deep', 'Plenty More Fish In The Sea', 'The Other Man's Grass', 'Knock, Knock, Who's There', 'Something Old, Something New', 'Alive And Kicking', 'Another One Bites The Dust', 'Head Over Heels' and 'Objects In The Rear View Mirror May Appear Closer Than They Are'.

Some titles are intriguing because of what they don't say: 'Because The Night' is grammatically incomplete. In the mid-1960s, Dylan had a penchant for adverbs in titles such as 'Queen Jane Approximately' and 'Positively 4th Street'. Other intriguing titles include 'Over Under Sideways Down', 'I'm Left, You're Right, She's Gone', 'I'd Do Anything For You (But I Won't Do That)', 'There! I've Said It Again', 'Sometimes When We Touch', 'Suddenly', 'Till' and 'Truth, Rest Your Head'. Titles with "if" arouse curiosity. 'Wedding Bell Blues' seems contradictory.

Repetition

Some lyrics are constructed on a repeated word or phrase: 'Blowin' In The Wind' ("how many" statements), 'Where Have All The Flowers Gone' ("Where have all the ... gone?'), 'It's Impossible' (to start so many verses with this phrase, it's just impossible), 'I Believe', 'Every Breath You Take' (count the everys), 'Ironic', 'This Old House', 'Plastic Man', 'King Of Pain', 'Just An Old-Fashioned Girl', 'Wonderful World' ("Don't know much about ... ") and 'Forever Young' ('May you ... '). The repeated word could reveal the deeper meaning and/or be the title. Some lyrics are constructed as lists, as with 'Reasons To Be Cheerful' and 'Inside Out'.

Before we venture into more complex, exotic chords, it is worth considering whether there is something more you can do with the basic chords we looked at in Section 2.

Voicings

Sometimes the simplest chord sequences can be made more effective by using different shapes, or voicings, of the same chords. Here are some ideas for alternate shapes. Some of them feature unison strings (where the notes are at the same pitch) to give a ringy, "12-string" tone on a regular 6-string guitar.

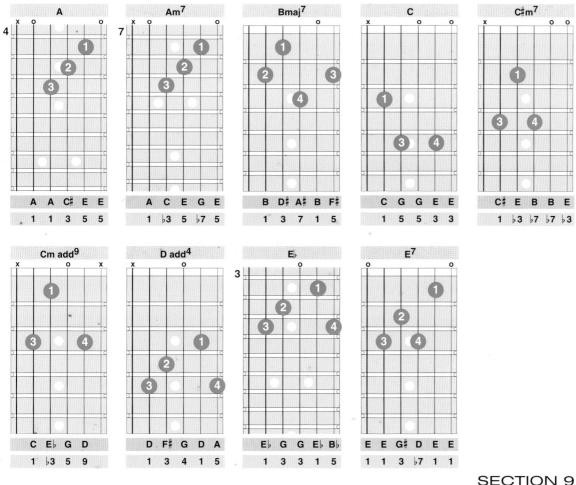

Chords continued from page 107

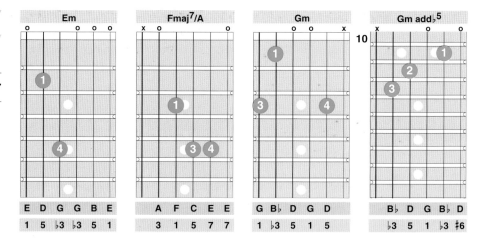

Em	Fmaj7/A	Gm	Gm add♭5
E D G G B E	A F C E E	G B♭ D G D	B♭ D G B♭ D
1 5 ♭3 ♭3 5 1	3 1 5 7 7	1 ♭3 5 1 5	♭3 5 1 ♭3 ♯6

Moving an Open-string Chord

One favourite songwriting trick of guitarists is to take an open-string chord and move it up the neck without turning it into a barre chord. What happens is that an unpredictable series of new chords is produced. The fretted notes retain their harmonic relationship, but the open strings change theirs in relation to the

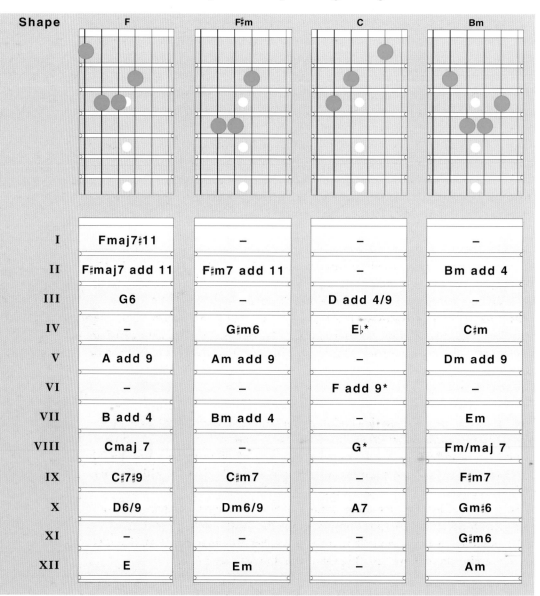

Shape	F	F♯m	C	Bm
I	Fmaj7♯11	–	–	–
II	F♯maj7 add 11	F♯m7 add 11	–	Bm add 4
III	G6	–	D add 4/9	–
IV	–	G♯m6	E♭*	C♯m
V	A add 9	Am add 9	–	Dm add 9
VI	–	–	F add 9*	–
VII	B add 4	Bm add 4	–	Em
VIII	Cmaj 7	–	G*	Fm/maj 7
IX	C♯7♯9	C♯m7	–	F♯m7
X	D6/9	Dm6/9	A7	G♯6
XI	–	–	–	G♯m6
XII	E	Em	–	Am

Asterisk means add
little finger to top string
at same fret as the
third finger

fretted. The following diagram illustrates this . The root note needs to be fretted, or you will be moving chords over a pedal note. You can hear this effect in songs such as 'Man On The Moon, 'Sugar Mountain', 'Miss World' and 'Love And Affection'.

Moving Chords over a Pedal Note

A pedal note is an effective compositional device. It's a note, usually in the bass, that remains the same while chords change above it. This creates a more ambiguous sequence than if the bass note changed for the root note of each chord. If the pedal note is the same as the key note, it is called a "tonic pedal"; if it is named after the fifth note of the scale, it would be a "dominant pedal".

Songs that use a tonic pedal include 'Alright' (Cast) v, 'One To Another' (Charlatans), 'Peaches' (Presidents of the USA), 'Gimme Some Lovin'', 'We Don't Talk Anymore' ch, 'Everything I Do' v 1, 'Everybody Wants To Rule The World' v, 'Express Yourself' ch, 'Dancing In The Street' v, 'The Sun Ain't Gonna Shine Anymore', 'You've Got Your Troubles', 'Everlasting Love', 'Substitute' and 'Let Me Entertain You'. Minor-key examples include 'I Know I'm Losing You', 'Green Manalishi', 'I've Never Met A Girl Like You Before' , 'Sweetness Follows', 'Running With The Devil' and 'Fire'.

'I'll Never Fall In Love Again' has a dominant pedal. One of the most unusual pedals I've ever encountered is in The Banshees' 'Nightshift', where over an A pedal the chords change from Am to G#m. 'To A Flame' has a Cmaj7 Fmaj7 Cm Am sequence over a C pedal.

The problem for the guitarist is that changing chords over a static bass note creates considerable fingering difficulties – unless the pedal note is the open E, A or D string. This is one instance where triads can help. You can form triads on the top three strings and have a D pedal, or strings 2-3-4 with an A pedal, or strings 3-4-5 with an E pedal. The key could be either major or minor. In guitar music, pedal notes are almost invariably on one of these three open strings. Triads often feature in the intros to songs. Examples would include 'Hold Your Head Up', 'Over The Hills and Far Away', and 'Blowin' Free'. For more information see page 14 for the triad boxes.

Inversions

A simple major or minor triad has three notes, 1 3 5 or 1 b3 5 (C E G or C Eb G). Most guitar chords are in root position, with the chord-name note lowest in pitch. But what happens if one of the other notes is lowest?

An "inversion" is a chord whose root note is not the lowest. The first inversion puts the third on the bottom: C E G becomes E G C. Compared to root chords, first inversions sound mobile. The bass note wants to either rise or drop back.

First Inversions

First inversions are useful in descending or ascending sequences and increase the possibilities for using only three chords in the harmony. Minor chords can also be inverted. C minor is C Eb G, so we can play it as a first inversion by making Eb the lowest note. Inversions are usually notated as "slash chords", with the bass note written after the root: C/E or A/C#.

To get a feel for the "tentative" sound of first inversions, compare a C to D change with C/E to D/F#. Also compare Em to F#m with Em/G to F#m/A.

Major-chord first inversions that are easy to play on guitar are C, D, F and G; for minor chords, they are Am, Bm, C#m, Dm, Em, F#m and Gm.

ABBREVIATIONS

Roman numerals I VII
indicate chord
relationships within a key.
m *minor*
maj *major*
Song sections:
br *bridge*
c *coda*
ch *chorus*
hk *hook*
i *intro*
pch *pre-chorus*
v *verse*
Most of the chord-sequence examples
are standardized for comparison
into C *or* A minor.
Famous songs referred to in C major
or A minor *are not necessarily in*
the key of the original recordings.

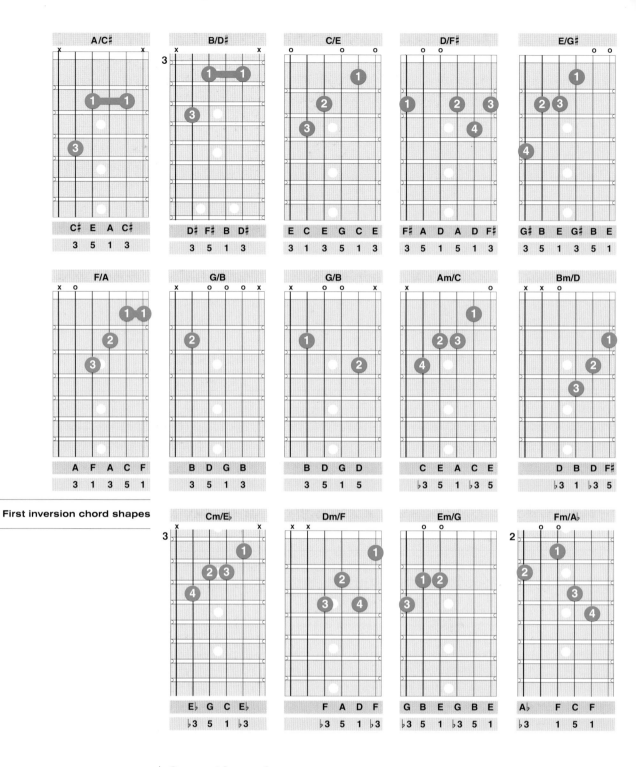

First inversion chord shapes

Second inversions

In the second inversion, the fifth of the chord becomes the bass note: C E G becomes G C E. Rarer than first inversions, they have something of the fluid nature of the first inversion but are more diffuse. Jimi Hendrix's 'The Wind Cries Mary' is introduced by an Eb-E-F progression, played first as second inversions and then as first inversions. There is a striking second inversion in the chorus of The Band's 'The Night They Drove Old Dixie Down', where the chords move between iiI and IV, and a descending link to the last choruses which also depends on inversions.

The number of possible inversions is always one less than the number of different notes in the chord. If a chord has more than three notes in it – C7, for example – then a third inversion is possible, with the additional note in the bass.

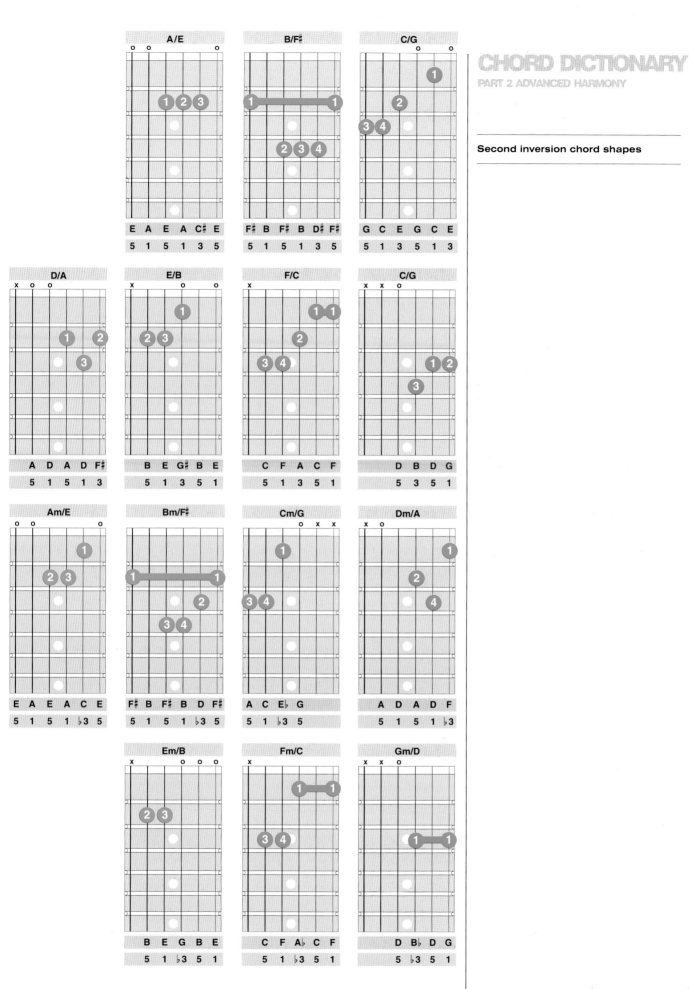

Second inversion chord shapes

A/E	B/F#	C/G
E A E A C# E	F# B F# B D# F#	G C E G C E
5 1 5 1 3 5	5 1 5 1 3 5	5 1 3 5 1 3

D/A	E/B	F/C	C/G
A D A D F#	B E G# B E	C F A C F	D B D G
5 1 5 1 3	5 1 3 5 1	5 1 3 5 1	5 3 5 1

Am/E	Bm/F#	Cm/G	Dm/A
E A E A C E	F# B F# B D F#	A C E♭ G	A D A D F
5 1 5 1 ♭3 5	5 1 5 1 ♭3 5	5 1 ♭3 5	5 1 5 1 ♭3

Em/B	Fm/C	Gm/D
B E G B E	C F A♭ C F	D B♭ D G
5 1 ♭3 5 1	5 1 ♭3 5 1	5 ♭3 5 1

Third inversions usually occur as passing chords. In the verse of Air's 'Remember' we find this:

I	iiiI7	iIV	V
Eb	Eb/Db	Ab/C	Bb

Inversions are not often used by songwriting guitarists. They can be difficult to finger, or it may be hard to find one that sounds as good as the equivalent root chord. One way round this problem is to have the bass guitar play the appropriate note to create the inversion while the guitar plays a root chord, as on the verses of 'Waterloo Sunset'.

Inversions are more frequently heard in the songs of writers associated with the piano, such as Elton John and Kate Bush. On a keyboard, an inversion can be created easily by moving the left hand up a few keys. 'This Woman's Work' gains much of its expressive power from its inversions; for example, a IV V I II progression becomes iIV iV iI II (Db/F Eb/G Ab/C Bbm). There are plenty of inversions in 'Everything I Do (I Do It For You)' and 'Heaven Can Wait'.

They also turn up in mid-period Dire Straits and in the verse of 'Cherish', where the synth bass moves onto some inverted notes.

Using Inversions

Inversions can enliven a simple three-chord trick: try E B A as E B/D# A/C#. Inversions also allow you to stretch a three-chord turnaround: C F G becomes C C/E F G over four bars. In 'Anchorage' Michelle Shocked extends a three chord change in a similar manner: G D/F# C D. In 'Novocaine For The Soul', there is frequent use of a I-IVm chord change; toward the end of the song, this alternates with I-iIVm, a first inversion of the F#m. The change is audible and expressive – a good example of attention to detail. Another example is the main theme for the film *Wag The Dog*, written by Mark Knopfler. The basic sequence is:

I	VII	IVmaj	VI	VII
Am	G	D	F	G

But the third chord is inverted to create a descending bass line:

I	VII	iIVmaj	VI	VII
Am	G	D/F#	F	G

Inversions play a significant role in the eight-bar verse of Gabrielle's 'Give Me Just A Little More Time':

I	iV	VI	V	IV	iI	iIImaj	V
Bb	F/A	Gm	F	Eb	Bb/D	C/E	F

Inversions are crucial to 'When A Man Loves A Woman', 'Baby Now That I've Found You', 'Stay With Me Till Dawn', 'Circle', 'What Becomes Of The Broken-Hearted', 'Mama', 'Perfect Circle', 'The Mighty Quinn', 'Say What You Want, the intro of 'Desperate People' and the coda of 'On Every Street'. It is especially worthwhile studying 'What Becomes Of The Broken-Hearted' for a whole string of inversions to hear what they can do.

Many of the Beach Boys' songs from the *Pet Sounds* era, written by Brian Wilson, make good use of inversions. The realisation that the bass did not always have to play roots, as demonstrated by these songs, was highly influential on Paul McCartney's input into The Beatles from the mid-1960s onward.

Ascending and Descending Chord Sequences

Inversions can play a significant role in creating ascending and descending chord sequences. Many popular songs have upward or downward progressions where the bass moves step-wise by a semitone (half-step) or tone (full step): 'Whatever', 'All You Need Is Love', 'I Am The Walrus', 'Our House', 'Bell Bottom Blues', 'Whiter Shade Of Pale', 'Go Now', 'Pictures Of Lily', 'Accidents Will Happen', 'Dear Prudence', 'Tales Of Brave Ulysses', 'White Room', 'Awaiting On You All', 'Turn Turn Turn'. 'Chestnut Mare' has two descending chord sequences in the same key; the first starts at I and goes down the scale; the second starts at IV and goes down the scale.

Let's take a look at how this can be done, beginning with these notes: C B A G F E D. If we harmonized this by using the primary chords of the scale and treating each note as a root note, the result would be:

I	VII	VI	V	IV	II	II
C	Bdim	Am	G	F	Em	Dm
c	b	a	g	f	e	d
r	r	r	r	r	r	r

Try strumming these chords at a medium tempo, two beats to each. This is a little stodgy and predictable, and the awkward diminished chord between C and Am would be horrible to sing over.

By using an inversion, we could play this:

I	V	VI	V	IV	III	II
C	G/B	Am	G	F	Em	Dm
c	b	a	g	f	e	d
r	1st	r	r	r	r	r

This is the most common way of harmonizing a bassline using these notes. In fact, it is possible to harmonize this bassline using only the three major chords:

I	V	IV	I	IV	I	V
C	G/B	F/A	C/G	F	C/E	D/G
c	b	a	g	f	e	d
r	1st	1st	2nd	r	1st	2nd

We could use this technique for a verse and introduce the minor chords for a chorus or bridge. Here's another possibility using just the three minor chords:

VI	III	VI	III	II	II	II
Am/C	Em/B	Am	Em/G	Dm/F	Em	Dm
c	b	a	g	f	e	d
1st	2nd	r	1st	1st	r	r

In this example, fewer chords are used:

I	V	VI	VI	IV	I	II
C	G/B	Am	Am7/G	F	C/E	Dm
c	b	a	g	f	e	d
r	1st	r	3rd	r	1st	r

The following is a variation with a chromatic passing note:

I	V	bVII	VI
C	G/B	Bb	Am
c	b	b flat	a
r	1st	r	r

Because that Bb suggests F major, it may sound good to treat VI as a first inversion:

I	V	bVII	IV
C	G/B	Bb	F/A
c	b	b flat	a
r	1st	r	1st

Here's an extended variation:

I	V	bVII	IV	bVI
C	G/B	Bb	F/A	Ab
c	b	b flat	a	a flat
r	1st	r	1st	r

Sometimes we can treat that the note Bb as a 1st inversion:

I	V	Vm	V
C	G/B	Gm/Bb	F/A
c	b	b flat	a
r	1st	r	1st

Here's an avant-garde harmony for this chromatic line:

I	VIImaj	bVII	VI	bVI
C	B	Bb	Am	Ab
c	b	b flat	a	a flat
r	r	r	r	r

Here's a static harmonization using the inversions of the major seventh and dominant seventh chords:

I	Imaj7	I7	VI (or IV)
C	Cmaj7/B	C7/Bb	Am (or F/A)
c	b	b flat	a
r	3rd	3rd	r

In the bridge of 'The Long And Winding Road', we find this:

I	IV	I	II	V
C/G	F	C/E	Dm	G
g	f	e	d	g
2nd	r	1st	r	r

Here's an ascending sequence from 'I'm Alive':

I	V7	I	IV	I	VI	I	VI	bVII
C	G7	C	F	C	Am	C	Am	Bb
c	d	e	f	g	a	g	a	b flat
r	2nd	1st	r	2nd	r	2nd	r	r

Let's try a minor key. This is a common turnaround:

I	VII	VI	V
Am	G	F	Em
a	g	f	e
r	r	r	r

With inversions:

I	III	IV	V
Am	C/G	Dm/F	Em
a	g	f	e
r,	2nd	1st	r

Here's an interesting variant:

I	V	VII	IVmaj	VI	III	IV
Am	E/G#	G	D/F#	F	C/E	Dm
a	g#	g	f#	f	e	d
r	1st	r	1st	r	1st	r

And an ascending progression:

II	I	IV	I	VI	V	I	VImaj
Dm	C/E	F	C/G	Am	G/B	C	A/C#
d	e	f	g	a	b	c	c#
r	1st	r	2nd	r	lst	r	1st

I hope these examples will encourage you to explore the musical possibilities offered by both inversions and scale-like bass lines.

Extended Chords

Now we can sample the musical shadings offered by more advanced chords. This is part two of the Chord Dictionary.

Seventh Chords with a Sharpened Fifth

An extended chord can be formed by *sharpening* the fifth of a dominant or major seventh chord – C7: C E G Bb becomes C E G# Bb; Cmaj7: C E G B becomes C E G# B. This is like superimposing an augmented triad on a major triad two tones (full steps) above. It has a mildly dissonant sound. There's a 7#5 chord at the end of each four-bar phrase in John Lee Hooker's 'The Healer'.

This chord imparts a mild blues/jazz feel and is used as a passing chord or as a means of changing keys. The raised fifth may lead to either the fifth or the sixth in a different chord. C7#5 might go to F or Am.

CHORD DICTIONARY
PART 2 ADVANCED HARMONY

Seventh chords with a sharpened fifth

Seventh chords with a flattened fifth

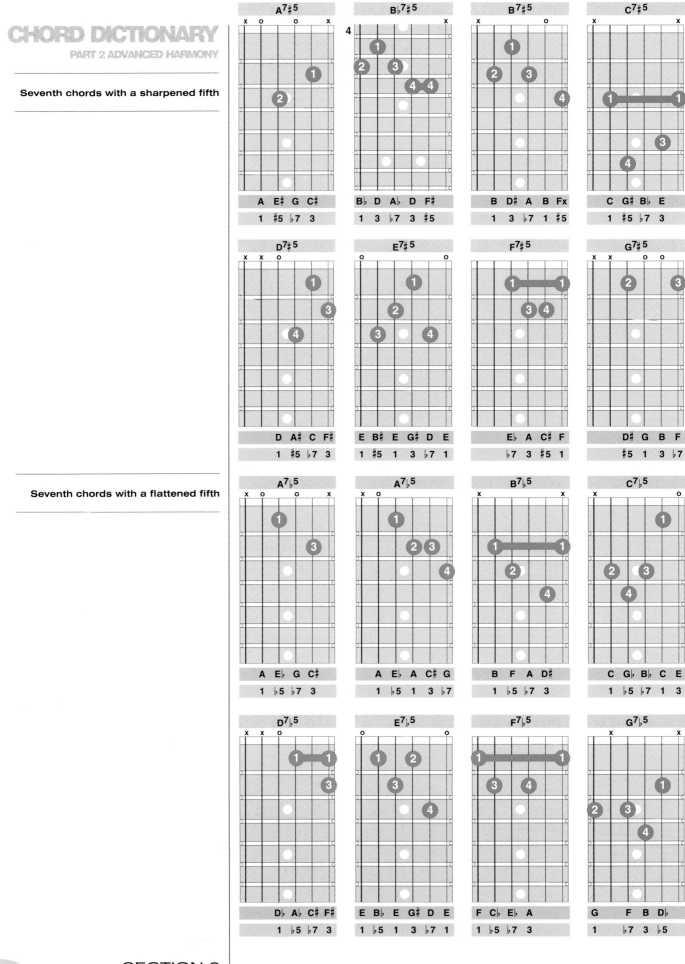

SECTION 9

Seventh Chords with a Flattened Fifth

Another extended chord is formed by *flattening* the fifth of a dominant seventh – C7: C E G Bb becomes C E Gb Bb. The 7b5 is close to a dom7 chord. Like the 7#5, it is used as a passing chord or to change key. There are several of these in 'Moon River' and one in Santana's 'Smooth'.

Chords of the Second Octave

To create these chords, the scale is extended over another octave:

C	D	E	F	G	A	B	C	D	E	F	G	A	B	C
1	2	3	4	5	6	7	8	9	10	11	12	13	14	15

Any notes that the ear cannot distinguish as making any harmonic difference to the chord can be eliminated. Therefore, 8 and 15 don't exist (because they duplicate the root note); neither does the 10 (which the ear hears as a third), the 12 (which it hears as a fifth), or the 14 (which it hears as a seventh). That just leaves the 9, 11 and 13.

C	D	E	F	G	A	B	C	D	E	F	G	A	B	C
1	2	3	4	5	6	7		9		11		13		

These chords are difficult to voice on the guitar, and in the case of the full 13th, impossible – because it has seven notes and the guitar has only six strings. Their harmonic complexity means they are sometimes unsuited to popular music (unlike jazz, where they are heard all the time). They are much easier to play on a keyboard, where, unlike the guitar, they can be voiced with the individual notes in sequence.

Major and Dominant Ninths

Ninth chords are formed by adding the ninth (that is, the secondof the scale an octave higher) to a seventh chord – C7: C E G Bb becomes C E G Bb D; Cmaj7: C E G B becomes C E G B D. There is also Cadd9: C E G D, where the seventh is missing.

These ninth chords are similar to their respective sevenths, if a little smoother. The dominant ninth is probably the most significant of the three in popular music. It was used extensively in 1950s rock'n'roll, in 1960s R&B, soul and funk, as well as in jazz. It is not quite as stark as the dominant seventh. The major ninth, compared to the major seventh, is less lush sounding. The ninth in both cases has a "diluting" effect. The add9 is tenser than either, with more emphasis

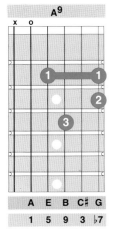
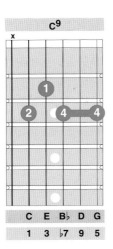
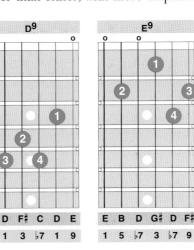

Dominant ninths

SECTION 9

117

Dominant ninths continued

Add ninth chord shape

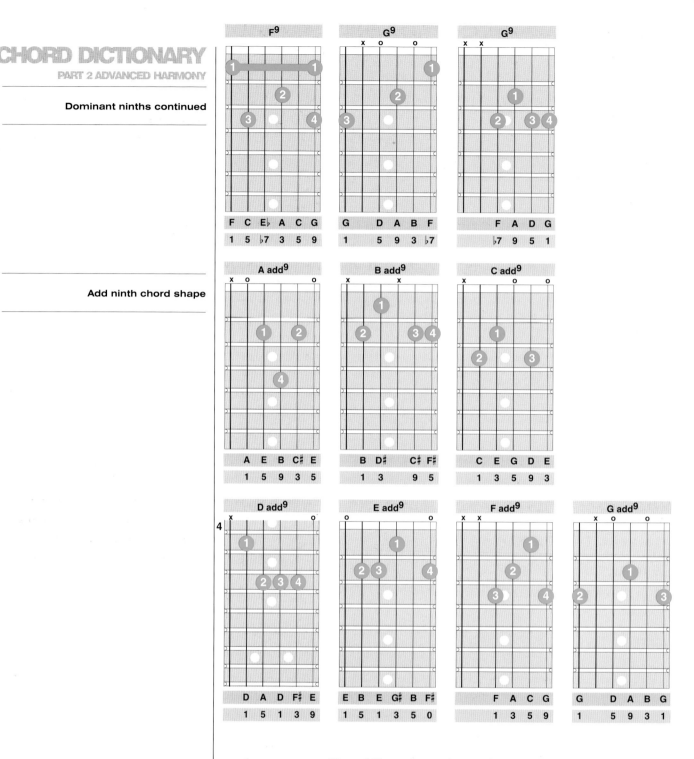

F⁹					
F	C	E♭	A	C	G
1	5	♭7	3	5	9

G⁹					
G		D	A	B	F
1		5	9	3	♭7

G⁹					
		F	A	D	G
		♭7	9	5	1

A add⁹					
A	E	B	C♯	E	
1	5	9	3	5	

B add⁹					
B	D♯		C♯	F♯	
1	3		9	5	

C add⁹					
C	E	G	D	E	
1	3	5	9	3	

D add⁹					
D	A	D	F♯	E	
1	5	1	3	9	

E add⁹					
E	B	E	G♯	B	F♯
1	5	1	3	5	0

F add⁹				
F	A	C	G	
1	3	5	9	

G add⁹					
G		D	A	B	G
1		5	9	3	1

on the extra note. The add9 can be an interesting variation to a straight major chord, and it is an easier chord to find on the guitar than the others. Both dominant and major ninths can also have altered-fifth forms, in which the fifth is flattened or sharpened. It should also be mentioned that it is possible to add a ninth on top of a fifth on the bottom three strings of the guitar (G D A). This was popularized by Andy Summers of The Police on songs like 'Message In A Bottle' (he also used add 9s on 'Every Breath You Take') and features prominently in Dubh Chapter's 'Palace Of Dreams'.

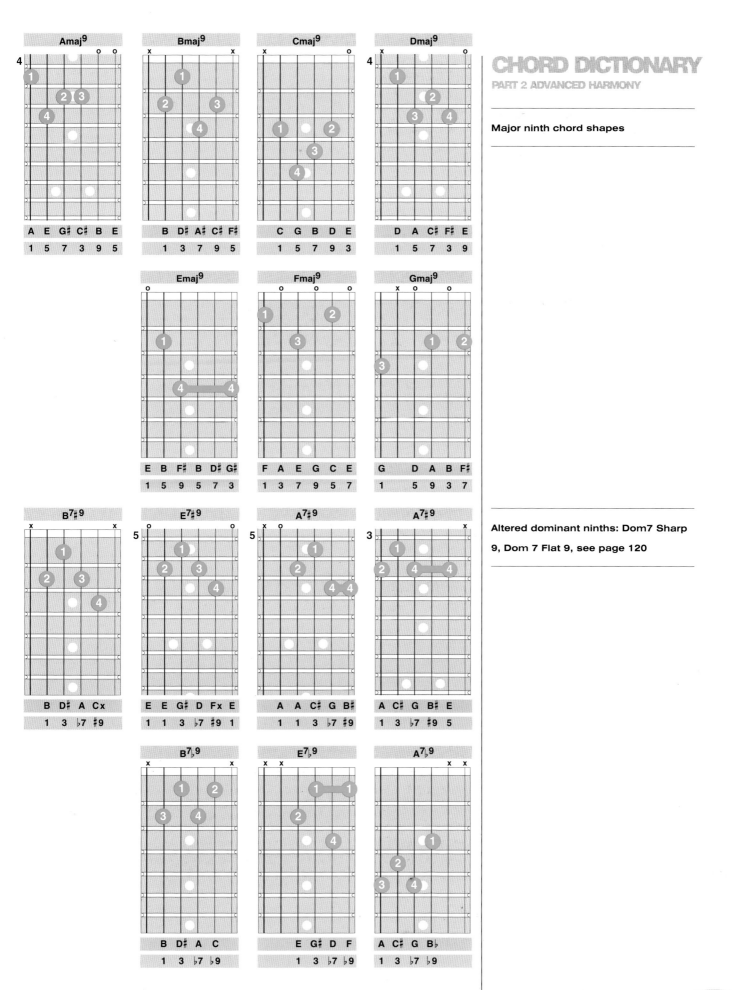

Major ninth chord shapes

Altered dominant ninths: Dom7 Sharp 9, Dom 7 Flat 9, see page 120

Altered Dominant Ninths: Dom7 Sharp 9, Dom7 Flat 9

The dom7 sharp 9 is popularly known as the "Jimi Hendrix chord" because of its use in songs such as 'Purple Haze', 'Stone Free' and 'Crosstown Traffic'. It should be noted that what Hendrix is sometimes playing (as in the case of 'Foxy Lady') is in fact only a minor seventh. The Stone Roses used this in 'Love Spreads'. It generates baggy-trousered Manchester-type funk very easily, especially if you put it through a wah-wah. It is also favoured among heavy rock bands for those Spinal Tap-ish thrash endings. The flat 9 chord is rare but turns up in blues and slower tempo songs if the harmony is sufficiently sophisticated.

Minor Ninths

If you add a ninth to a minor seventh chord, you get a minor ninth – Cm7: C Eb G Bb becomes C Eb G Bb D. There is also Cmadd9: C Eb G D, without the

minor add ninth chord shapes

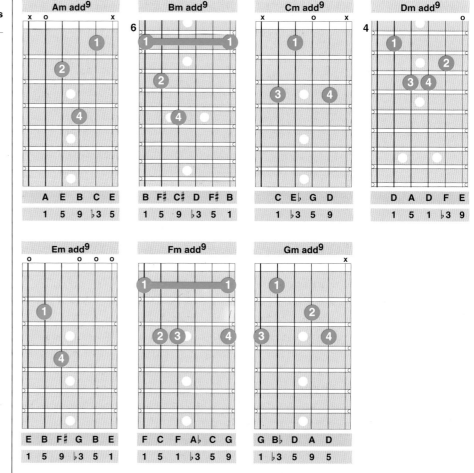

seventh. The min9 is similar to the min7 in sound. It is often heard in soul and MOR ballad material as a substitute for the min7, and it has the effect of intensifying the minor chord. It can be found in some rock and folk. There are wonderful examples of the minor9 chord in 'I Remember California', 'Badge', 'Alone Again Or', the intro to 'Achilles Last Stand', and in many songs by All About Eve.

Minor ninth chord shapes

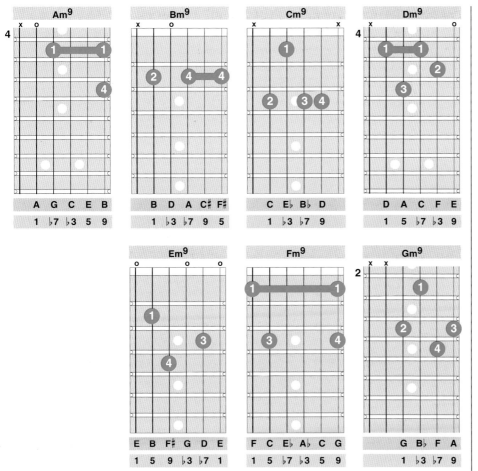

A G C E B	B D A C# F#	C E♭ B♭ D	D A C F E
1 ♭7 ♭3 5 9	1 ♭3 ♭7 9 5	1 ♭3 ♭7 9	1 5 ♭7 ♭3 9

E B F# G D E	F C E♭ A♭ C G	G B♭ F A
1 5 9 ♭3 ♭7 1	1 5 ♭7 ♭3 5 9	1 ♭3 ♭7 9

Major and Minor 11ths

Adding the 11th note (the fourth an octave higher) to a dominant seventh chord or to a major or minor ninth chord produces an 11th chord. C11 is formed when C E G Bb D becomes C E G Bb D F; Cmaj11 is formed when C E G B D becomes C E G B D F; Cmin11 is formed when C Eb G Bb D becomes C Eb G Bb D F. Dominant and major sevenths can also become add11s by the addition of just the 11th. The former can be thought of as two major chords a tone (full step) apart added together; the latter a major chord with a diminished triad on top.

These are complex chords with a subtle colour. Their use on the guitar is compromised by the fact that they are difficult to voice in an effective way. The more different notes there are in a chord, the harder it is to find a satisfactory

Eleventh chord shapes

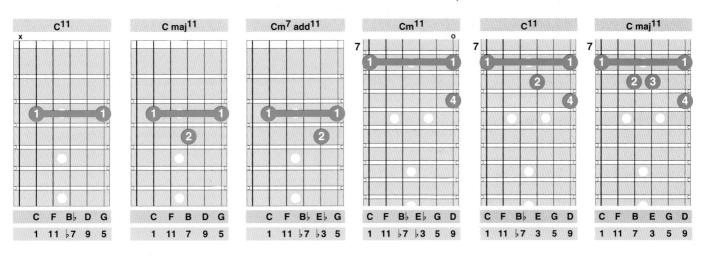

C F B♭ D G	C F B D G	C F B♭ E♭ G	C F B♭ E♭ G D	C F B♭ E G D	C F B E G D
1 11 ♭7 9 5	1 11 7 9 5	1 11 ♭7 ♭3 5	1 11 ♭7 ♭3 5 9	1 11 ♭7 3 5 9	1 11 7 3 5 9

fingering. On the piano Cmaj11 (C E G B D F) is easy to play. The notes can be voiced in ascending order, three in each hand. If you try to do that on the guitar, look what happens: C is sixth string, fret eight; E is fifth string, fret seven; G is fourth string, fret five. Holding these down will use up your first, third and fourth fingers – but you've got only half the chord. What about B (third string, fret four), D (second string, fret three) and F (first string, fret one)? Very often one of the notes has to be left out – usually either the fifth or the ninth - to make an 11th chord playable. They do turn up, though: an 11th is heard at start of 'I'm Not In Love', resolving to a straight major chord.

Major and Minor 13ths

All 13th chords on the guitar are a compromise. As with the 11th, they are difficult to finger and some notes have to be left out. These chords are formed by adding the 13th (the sixth an octave higher) to a dominant or a major or minor 11th. Cdom13 is C E G Bb D F A; Cmaj13 is C E G B D F A; Cm13 is C Eb G Bb D F A. The formation of the minor 13 is affected by which minor scale is used, Aeolian or Dorian. One variant that does sometimes appear is the dom7add13 (C

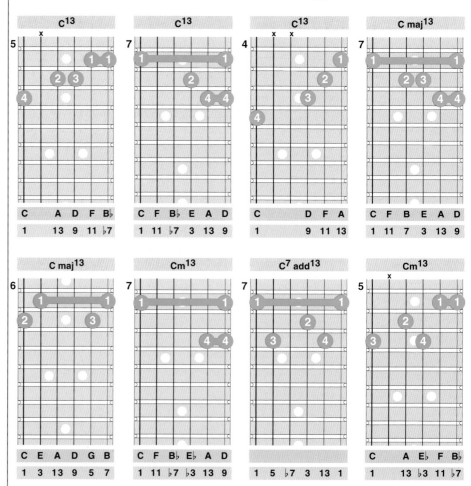

E G Bb A) because it is easy to play. There are a number of these in 'Oblivious'.

Complex chords such as these have little function in popular songwriting because their tone colours are too indistinct. The relationships of the chords you choose are much more important than the types, as long as the ones you're using generally fit the style in which you're writing.

Slash Chords That Are Not Inversions

Take an ordinary F major, top four strings only: F A C F. If we add the open fifth

string, we get F/A – a first inversion; if we hold down C on the fifth string – C F A C F – it's a second inversion. But what happens if we play a G on the sixth string and mute the fifth string, so we have G (x) F A C F? We have F/G. Depending on the musical context, we could stop thinking of the F chord as a chord in its own right and analyze it as if G were the root note. If so, F becomes the flat seventh, A the ninth and C the 11th. (The third, B, and the fifth, D, are both missing.) Strictly speaking, we need a third to tell us whether the chord is major or minor, but context might do that. So this F/G could be used in either a major or minor context as a G dom11. This approach suggests the following:

1 Take a major chord and add a bass note a tone (full step) above its root to make a passable dominant11th.

2 Take a major chord and add a bass note a fourth above its root to make a ninth chord (C under G B D = 1, 5, 7, 9).

Using Extended Chords

In most pop, rock and soul songwriting these more complex chords are not used very often. Fascinating as they are, try not to get carried away with them. It is a fatal habit among keyboard players who write songs that because it is easy for them to play extended chords they have to use them all the time. I have known keyboard players who seemed incapable of playing a simple C Em Am G progression without turning it into C11, Emadd9b5, Am7b5 and Gdom11(no 3rd). This is as beside the point as guitarists who insist that every song has to have at least two long guitar solos! Of course this stuff is interesting to play. But songwriting is not about giving yourself *interesting* things to play. The individual instrumental parts of a song may be rather dull, or at least not taxing, but the magic of the song is in the whole being greater than the sum of the parts.

So use extended chords carefully, just to add a touch of colour here and there. One ninth chord placed at a telling position in a chord progression can add far more than half a dozen. One way to try this out is to take some of the turnarounds in section 3 and change one of the chords into a more complicated form.

Now it is time to explore one of the most exciting areas of songwriting craft. Got your backpack, provisions, suncream and maps? We are going travelling - into the world of key changes.

What Is a Key?

A key is a structural device of music. It is derived from a major or minor scale, which in turn creates the chords that belong to that key. In terms of our experience of music, keys are a fundamental aspect of the way we hear and organise it in our minds. A key is a tonal center, with the key note and key chord at its core. Whenever we land on the key chord (chord I), it feels as though we have reached "home", or the center of the music – or, to use a physical analogy, regained our balance. In a major key, this is usually a satisfactory, secure place to be; in a minor key, it will feel sadder.

Even within one key, the progression of chords represents a departure from the center. To use a geographical metaphor, the chords within a key are like the different districts of your home town, with happy and sad associations. Changing the chord within a key is like making a short journey. By analogy, a key change is like a visit to another county or state, which could be nearby and therefore have similar terrain, or distant and have a very different landscape. A key change is called a "modulation".

Why Is Modulation Important?

In longer pieces of music, key changes are essential to avoid monotony. Consider the symphony. Most 19th- and early 20th-century symphonies last, on average, 30 to 45 minutes. A symphony that remained in one key would certainly require extraordinary invention to prevent boredom setting in even during its first movement. That's why expansive forms such as the symphony make extensive use of modulation, and that modulation itself often expresses meaning or dramatizes an inner journey.

Some composers have even used keys as though they possessed intrinsic extra-musical qualities or values. In Baroque music, some composers viewed the keys as a sort of hierarchy: flat keys were associated with the realms of earth, suffering and hell; sharp keys represented increasing happiness and bliss, culminating in the "heavenly domain" of E major (the sharpest key in common use at that time). For more on the symbolic possibilities of keys and key changes, read Wilfred Mellors's excellent *Vaughan Williams and the Vision of Albion* (1997).

A song is a short musical form. Modulation is therefore not as crucial – but it may be desirable, to add interest and contrast. Even in the microcosmic world of the popular song, key changing can be used to fine effect. Modulation can certainly be found in much popular songwriting, though noticeably less so toward the end of the 20th century, as popular music became increasingly rhythmic and devoid of harmonic colour.

Modulations may be fleeting or more secure. A piece of music might move through several keys in a matter of bars with none of the keys given sufficient time to become established. Tonality can be blurred, and it is not always easy to say what key certain bars of music are in – or even if they *are* in a defined key.

The Magic of Distance

All major keys have identical internal structures; they are simply built on key notes (roots) of differing pitch. But a piece that changes key from G to C *subjectively* sounds as though it has "gone somewhere". From the perspective of C major, G major seems to be a different 'place'. The sense of difference is even more profound if we move from C major to, say, Bb minor.

Modulation may support the lyric content – or undermine it. Imagine you are writing a love song in which the speaker sings of the sorrow left behind, in a major key, and the happiness ahead, in a minor key. The keys are the reverse of what you might expect, which suggests that the song is about something more than what the lyric is explicitly saying.

A key change can have a subtle effect that perhaps represents uncertainty or an emotional dislocation. Or it can be crude, as when it is used to ratchet up the final choruses for added excitement.

Keys and Singing

When you write songs for yourself to sing, take into account the keys that suit your voice. Find your lowest note and your highest note for comfortable singing, and then any higher notes you could get by pushing your voice, and finally high notes that are reachable by singing falsetto. Relate the highest comfortable note to the scale of the key in which you want to write a song. Check to see if this note is an important one in the scale, like the root, third or fifth. You can plan your melody to take that into consideration.

A well-known recording trick is to pitch a song in a key that is slightly too high for the singer, so the straining for notes becomes part of the performance. Motown writers like Holland-Dozier-Holland used to pitch songs in keys that were just a bit too high for Marvin Gaye or Levi Stubbs of The Four Tops, to bring out more passion in their voices. But if you're going to sing your songs live, don't use this technique on too many – or you'll never get through a set with your voice intact. The opposite effect is not so common, but worth considering. 'Perfect Circle' gains something from Michael Stipe singing at the low end of his range, and as for Lee Marvin's 'Wanderin' Star'. . . .

With age, the voice naturally loses some of its range. This has had an interesting consequence for a singer-songwriter like Joni Mitchell who has relied on altered guitar tunings. Over the years her tunings have had to move down to match the drop in her voice – causing some intonation problems as the guitar strings have got slacker.

Near Keys and Far Keys

Some keys are "closer" to each other than others – we can speak of "related" keys, or "near" and "far" keys. Adjacent keys (one sharp or one flat away) are close. Each key has a relative minor or major that is three semitones (half-steps) from the root note; that is a near key. These can be seen on this figure:

Cb	Gb	Db	Ab	Eb	Bb	F	C	G	D	A	E	B	F#	C#
Abm	Ebm	Bbm	Fm	Cm	Gm	Dm	Am	Em	Bm	F#m	C#m	G#m	D#m	A#m

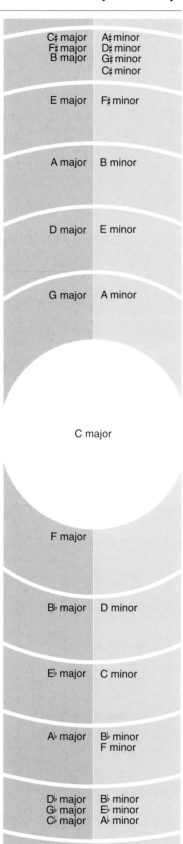

C♯ major	A♯ minor
F♯ major	D♯ minor
B major	G♯ minor
	C♯ minor
E major	F♯ minor
A major	B minor
D major	E minor
G major	A minor
C major	
F major	
B♭ major	D minor
E♭ major	C minor
A♭ major	B♭ minor
	F minor
D♭ major	B♭ minor
G♭ major	E♭ minor
C♭ major	A♭ minor

From C major, the closest keys are F, G, Am, Dm and Em – chords IV, V, VI, II and III of the key. Next would come C minor, the tonic minor – the minor key that shares the same root note.

You'll notice that there are 15 major and 15 minor keys on this diagram. If Cb = B, Gb = F# and Db = C#, that makes the number 12, the same as the number of notes. The number of possible modulations and key-changing effects within this apparently limited number is extraordinary. There are a number of ways in which the relative distance of keys can be assessed. Here is one:

As you can see from this table, adjacent near keys tend to have three or four chords in common, making it easy to change from C major to any of them. Use the chord table in Section 3 to find common chords.

Key Changing for Guitarists

Changing keys is more problematic for guitarists than pianists because of the fingering problems that may arise. This is one reason why songwriter-guitarists tend to use less modulation than songwriter-pianists. For example, take a song whose verse and chorus are in A, with plenty of open-string chords. If you raise the key a semitone (half-step) to Bb, five of the six primary chords turn into barre chords. Guitarists would therefore tend to favour changing to a key that has easier chord shapes.

You can exploit this characteristic of the guitar by reversing the scenario. Start in a key that requires barre chords and then modulate up a semitone (half-step) to a key with open-string chords. The change in the timbre of the chords can be striking. Try B into C or F# into G or D#m into E minor. The effect is further complicated by the resonance of certain chords against others – according to how many strings are in the chords. If you write an introduction in an awkward key, at least you won't be stuck in it for very long.

Keys and Their Associations

On the guitar, A major and E major are both associated with rock, the latter especially with heavy rock, with B and F# as also-rans. The keys of D, G and A are popular in indie/"jangle" styles because of the ringing open strings. R.E.M. had a long-standing love affair with E minor. Oddly, C has never been a popular rock key.

Some players have marked preferences for certain keys. Mark Knopfler's early songs were often in F and D minor. Blues players who detune a semitone (half-step) often end up in Eb and Ab by default, as in 'Voodoo Chile (Slight Return)' and some of Stevie Ray Vaughan's songs. Songwriters sometimes build up personal associations with keys – they have "hot" keys and "cold" keys, "summery" keys and "wintery" keys.

The keys of Eb and Bb are suited to brass instruments and are associated with 1960s soul/Motown. The Celtic harp is usually tuned to C minor, so it has Celtic folk associations (listen to the music of Breton harpist Alan Stivell). F minor is a favoured key for James Bond music – session trombonist Don Lusher once said, "If we got a booking for a Bond session with John [Barry], it'd be, 'Oh yes. That'll be another week of F minor then.' It was always F minor. You could bet on it!". This came true yet again with 'The World Is Not Enough'.

Which Keys Suit the Guitar?

The natural keys for the guitar are those in which the open strings can be maximised. These range from F to E, with their attendant minors. Here are the major keys, with the number of open-string chords in each (this covers chords I-VI plus the bVII):

Cb	Gb	Db	Ab	Eb	Bb	F	C	G	D	A	E	B	F#	C#
2	1	0	0	0	1	3	5	5	5	4	3	2	1	0	0

Odd Keys and the Capo

Guitarists often employ a capo (capodastro, from the Italian *capo tastro*, meaning "head stop") when playing in flat keys, to make it possible to use open-string chords. A capo can also be used to lower the action and string tension. Some players like to tune their 12-strings a semitone (half-step) or tone (full step) below concert pitch and then capo at the first or second fret, to lessen the tension on the neck. A capo makes it easy to try a song in different keys with the same chord shapes till you find one that suits your voice. They're great for recording more than one guitar part or in a duo to get a fuller sound.

Here is a table for using the capo. Simply find the key you are playing in and read up to the shapes at the top and the capo position at the side.

Famous Songs That Use a Capo

I 'Three Steps To Heaven', 'Show Me Heaven', 'Day After Day', 'Kiss Me' 'She Said', 'Changing Of The Guard', 'Jokerman'.

II 'Mrs Robinson', 'Wonderwall', 'Let's See Action', 'Fast Car', 'One Of Us', 'Love Is The Law', 'Julia', 'Norwegian Wood', 'Why Does It Always Rain On Me', 'Run To You', 'And Your Bird Can Sing', 'For No One', 'Julia', 'Nowhere Man', 'Wait', 'Sisters Of Mercy', 'A Hard Rain's Gonna Fall', "All I Really Want To Do', 'She Belongs To Me'.

III 'Debora', 'Homeward Bound', 'Long Long Long', 'No Surprises', '5:15', 'Getaway'. 'Magic Blue' 'Mr Tambourine Man' (Dylan), 'By The Light Of A Magical Moon', 'One Inch Rock', 'Martha My Dear', 'Hurry Up and Wait', 'More Than Us', 'Every Grain Of Sand', "I Want You (Dylan)', 'Things Have Changed'.

IV 'Catch The Wind', 'Ride A White Swan', 'Holy Mother', 'That's Entertainment', 'Ironic', 'Tumbling Dice' (with open G tuning'), 'It's All Over Now, Baby Blue', 'All Along The Watchtower' (Dylan) 'Positively Fourth Street'.

V 'I Am The Resurrection', 'Torn', 'It's Only Love' (The Beatles), 'For You Blue'. 'Telegram Sam', 'Daisies Of The Galaxy', 'Michelle'

VI 'Halleluja,' 'Piggies'.

VII 'Here Comes The Sun', 'Blowin' In The Wind', 'Tramp The Dirt Down', 'Driftwood', 'Hotel California'.

VIII 'Girl'.

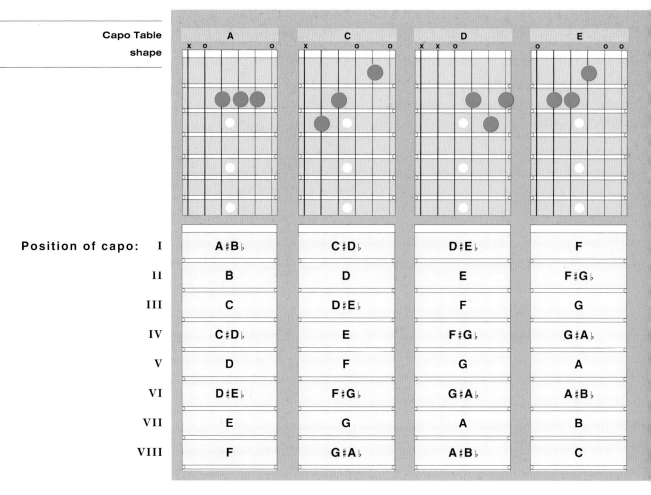

Capo Table
shape

Position of capo:	A	C	D	E
I	A♯/B♭	C♯/D♭	D♯/E♭	F
II	B	D	E	F♯/G♭
III	C	D♯/E♭	F	G
IV	C♯/D♭	E	F♯/G♭	G♯/A♭
V	D	F	G	A
VI	D♯/E♭	F♯/G♭	G♯/A♭	A♯/B♭
VII	E	G	A	B
VIII	F	G♯/A♭	A♯/B♭	C

How Do I Change Key?

There are many ways of changing key – the one you use depends partly on whether you are going to a near or far key.

Using Chord V

The simplest way is to play chord V of the key you want to get into and from that chord proceed to chord I of the new key. So if you wanted to go from C major to G major, chord V of G is D (instead of Dm as in C). If this chord V is played as a dominant seventh, the change is strengthened. That gives us this chord progression:

C F G F C Dm D7 G

At the end of this, we are in G major. If that last chord then becomes a G7, we can go straight back to C because G is chord V of C major. Remember that any dominant seventh can also take you into a minor key, as G7 is the dominant seventh of C minor as well as C major. The key chord to which you're heading can also be approached from the new chord IV, but the effect is weaker and in the case of going from C to G ambiguous, since C (I in the old key) is IV in the new key (G).

A sequence of dominant seventh chords can create a sense of passing through a series of keys. Take this sequence, starting from A major:

F#m B E A D Bm A

G	Am	Dm	Em
G♯A♭	A♯mB♭m	D♯mE♭m	Fm
A	Bm	Em	F♯mG♭m
A♯B♭	Cm	Fm	Gm
B	C♯mD♭m	F♯mG♭m	G♯mA♭m
C	Dm	Gm	Am
C♯D♭	D♯mE♭m	G♯mA♭m	A♯mB♭m
D	Em	Am	Bm
D♯E♭	Fm	A♯mB♭m	Cm

Notice how several of these chords have a dual harmonic function. The fourth chord establishes E as the new key, but the next A takes us briefly into D before returning to A. Try strumming the following version and listen to the difference:

After B7, we expect E to be the new key – but E7 (a dominant seventh) suggests that it is chord V of A. But when we land on A, the same thing happens. It's a dominant seventh, suggesting that the new key is D. And then it happens again. D is another dominant seventh, but instead of going to G we go to Bm and then to A as the new key. We are never allowed to settle on any chord as a new key; the succession of dominant sevenths insists that we move on to the next. This was used as a bridge in Badfinger's 'No Matter What'; 'Crosstown Traffic' and the chorus of 'Sunny Afternoon' have similar sequences.

Consider this progression from the verse of 'Now I'm Here' for a series of V-I changes:

V	I	V	I	V	I	V	I
G	C	A	D	B	E	F#	C#

Apart from chord V, you can use another chord that is common to both keys, approach it as you would from the home key with a home-key chord, but leave it with a chord that is only in the new key. This should either be chord V of the new key or should lead to chord V of the new key.

Same Chord, Different Role

It's important to remember that a single chord can have a different role in different keys, even though its pitch (and its fingering on the guitar) remains the same. The analogy would be with an actor and his or her various film roles. A chord has the ability to play different roles according to whether it is chord I, II, III, IV, V, VI or VII of the key. Consider the function of C in the following keys:

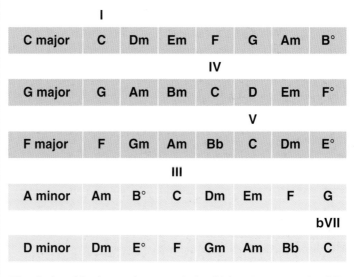

	I					
C major	C	Dm	Em	F	G	Am	B°

			IV			
G major	G	Am	Bm	C	D	Em	F°

				V		
F major	F	Gm	Am	Bb	C	Dm	E°

		III				
A minor	Am	B°	C	Dm	Em	F	G

						bVII
D minor	Dm	E°	F	Gm	Am	Bb	C

The C chord is always the same in itself, but it appears in different roles.

Shortcut Key Changes

Key changes in pop songs usually have to be achieved very quickly. Here are some typical "shortcuts" to near keys. Remember that in each instance you could end up in the minor key of the last chord if you wanted.

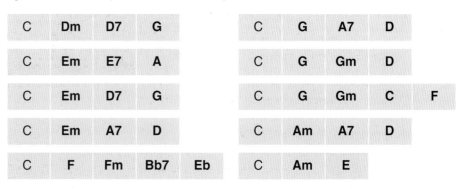

C	Dm	D7	G		C	G	A7	D
C	Em	E7	A		C	G	Gm	D
C	Em	D7	G		C	G	Gm	C	F
C	Em	A7	D		C	Am	A7	D
C	F	Fm	Bb7	Eb	C	Am	E

Notice that IImaj, IIImaj and VImaj all have possibilities for modulation. In the verse of 'I've Got To Get A Message To You', we have a I II V I progression that becomes I II V VImaj (G instead of Gm) to lead from Bb to a C chorus. This is a strong modulation because V in Bb (F) is IV in C. In the verse of 'Stop! In The Name Of Love', the progression goes:

I	Imaj7	Vm	VImaj/7	IV	V	IV	V
C	Cmaj7	Gm	A7	F	G	F	G

This is clever because Gm and A7 are chords IV and V in D minor, so we expect to go to D minor, but instead the music turns back to F – chord IV in C. (To hear a song in C major that does have an A7 leading into D minor, listen to the verse of 'Baby Love'.)

Travelling to distant keys

If you want to go to a distant key, you can choose an intermediary key to help you make the change. For example, imagine going from C major to B major – two keys that have no chords in common.

	I	IV			
Old key	I	IV			
Crude semitone shift	C	F	F#	F#7	B
New key			V	V7	I

	I	III		
Old key	I	III		
Abrupt romantic	C	Em	B	
New key		IVm	I	

	I	III		
Old key	I	III		
Crude semitone shift	C	Em	E7	B
New key			IV7	I

	I	IV	IImaj			
Old key	I	IV	IImaj			
Climbing + secondary key	C	Dm	D7	G	A	B
New key			[V	I]		
				bVI	bVII	I

	I	IIImaj				
Old key	I	IIImaj				
Intermediate key	C	E	A	F#m	F#7	B
New key		[V	I	VI]		
					V7	I

	I	VI	bVImaj			
Old key	I	VI	bVImaj			
Semitone shift+ middle key	C	Am	Ab (G#)	C#m	F#7	B
New key			[V	I]		
				II	V7	I

Remember the possibility of enharmonic chords, which may be written as flat in one key but sharp in another – like the Ab/G# in this example.

Key Changes with Diminished Sevenths

The diminished seventh chord is important for key changing. Each note within a diminished seventh can be the leading note (seventh) for a new tonic. Take G dim7: G Bb Db Fb (E). You can get to this chord from any key whose scale includes one of these notes.

G is the 7th of Ab
Bb (A#) is the 7th of B
Db (C#) is the 7th of D
Fb (E)is the 7th of F

Therefore, G dim7 could take you into the keys of Ab, B, D or F, or their minors. Try changing from Gdim7 to any of these key chords, and you will hear that it works.

Classic Pop Modulation #1: The Semitone Shift

The most common (and slightly vulgar) use of a key change in popular music is to avoid monotony in the repetition of the chorus at the end. Pop songs revolve around the immediate appeal of a repeated chorus, so by shifting the chorus into a new key it can be repeated with a sense of the familiar somehow freshened.

This has tended to be done in two main ways. One is brutally direct: shift up a semitone (half-step).

[C major]	I	II	IV	V				
Old key	C	Dm	F	G	C#	D#m	F#	G#
New key					I	II	IV	V	[C#maj]

Although C major and C#major are only a semitone apart, this is a shift to a distant key. What was a scale of seven natural notes (C D E F G A B C) has become a scale of seven sharps (C# D# E# F# G# A# B#). The chord change from G to C# is inelegant, and usually only the speed of the change and the brio of the arrangement will disguise the dissonance. Even so, the ear accepts the semitone shift as a small step in pitch. And because all the musical material – the melody, the words, the chords, the rhythm, the parts – remain the same, this is enough to make it acceptable.

This key change is an act of musical bravura rather than an approach that is musically smooth. If C is the last chord of the sequence, chord I of C major merely slides up to chord I of C#major. If the sequence ends on chord V, G, that could slide to G#(7) for a V-I into the new key. The problem is that the two keys have no chords in common. Another approach might be via the IIImaj chord and a temporary modulation to A major:

[C major]	I	III	IIImaj				
Old key	C	Em	E	A	G#7	C#	
			[V	I]			
New key				bVI	V	I	[C#maj]

Here's another way of doing it:

Old key	I	III	IIImaj				
	C	Em	E	F#	G#7	C#	
			[I	IImaj]			
New key				IV	V7	I	[C#maj]

Here are some songs that use a semitone shift: 'I Try' D-Eb, 'Glad All Over' D-Eb v, 'Baby Love' v, 'The Onion Song' Ab-A, 'Heaven Help Us All' Ab-A, 'I Got You Babe' F-F#, 'Always Something There To Remind Me' Ab-A, 'Silence Is Golden', 'Harlem Shuffle' Am-Bbm, 'Don't Stand So Close To Me' v Eb ch D, 'The Happening', 'Farewell Is A Lonely Sound', 'For Once In My Life', and 'C'mon C'mon C'mon' (C#m-Dm).

'And I Love Her' starts in F#m (or E), goes to Gm (F) and ends on a D. This is reached by a sudden dislocating leap from E to Gm at the guitar solo. 'I Get Around' starts in G, moves to A for the guitar solo and then to Ab for the last verse and chorus. 'My Cherie Amour' moves from Db to D on a swooning "maybe some day". In 'You Keep Me Hanging On', the home key of Ab contrasts with B and F#. 'I'll Pick A Rose For My Rose' goes from Bb to B to C and does this shift twice. The change from A to Bb in 'Shake Me Wake Me' only serves to pitch Levi Stubbs's agonised vocals to a higher degree of eye-watering anguish.

By the mid-1960s Holland-Dozier-Holland were often willing to exploit the semi-tone shift to dizzy extremes. 'I Guess I'll Always Love You' starts in C but near the end it suddenly shifts up to Db and after only one hook moves up again to D just before the fade. They went further with 'I Hear A Symphony', where the song shifts a semitone (half-step) at least four times and does so somewhat abruptly, causing difficulties for the pitching of the melody (a classic problem of this modulation). It starts in C, moves to Db, then to D and finishes in Eb. Diana Ross copes well with the first three key changes but is audibly off-pitch for a bar on the last one. The ratcheting up, key by key, has significance lyrically in expressing the ecstasy of the lovers. The excessive modulation may also be a nod to the word "symphony" in the title.

Classic Pop Modulation #2: The Tone Shift

After the semitone (half-step) shift comes the tone (full step) shift. This is a key change to a closer key. If a song is in C major, a tone shift will take it to D major, so what was a scale of seven natural notes (C D E F G A B C) becomes a scale of two sharps (D E F# G A B C#).

Like the semitone shift, this key change is usually performed with an act of musical assertion rather than an approach that is musically smooth. In fact, though, there are plenty of common chords with which to make the approach: namely, Em, G and C (as a common bVII chord in D) as well as F (as bIII in D).

Sometimes this modulation is used not only for repeats of a chorus but to contrast a verse and a chorus, giving each chorus a "lift" in relation to the verse. A IV-I change into the new key can easily do the trick:

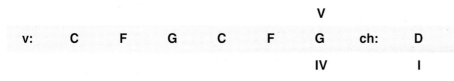

```
                                    V
v:   C      F      G      C      F      G   ch:   D
                                              IV          I
```

Examples of songs that use a tone shift include: 'My Girl' C-D, 'Up The Ladder To The Roof' Bb-C, 'What Becomes Of The Broken-Hearted' v Bb ch C, 'Baby I Need Your Loving' v Bb ch Ab, 'So Lonely' C-D, 'Going Underground' B-C#, 'If You're Going To San Francisco' Em-F#m (partial final v), 'Young Girl', 'Something In The Air' E-F#, 'Londinium' v A ch B s C#, 'She's Waiting' G-A, 'Fox On The Run' C ch Bb v (drops back), 'See My Baby Jive' v D ch E, 'I've Just Got To Get A Message To You' v Bb ch C, 'Don't Worry Baby' E to F#, 'The Best Of Me' E-F#, 'My Sweet Lord' E-F#, 'See Emily Play' v G ch A, 'Dance Away' v Eb ch F, 'Anarchy In The UK' 2nd gtr break C-D then back, 'God Save The Queen' A-B, 'Instant Karma' v A ch G, 'Only Happy When It Rains' (Garbage) v B ch C#, 'Please Forgive Me' v A ch B and 'Exhuming McCarthy' Ab-F#(Gb).

Other Modulations

1 (C-Eb or Ebm)
'Children Of The Revolution' v E ch G, 'Get Ready' v D ch F, 'Shoplifters Of The World', 'You're Going To Lose That Girl', 'Don't Sleep In The Subway' v C ch Eb, 'Goodbye Yellow Brick Road' A C, 'Pretty Woman' F-Ab, 'Summer Of 69' br D-F, 'When You're Young And In Love' C-Eb, 'Tears In Heaven' A-C.

2 (C-E or Em)
'Needles And Pins', 'Message In A Bottle' v C#m ch A, 'There's A Place' v A ch C#m, 'Bus Stop' starts in Em br goes G F#7 Bm (momentarily in Bm).

3 (C-F or Fm)
'Mull Of Kintyre' v A v D, 'You've Got Your Troubles' v Ab D, 'Octopus' Garden' E A, 'Roadrunner' C F, 'Sidewinder' v C ch G, 'I Can See For Miles' v E br A, 'Yes

It Is' in E br A, 'Wishing Well' Em Am, 'Candyman' Gm Cm, 'Badge' v Am br D, 'Someone Saved My Life Tonight' v G ch C, 'Everything I Do (I Do For You)' Db-Gb br.

4 (C-G or Gm)

'Make It Easy On Yourself' v A ch E, 'Crush With Eyeliner' v A ch E, ' Great Things', 'Yeh Yeh', 'The Sidewinder Sleeps Tonite' (v C ch G). 'Wonderful World' v/ch C br goes to G.

5 (C-Ab or Abm)

'Walk This Way' riff E V C v, 'Can't Stop This Thing We Started' A goes to F for br and part of penul. ch.

6 (C-A or Am)

[To A] 'Pictures Of Lily', 'Walk On By' v Am ch F, 'Bell Bottom Blues' v C ch A, 'Bungalow Bill' ch v in relative minor, 'Something' v C br A, 'Things We Said Today' v starts in Am goes to F. 'Don't Leave Me This Way' v in Db, ch in Bb.

[To Am] 'Blackberry Way' v Em ch Gb Am, 'You Don't Have To Say You Love Me' v Dm ch D, 'Fool On The Hill' v D ch Dm, 'Standing In The Shadows Of Love' D Bbm, 'While My Guitar Gently Weeps', 'Roxanne' v Gm ch Bb, 'When I'm Sixty Four' C-Am at br, 'I Should Have Known Better' v ends on a IIImaj and the br is on VI. 'Wild World' v Am ch C.

An unusual variation on this key change is 'Before The Beginning', where Bbm goes down to Gm for the coda.

7 C-Cm or vice versa

'Fool On The Hill', 'While My Guitar Gently Weeps', 'Shakin' All Over' v Em s E, 'Matthew And Son' (v Em ch E) 'Runaway' v Bbm ch Bb, 'Ha! Ha! Said The Clown', 'Part Of The Process' and 'I Am A Child' all three v Dm ch D, 'Come Round Here' G-Gm, 'Seven Rooms Of Gloom' split between F# and D#m, 'Telegram Sam' v A ch Am, 'December Will Be Magic Again' v Cm ch C, 'No Milk Today' v Am ch A, 'Runaway' v Fm ch F, 'Live And Let Die' (starts in G, riff section Gm), 'Lonely Days' v Cm ch C, 'Kiss From A Rose' Gm-G, 'It's Wonderful To Be Loved By You' (Bbm-Bm).

Using Modulation to Contrast Different Sections

Modulation can effectively contrast different song sections. 'You Never Give Me Your Money' starts in A minor, goes to C major for the bridge and then to A for the last verse. The contrasts are enhanced by tempo and arrangement features. Other multiple key songs include 'Lucy In The Sky With Diamonds' (A, F, G), 'Days' (D, F, Dm), 'Band On The Run' (D, Am, C), 'Jungleland' and 'Word On A Wing'.

'Fortress Round My Heart' has a verse in Gm, Eb, F#m but the chorus is in Em. 'Something In The Air' moves from E to F# to C to Ab. 'Londinium' goes from A in the verse to B in the chorus to C# in the last chorus. 'Pinball Wizard' has an intro in Bm, goes to B and D and has a final verse in A. A lover's exuberance is depicted in 'The Happening' by a mid-verse jump from G major to Bb major, a bridge modulation to E minor and a last verse that goes up a semitone (half-step) from the first verse in order to go Ab major and then to B.

Unsettled or Ambiguous Key Centers

Techniques such as displacing, suppressing or delaying the key chord, or using chords that don't belong to any one key, can create tonal ambiguity. Consider this sequence from the verse of 'Step Inside Love':

C	Gm7	Gb9	Gb7	F	Fm7	E7	Eb	F	G7	Dm7	G7

This progression keeps us guessing as far as key is concerned. The emotional effect is to arouse a complex emotion rather than a simple one.

Using Transposition

'My Generation', 'All Of The Day And All Of The Night' and 'You Really Got Me' are songs that use a simple chord change and transpose it into different keys. The chorus of 'California Girls' pushes a melodic idea through B to A to G. Semitone (half-step) or tone (full step) shifts often occur with this technique, though its aim is often not to change key but to preserve the melodic material. 'House Of Fun' starts in D and goes to Em and F#m on the chorus as the hook line is transposed up a tone.

Of all the techniques covered in this book I would say that currently modulation is the most neglected technique in popular song. It can take planning and a bit more trial-and-error with progressions, but a well-judged key change can greatly deepen a song. For more detailed discussion of the emotional effects of modulation see some of the songs discussed in section 14.

GUITAR RESOURCES SECTION 11
Part 1

There are many ways that you, as a guitarist, can get the most from your instrument when writing and recording songs. Here are some tips on how to use the guitar effectively in song arrangements.

Get More from One Guitar

Try these methods to get a fuller recorded sound from a single guitar part:

- Use stereo delay recorded onto two tracks.
- Use stereo delay onto two tracks, with one side also going through chorus, distortion, phasing or similar processing.

● When recording an acoustic, put a pickup on it and send that signal to one track; use a microphone to capture the pure acoustic sound and send that to another track.

Make Two Guitars Work Together

If you perform live with another guitarist or make multi-track recordings, you have the opportunity to use more than one guitar part. The traditional divide between rhythm guitar and lead guitar doesn't always apply in a song, because the lead will usually be confined to a short break in the bridge or middle eight, unless you play counterpoint to the melody in a disciplined way.

Here are some effective guitar combinations. The trick is not to duplicate a part but to create contrasted guitar tones to get a fuller and more interesting sound.

● Use one guitar with single-coil pickups and another with double-coil pickups – for example, a Fender Stratocaster and a Gibson Les Paul. Take advantage of the recently reissued guitars by companies such as Danelectro and Godin that have lipstick-tube pickups or mini-humbuckers.
● Try these pairings: electric + electric, electric + semi-acoustic, electric + acoustic, 6-string + 12-string, nylon + steel.
● Try clean with distorted, standard tuning with open tuning, capoed and non-capoed, standard and detuned standard. Clean guitars provide harmonic definition; overdriven guitars give punch and aggression.
● Make the guitars dynamic by taking care where you bring them into a mix and where you take them out. Play full chords and triads; balance strumming with arpeggios. Remember that fifths strengthen. Other possibilities include rhythmic interweaving, twin lead, contrasted voicings and low on the neck versus high on the neck.

Part Playing

One of the basic principles of making guitars work in a recording is part playing. If you have played a lot of rhythm guitar or sung your songs solo, you will be accustomed to strumming chords constantly to get a full sound. If you like jamming lead guitar, you will be accustomed to having the freedom to constantly whack out endless streams of notes. Neither of these approaches will do for arranging songs.

Phil Manzanera of Roxy Music once told me, "We had a very good producer from the second album onwards, Chris Thomas, who had worked with The Beatles, had done *Dark Side Of The Moon* and subsequently worked with The Sex Pistols. I learned an incredible amount from him about part playing in recording. With Chris it was: 'Look for the gap, don't play over the vocal, less is more.' You learned how to position things – just as all the great Motown stuff has incredible position and texture. All the parts add up to something greater. It all locks in."

To understand part playing requires, first, the realization that the overall sound of a mix will generate the harmony, so you don't have to strum chords all the time. Drums and bass create rhythm, so you don't have to keep strumming for that reason either. Sometimes all that is needed from a lead guitar during the verses is three or four well-chosen notes to add a little melodic interest between gaps in the singing. If you find your multi-track recordings feature more fragmentary guitar parts, then you're probably on to the right thing.

Guitar Effects

Modern technology has made a vast palette of tones available to the electric guitarist. Rock arrangements require a touch of overdrive, distortion or fuzz for an authentic 1960s sound. Remember that distortion tends to soak up frequencies – even on a hard HM track, you may not need as much as you think, let alone as much as is available with most multi-effects processors.

Chorus, delay, flanging and phasing thicken a clean guitar sound and are suitable for rhythm parts. Some of the latest processors offer speaker cabinet, mike placement, vintage amp and guitar simulations to further widen your sound. Synth and MIDI guitars open up a new world of sound triggered from the guitar.

Delay and Counterpoint

Fast delays thicken a sound; longer ones lend depth and interest to lead breaks, even if the delay is quieter than the "dry" signal. Multi-tap echoes allow you to generate rhythms in time with the echo, so it sounds as if there are two guitars playing at the same time. U2's The Edge is a master of this approach. The live recording *Under A Blood Red Sky* gives a good indication of how effective this can be. '11 O'Clock Tick Tock' has a guitar part that acts as counter-melody to the vocal at the same time it outlines the harmony. The Edge's parts often feature open strings ('I Will Follow' and 'Gloria'), and in solos such as the one in 'Sunday Bloody Sunday' he will move up and down a string whilst hitting the adjacent one. 'Pride' also features this sound, along with effective harmonics. Songs such as 'Where The Streets Have No Name' and 'I Still Haven't Found What I'm Looking For' are classics of rhythmic playing with delay, where a simple phrase is transformed by the notes bouncing back.

Working with Sustain

Even the finest acoustic guitars have comparatively short sustain, a factor that has shaped guitar technique. Strumming and fingerpicking are techniques that ensure a wash of sound, and, in the case of fingerpicking, a harmonic backdrop for a melody.

To increase sustain, guitarists have experimented with string gauges (heavier strings = more sound), altered tunings and feedback. A compressor enhances sustain because it boosts the level of a decaying note. Electric players can get extra sustain with distortion and overdrive. The E-Bow is a hand-held gizmo that, when positioned close to the string, produces a sustained note. Fernandes have developed a guitar with a similar sustain device built into it.

You can use the volume control on an electric guitar to do this trick: turn off the volume pot, play a note and then turn the pot up – the note starts out inaudible and fades up. There's no percussive "click" when the note is struck, and the ear is more conscious of the sustain in the sound. This technique is favoured by country players because it simulates the sound of steel guitar. How easy it is to manipulate the volume pot depends on the physical layout of your guitar. (If it's difficult or impossible, a volume pedal can be used to do the same thing.) This trick works well with reverb and delay, especially if you come in with a bend, and it can give an expressive quality to chords. Two fine examples of this type of guitar playing are 'Dreams' and 'Well I Wonder'.

Solos

If you are going to play a solo in a song, think hard about its length and make sure that it serves a purpose. Solos should have a strong thematic interest even when they're not melodic. Some songs need something more atmospheric than a few favourite pentatonic blues licks – think of Andy Summers's celebrated solo on 'Bring On The Night', which amounts to feedback, a fourth and two sixths.

The songwriting guitarist's basic tool kit for lead breaks and fills consists of: the major scale, the natural minor scale, major and minor pentatonic scales, the blues scale, and the Dorian and Mixolydian modes. That will get you through most situations.

A quick guitar solo can often be turned out using the pentatonic major or minor scale. The pentatonic major will fit major keys but not minor ones. The pentatonic minor will fit minor keys, and it can also be used in a major key if the song has a strong blues element. In chord terms, this means it will sound acceptable over I, IV, V and bVII, or if you use the hard rock formula it's I, IV, V plus bVII, bVI and bIII. It won't sound as good over the major key's minor chords (II, III, VI).

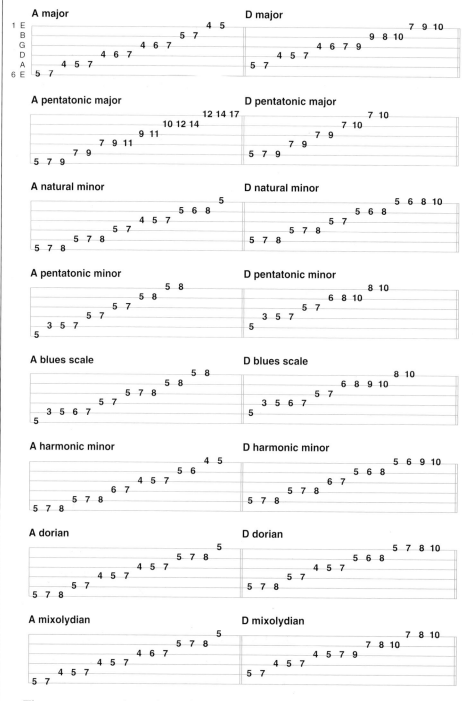

There are songs where the guitar acts as a kind of second voice to the vocal – 'Ten Storey Love Song', for example. In 'Sultans Of Swing', 'You And Your

Friend' and 'Brothers In Arms', Mark Knopfler seems to be sharing the vocal part with the guitar. 'Big Log' is another example – half vocal, half instrumental.

Beyond Scales: Thirds, Fourths, Sixths and Octaves

Guitar breaks and fills do not have to be scale oriented. You can also use triads, arpeggios and intervals. These have the advantage of thickening the sound more than single notes.

Major and minor thirds (C-E, C-Eb) provide a "sweet" sound. They were used a lot by Johnny Marr with The Smiths – listen to 'This Charming Man'. Marr also showed masterful imagination when he placed dissonant thirds over the main chord change in 'How Soon Is Now?' The famous break on The Beatles' 'Twist And Shout' is in thirds. Thirds sound great on strings 1+2 or 2+3, but get progressively less effective as you go down the strings. There is a fabulous guitar break on 'Everybody Wants To Rule The World' using thirds and fourths instead of a scale. When moving them up and down, it is important to have a guide finger to facilitate smooth changes.

If you turn a third upside down, you get a sixth. A minor third (C-Eb) becomes a major sixth (Eb-C), and a major third (C-E) becomes a minor sixth (E-C). Sixths are similar in sound to thirds, though not quite as sweet. They are common for fills, and many blues 12-bars finish with a sequence of sixths. Soul man Steve Cropper used sixths on many classic recordings. They are usually played on either strings 1+3 or 2+4.

Octaves are mainly deployed in solos for strengthening a phrase. Jazz guitarists like to use octaves, especially to thicken a melody. In his last years, Jimi Hendrix made plentiful use of octaves in songs such as 'Freedom' and 'Dolly Dagger'.

Perfect fourths (C-F) have a distinctive "bare" Oriental sound. On the top two strings they occur at the same fret, so they can be held down with one finger. Let's say we are playing a sequence of fourths in D major, commencing at fret three. The sequence goes DG - EA - F#B - GC - AD - BE - C#F#. If we treat the top note (G) as the key, you will find one position always sounds wrong. That's because G major does not have a C#. To adapt the pattern for a key whose root note is on the top string, simply flatten the second string note when you get to the next-to-last position. If you play the original sequence as DG - EA - F#B - AD - BE in D major, you have a pentatonic major scale harmonized in fourths.

Fourths can be heard in Chuck Berry's music, and their exotic sound is exploited in The Vapors' 'Turning Japanese', The Beatles' 'Don't Let Me Down', Pulp's 'A Little Soul', Bowie's 'China Girl', The Cranberries' 'Zombie', Led Zep's 'Ten Years Gone' and the intro to 'Band On The Run'.

```
 2  3  5  7  9 10 12 14
 ❸  5  7  8 10 12 14 15        7  8 10 12 14 15 17 19
                               ❼  9 11 12 14 16 18 19



❸ = ROOT NOTE                 ❼ = ROOT NOTE
```

Thirds in D major

```
 ❸  5  7  8 10 12 14 15        3  5  7  9 10 12 14 15
 3  5  7  8 10 12 13 15        ❸  5  7  8 10 12 14 15



❸ = ROOT NOTE                 ❸ = ROOT NOTE
```

Fourths in G major and D major

```
 ❶  3  5  6  8 10 12 13        ❸  5  7  9 10 12 14 15

 2  3  5  7  9 ❿ 12 14         4  5  7  9 11 ⓬ 14 16



❶ & ❿ = ROOT NOTES           ❸ & ⓬ = ROOT NOTES
```

Sixths in F major and G major

Open Strings

Open strings generate bigger sounds. Play the right scale for the key or progression up and down one string (instead of across the fretboard) and hit an open string above or below it. Treat the open string as the root note of a major or minor chord. If soloing over an E chord (major or minor), the top open E is available as a drone. The open B will work for B major or B minor, and the open G string for G major or minor. The fretting hand then plays the right scale up and down an adjacent string. Since the top three strings make an E minor chord and the second, third and fourth make an open G, if you are playing in either of these keys you could have two drones sounding rather than one.

The open strings can also function in chords as the third or the fifth: E is the third of C major and C#minor; B is the third of G major and G# minor; G is the third of Eb major and E minor. E is the fifth of A major/minor; B is the fifth of E major/minor; G is the fifth of C major/minor.

Droning open strings work well not only as lead ideas but also as riffs. For riffs, try any of the lower three strings (E, A or D) and move a scale or even a sequence of intervals such as thirds on the string above it.

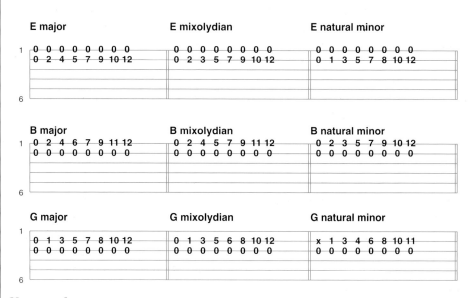

Harmonics

As noted above, the open strings offer two triads – one major, one minor: strings 2, 3, 4 (BGD) make a G major chord (GBD); strings 1, 2, 3 (EBG) make an E minor chord (EGB). With the finger lightly held against the strings over the 12th fret, you can play a G major or E minor triad in harmonics. At the fifth fret, the same harmonics sound an octave higher. At the seventh fret, the harmonic chords become D major and B minor, respectively.

In a song with the chord sequence G Em D Bm, you could play the entire sequence in harmonics for an ethereal second guitar part. If you're in a different key, a capo can make the right harmonics available.

Slide in Standard Tuning

The harmonics triads also apply to slide (bottleneck) guitar in standard tuning. By using these triads, you can play a major or minor chord with the slide alone and not have to worry about fretting notes. For a 12 bar in C, chords C, F and G can be played at the fifth, 10th and 12th positions with the slide. If there's a minor chord in the sequence, just play the top three strings at the right fret.

12-String Guitars

Your first close encounter of the 12-string kind can be a startling experience. It's probably bigger than what you're used to, and there doesn't seem to be any room between the strings. Fingerpickers will notice this even more and have the additional problem of trying to pluck two strings at once. The 12-string acoustic has a bright, shimmering sound with loads of high notes where you don't normally get them. It produces its own "chorus" effect by never being precisely in tune. (Listen to Dave Mason's 12-string contribution to Hendrix's 'All Along The Watchtower'.) If you fall for the 12-string's charms, you may feel you will never be able to look a 6-string in the soundhole again. Fortunately, this passes.

On a 12-string, the bottom three strings alone generate a chord similar to what you would get on a 6-string. Triad shapes become the equivalent of a 6-string chord. For example, hold C on the fifth string, third fret; Eb on the fourth string, first fret; and play the G string open. On a 6-string, this produces a C minor triad. On a 12-string, it produces the rough equivalent of playing a standard C minor barre chord at the third fret. Out of the movement of these triads can come different harmonic progressions and ideas. If you want to get really adventurous with a 12-string, try tuning it so the first string of each pair is a fourth below its partner: bE, eA, aD, dG, f#B, bE. This can produce some wonderful chords.

The Beatles, The Byrds and R.E.M. have all benefitted from the "chimes of freedom" of the electric 12-string, which can be a welcome addition to a recording. The classic way to play the electric 12-string is to pick chords in rapid arpeggios. It's unusual to attempt to play a guitar solos on an electric 12-string, and string-bending is difficult if you push any further than a semitone (half-step).

The twin-neck electric 6+12 has certain unique musical possibilities – and with one neck on and one off, you can explore the wonders of sympathetic resonance.

Harmonized and Non-Harmonized Lead Breaks and Fills

Quite a few bands, including Queen and Thin Lizzy, have featured twin-guitar breaks that are carefully harmonized. (Nowadays, intelligent pitch-shifters will allow you to create harmonized lines from a single guitar part.) The standard intervals for such harmonizing are thirds, sixths or octaves, though a few fourths add interest providing that they are in keeping with the harmony. Examples include the guitar lines on 'Whisky In The Jar', 'Don't Believe A Word', 'The Boys Are Back In Town' and 'The Dean And I'.

Non-harmonized combinations of lead guitars are harder for the ear to keep track of because the focus of attention keeps moving back and forth. As a result, there is built-in unpredictability, and each listen often reveals something never heard before. The effect of two guitars independently soloing can be heard on Wishbone Ash's 'Throw Down The Sword', Janis Joplin's cover of 'Summertime' (part of which is free form and part of which is arranged), Love's 'A House Is Not A Motel' and in many places on *Layla And Other Assorted Love Songs*.

To try this, set up the track for your solo and record a take. Do another pass without listening to the first take in your cans. Play both back and pan left and right. If you retained any ideas from take 1 for take 2, it is possible they may coincide, which will give moments of reinforcement. Some phrases could be deliberately played a couple of times if you want three or four guitars at once.

The 'Telegraph' Figure

This is a repeated note played high up (like a pedal in reverse) and is good for creating a sense of drama. Examples can be heard in 'S.O.S.', 'The Happening', 'Melting Pot' and 'You Keep Me Hanging On'.

ALTERED TUNINGS

Sometimes it seems as if the people who write songs on the piano have all the advantages. Just think: no barre chords; the ability to play chords with 10 notes; perfectly ordered ninths, 11ths and 13ths; easy inversions; melody in one hand, chords and bass in the other; weird chord changes at the slip of a finger; a seven-octave range ... and so on.

Well, there is one big exception, and that's the wonderful world of altered and open tunings. Many guitarists have written a couple of songs in a tuning that is not E A D G B E; others have done almost nothing else but play in altered tunings. For some, this was a case of necessity being the mother of invention: no one showed them how to tune the guitar, so they tuned it themselves until it sounded "right" – which usually meant, had a musical sound – and what they ended up with was an open chord, the simplest altered tuning.

Purists say the guitar has only one "proper" tuning. Ignore them. I once took a guitar into a shop for repair, and that guitar happened to be in an open tuning. I was told by the ignoramus behind the counter that guitars were meant to be played only in one tuning. Wrong! What matters is the music you make, not how you make it. When Moses came down from the mountain with the stone tablets, there wasn't an eleventh commandment that said, "Thou shalt tune E A D G B E."

Originally, altered tunings were used mostly by folk and blues players, but they are now deployed by guitarists in almost all genres. Well-known players who have made altered tunings integral to their style include Joni Mitchell, Nick Drake, Bert Jansch, John Renbourn, Jimmy Page, CSN&Y, Sonic Youth and Soundgarden. In connection with songwriting, the appeal is not hard to fathom:

● Songwriting is driven by inspiration. If you get tired of E A D G B E, an altered tuning can motivate you because of the way it changes the sound of your guitar. It takes only a couple of superb chord shapes to set off a song.

● Commonplace chord sequences can sound fresh in an altered tuning. Sometimes you will write a song and only later realise what a common sequence it would be in standard tuning.

● Altered tunings facilitate fingerpicking.

● For solo singer-songwriters, altered tunings help create a fuller sound.

- Open strings provide for drone effects, consecutive octaves or playing the melody while you're singing.

- Unison voicings give a "12-string" quality to some chords.

- Altered tunings allow you to play chords that are impossible in standard tuning.

- Open tunings are better for slide-guitar playing in blues songs.

- To the more devious and image-conscious, altered tunings offer an opportunity to puzzle the hell out of other guitarists, who may not be able to figure out what you're doing from the shapes.

Alas, altered tunings also have some drawbacks:

- There's more danger of breaking strings.

You must re-tune in live performance (unless you have several guitars).

- Chord shapes can be hard to remember. Write them down. (They are hard to transcribe, even from your own demos, once a few years have passed.)

- Key changing is more difficult, and you may find yourself trapped in one key.

- Sometimes the open top strings dominate the chord shapes, giving a certain sameness to the overall sound.

Types of Altered Tunings

Altered tunings can be divided into the following groups:

Detuned Standard

This is not much of an altered tuning, *per se*, but it is worth mentioning. It is common for guitarists to tune down a semitone (half-step), especially in hard rock/blues and HM. The lower pitch can make it easier for the singer to pitch a melody and the lead guitarist to bend strings. It's popular with heavy bands because of the lower frequencies. If you are writing a song pitched in Eb, Bb or Ab, it can make sense because you get fuller open-string chord shapes, especially if you're working with another guitar part. Also, it is not uncommon to find 12-string acoustic guitar recordings that are detuned a semitone to ease tension on the guitar's neck. 'The Boxer' is down a semitone so B major can be played as if it were C major and matched with a standard-tuning guitar capoed at the fourth fret, where B is a G shape:

Chord	I	II	III	IV	V	VI	bVII
Actual pitch	B	C#m	D#m	E	F#	G#m	A
Semi-detune shape	C	Dm	Em	F	G	Am	Bb
Capo IV shape	G	Am	Bm	C	D	Em	F

'Blackberry Way' and 'Yellow Submarine' are also down a semitone (half-step). Sometimes guitars are detuned by a tone (full step). Paul McCartney did this for 'Yesterday', All About Eve on 'Martha's Harbour' and Hendrix for the longer version of 'Voodoo Chile', and it has also been used by Jeff Healey and many grunge bands. This detuning creates some effective timbral changes in an acoustic guitar that complement a guitar in standard tuning. Let's say you are recording a song in C major. Compare these two guitar parts, one with a capo at the eighth fret and the other standard detuned by a tone:

Chords	I	II	III	IV	V	VI	bVII
Actual pitch	C	Dm	Em	F	G	Am	Bb
Tone-detune shape	D	Em	F#m	G	A	Bm	C
Capo VIII shape	E	F#m	G#m	A	B	C#m	D

Conversely, on the first album by The Smiths, Johnny Marr tuned a tone *above* standard pitch to get a brighter tone. With regard to string tension, this is not a good idea – unless you can afford lots of strings and/or replacement guitars.

Single-String Alterations

The easiest form of altered tuning involves retuning only one string. Even such a small change can produce effective new chord shapes.

The most popular way to do this is to detune the low E to D, which is slightly misleadingly called "dropped D" tuning. Fingerpickers like this because it provides an octave in the open bass strings (6 and 4) for an alternating-thumb pattern, leaving the fingers free to play a melody. It gives you deeper-sounding D and Dm chords than in standard tuning. It permits you to use the bottom D as a pedal note and move shapes over it, or play the bottom three strings as a drone and move triad shapes on the top three [see diagrams]. This tuning is also favoured by writers who want to play really low, heavy riffs. A power chord can be played on the bottom three strings with just a first-finger barre, and the famous "boogie rock" rhythm figure is easier to finger than in standard tuning. Dylan's

DADGBE tuning

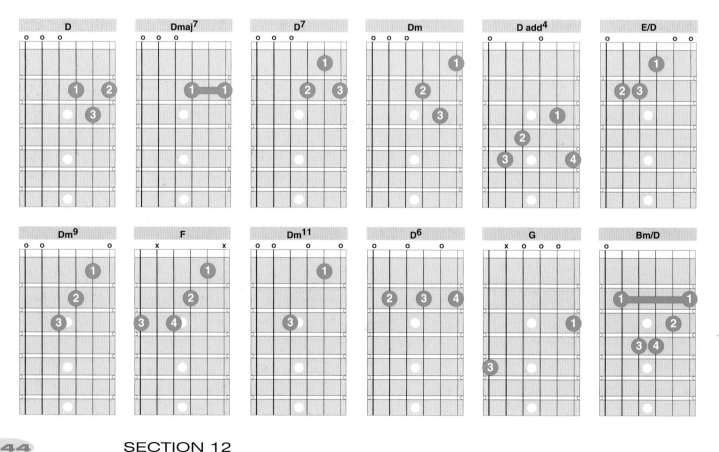

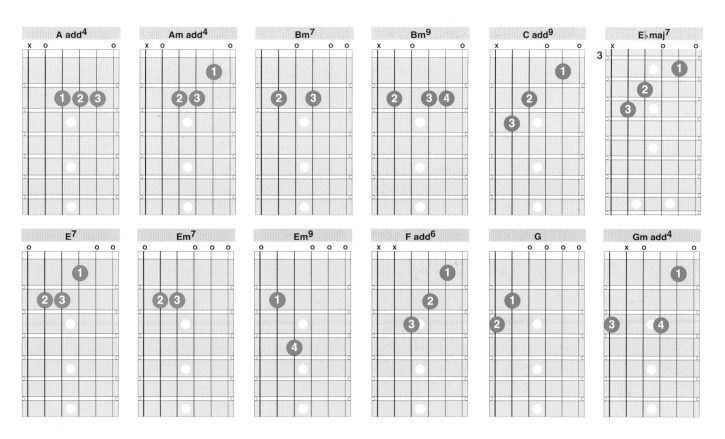

'Mr Tambourine Man' uses dropped D tuning.

Other single-string alterations include detuning the high E string down to D; the G string down to F# (so-called "lute tuning"); and the A string down to G to make E G D G B D, an open Em7 chord.

EADGBD tuning (above) and

EADF#BE tuning (below)

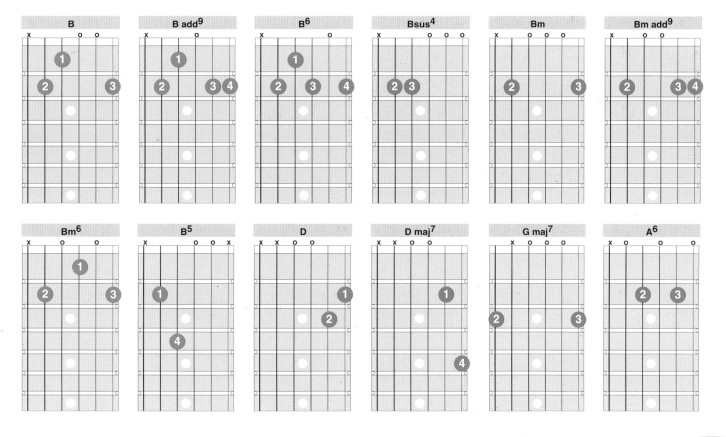

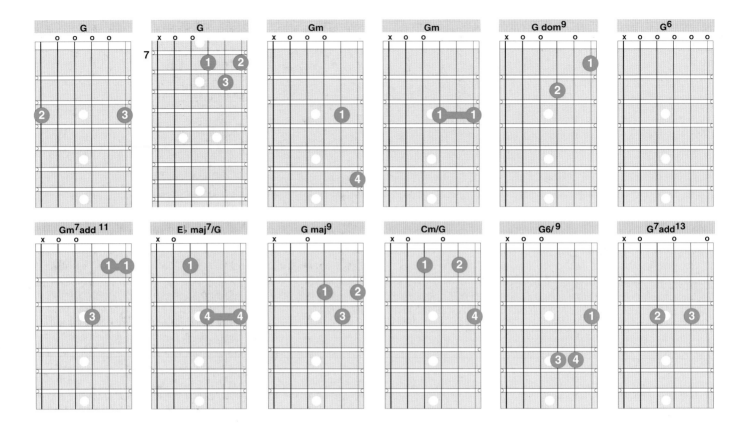

EGDGBD tuning

It's great fun to experiment with single-string alterations. They instantly mess up all your normal chord shapes, but not so drastically that you can't figure out where you are. And if you don't like the sound, it is easy to make a small adjustment and try something different. 'It's All Over Now, Baby Blue' has a capo at IV and the bottom string two tones down.

Open Tunings

An open tuning is one where the strings have been tuned to the notes of a major or minor chord. This means that when you lay a finger across the neck, the barre creates another chord. The other fingers can then add notes to that chord. In an open minor tuning, a major chord can be played by identifying the string(s) tuned to the third and putting a finger on that string one fret up.

Open major and minor tunings have certain things in common. For example, the chord on which the tuning is based will repeat itself at the 12th fret. Chord IV is played as a barre at the fifth fret, and chord V as a barre at the seventh. These, in combination with the open strings, will give you the three-chord trick. Minor open tunings are the same, except IV and V will be minor. The fifth, seventh and 12th frets will also provide resonant harmonics.

Open G – D G D G B D – is a popular tuning, favoured by Keith Richards, that is suited to both electric and acoustic uses. You can hear open G on 'Blackbird', 'That's The Way' (a semitone lower at open Gb) and 'Black Country Woman'. Since the root note is on the fifth string, some players don't bother to tune the low E down to D but find it more useful to leave it as is. Another option would be to tune the bottom string up three semitones to G. A tone (whole step) higher, open G becomes open A – E A E A C# E – a tuning favoured by electric slide players. But be careful, as this increases tension on the neck.

Open D – D A D F# A D – is a tuning used by Joni Mitchell, Bob Dylan on *Blood on the Tracks*, and in its electric version of open E – E B E G# B E – by Ron Wood. Open D has a deeper sound than open G because the root note is on the

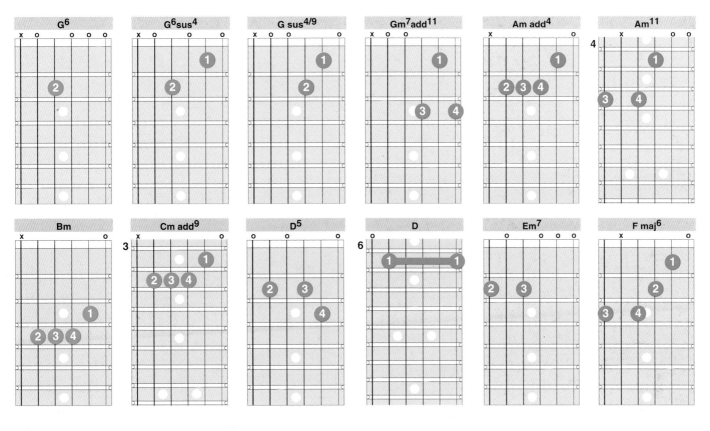

bottom string. John Squire used this for slide on 'Love Spreads'. Open C – C G C G C E – is an even deeper-sounding open tuning, though not as common as open G or D.

Open minor tunings are not as common as the majors. In some ways this is

DGDGBD tuning (above) and
DADF#AD tuning (below)

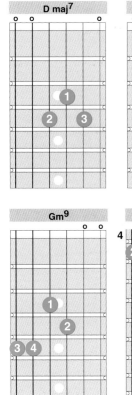

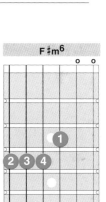

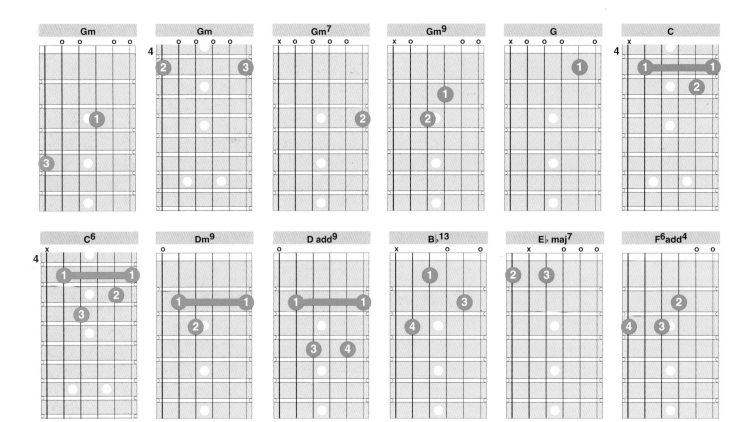

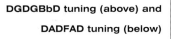
DGDGBbD tuning (above) and

DADFAD tuning (below)

surprising, because they can be more flexible when it comes to getting strong minors and majors. In open major tunings, it is sometimes hard to find a good fingering for a minor chord. Standard tuning requires only two alterations to create open Em – E G B G B E. Folksinger Michael Chapman used open Gm –

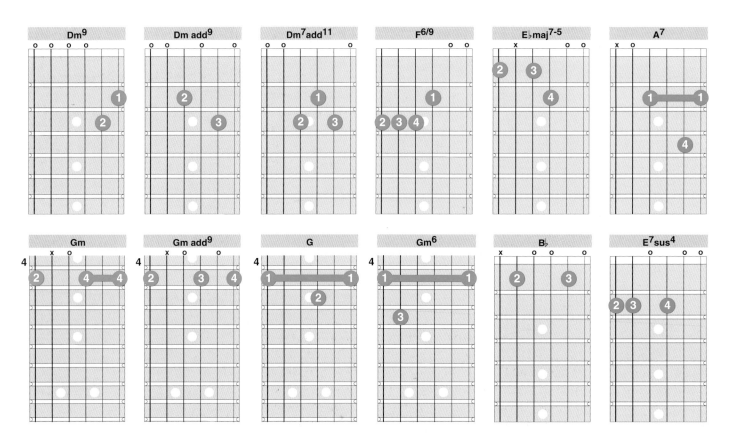

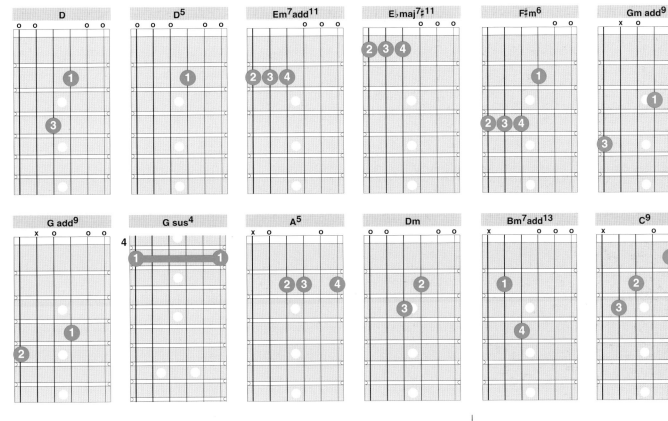

D G D G Bb D – which is a single-string alteration from open G. Flattening the third string of open D – D A D F# A D – makes D A D F A D, which is open D minor.

Remember that putting a capo on an open tuning will enable you to use it for different keys. Keith Richards capoed open G at the fourth fret to play open B for 'Tumbling Dice'. And there's nothing to stop you from writing a song in open G that is actually in another key, say C, as the Stones did with 'Start Me Up'.

Altered Tunings

It is helpful to reserve the name "altered tuning" for any tuning that does not make a simple major or minor chord. Some are seventh chords or are derived from the open majors. They are sometimes called "modal tunings". They are not as easy to work with as straight open tunings and are less suitable for slide guitar. It takes a little patience to get the best from these. Here are some examples:

- D A D G A D can be thought of as Dsus4 and has been used by Pierre Bensusan and Jimmy Page.
- "Double Dropped D" – D A D G B D – was famously used by Neil Young for 'Cinnamon Girl'.
- D A D F# B D is Dmaj6.
- D G D G C D is Gsus4.

Players have also tuned to a fifth chord: two possibilities are D A D A A D and E B E E B E. The Indigo Girls used D A D G B D for 'Chicken Man', D A D G B C for 'Galileo', and 'Virginia Woolf', and D A D G A D for 'Love Will Come To You'.

Alternative bands such as Sonic Youth have pioneered the use of altered tunings (some of them almost atonal) in rock. If you happen to have a double-neck guitar, you could write a song that is played with one of the necks in

DADGAD tuning (above)

standard tuning and the other in an altered tuning, so you could play the verse on one and the chorus on the other. Jimmy Page did this on 'Wonderful One'.

Creating Your Own Tunings

If you want to make up your own tunings, here are some tips:

- If possible, tune down rather than up, to lessen the risk of breaking strings and ease the tension on the neck.
- Try to keep at least one of the open strings of E A D G B E as part of your new tuning.
- Find which of the open strings has the root note. The lower, the better.
- If you create an open major tuning, locate the third of the chord. Fret this string at the first fret for a sus4; go two frets higher for a fifth chord. Lower this string a semitone (half-step) for an equivalent open minor tuning.
- Be sensitive to the balance of roots, fifths and thirds in your tuning, and to the intervals between the strings.
- Look for strings tuned an octave, third or sixth apart. These can be valuable for consecutive interval figures.

DGDGBD tuning

Octaves

Octaves

Tenths (octave + 3rd

Tenths (octave + 3rd

Thirds

Thirds

DADF#AD tuning

Octaves

Octaves

Tenths

Tenths

Thirds

Thirds

- It is useful to find movable major and minor shapes in case a chord sequence requires a chord that does not occur as an open-string voicing.
- If you detune more than a tone (full step), you may need to use a heavier-gauge string to compensate for the lack of tension.

- Always write down any good chord shapes that you find in an altered tuning.
- If you use an open or altered tuning in a recording with more than one guitar part (and possibly keyboards), remember that such tunings are "ensemble fragile". The distinctive quality of the chord voicings can be lost, as they tend to be obscured by the other harmonic instruments in an arrangement.

Some Alternative Tunings

It is possible to create different versions of the same open tuning by changing the mixture of roots, thirds and fifths. Let's take E major as an example. The standard open E is:

String	6	5	4	3	2	1
Note	E	B	E	G#	B	E
Inc/Dcr	-	+2	+2	+1	-	-
Part of triad	r	5th	r	3rd	5th	r

This tuning increases the tension on the neck. Is there a way of doing it by tuning down instead? Here's a solution I devised:

String	6	5	4	3	2	1
Note	E	G#	B	E	B	E
Inc/Dcr	-	-1	-3	-3	-	-
Part of triad	r	3rd	5th	r	5th	r

The same thing can be done with open A. The standard version (used on 'In My Time Of Dying') is:

String	6	5	4	3	2	
Note	E	A	E	A	C#	E
Inc/Dcr	-	-	+2	+2	+2	-
Part of triad	5th	r	5th	r	3rd	5th

This is my version:

String	6	5	4	3	2	1
Note	E	A	C#	E	A	E
Inc/Dcr	-	-	-1	-3	-2	-
Part of triad	5th	r	3rd	5th	r	5th

Now let's try open C. The standard version is:

String	6	5	4	3	2	1
Note	C	G	C	G	C	E
Inc/Dcr	-4	-2	-2	-	+1	-
Part of triad	r	5th	r	5th	r	3rd

But it could be done:

String	6	5	4	3	2	1
Note	C	G	E	G	C	E
Inc/Dcr	-4	-2	+2	-	+1	-
Part of triad	r	5th	3rd	5th	r	3rd

The same principle can be applied to minor tunings. Here's a standard E minor:

String	6	5	4	3	2	1
Note	E	B	E	G	B	E
Inc/Dcr	-	+2	+2	-	-	-
Part of triad	r	5th	r	3rd	5th	r

Here's a variant with a deeper sound and less tension on the neck:

String	6	5	4	3	2	1
Note	E	G	B	E	B	E
Inc/Dcr	-	-2	-3	-3	-	-
Part of triad	r	3rd	5th	r	5th	r

You can build more unusual tunings around one of the open strings of standard tuning. Let's use D: D is the root of D and Dm, the third of Bb and Bm, and the fifth of G and Gm. So we could construct a tuning for any of these in which that string would not change. In Bb, that would work like this:

String	6	5	4	3	2	1
Note	D	Bb	D	F	Bb	D
Inc/Dcr	-2	+1	-	-2	-1	-2
Part of triad	3rd	r	3rd	5th	r	3rd

Or how about B minor? That would be:

String	6	5	4	3	2	1
Note	D	B	D	F#	B	D
Inc/Dcr	-2	+2	-	-1	-	-2
Part of triad	3rd	r	3rd	5th	r	3rd

With altered tunings the only limit is your musical imagination and your patience at working out the potential of a tuning. But don't forget to put the song first, otherwise you will move into composing instrumentals.

"There are records I love that are not good songs but are great records ... People were making significant records from the beginning of rock and roll. Elvis's records, all the Motown records. Motown made those records the way they made the '55 Chevrolet. It's still beautiful and it still drives." - Jackson Browne, quoted by Dave Marsh from Bill Flanagan's *Written In My Soul.*

A Great Song Versus a Great Record

It is important to distinguish between writing a great song and making a great record. The latter calls for a different set of skills – which is where engineers and record producers come into the picture. Great songs do not always become great records, and some great records have been made of less-than-wonderful songs. The ideal is, of course, to have both. If you took 'Erotica' and played it on an acoustic guitar, you would not think it's a very good song. The record itself is another matter. Conversely, if you play 'Don't Dream It's Over' on an acoustic guitar, you can hear it's a great song right away. But is Crowded House's recording of it a great record? Personally, I feel the arrangement is merely adequate – it doesn't add anything to the song. It is a testament to the quality of the song that it survived such a flat presentation.

Home Demos

Most songwriters want to hear what their songs would sound like played and recorded in a proper arrangement. The advent of the 4-track cassette recorder in the 1980s made it possible to experience the joys of multi-tracking without the expense of buying a reel-to-reel tape recorder (or booking studio time). Songwriters could make demos and mix them on a single portable machine. Even though the sound quality left much to be desired, the 4-track cassette was a clever sketchpad. In the 1990s, the advent of digital hard-disk recording led to the first 8-track digital recorder/mixer. By 2000, for less than the cost of an old 8-track tape machine you could buy a digital mini-studio that combined 8-track recording, CD quality, editing, mixing and sound effects – all in one compact package. Some musicians now record directly onto computers.

If you are seriously interested in songwriting, I recommend that you make your own 8-track recordings in whatever medium – analogue or digital – suits your taste, wallet and available space. A couple of guitars, a drum machine and an electronic keyboard give a range of sounds and possibilities. Recording 8-track demos will improve your musicianship, teach you about production and arrangement, and sharpen your appreciation of the finer parts of songwriting.

ABBREVIATIONS

Roman numerals I VII
indicate chord
relationships within a key.

m *minor*

maj *major*

Song sections:

br *bridge*

c *coda*

ch *chorus*

hk *hook*

i *intro*

pch *pre-chorus*

v *verse*

Most of the chord-sequence examples
are standardized for comparison
into C *or* A minor.

Famous songs referred to in C major
or A minor *are not necessarily in*
the key of the original recordings.

Virtuoso technique on bass or keyboard is not necessary to play simple parts that work in the context of a song. The trick here is "part playing" – more about that in a moment.

If you want to submit your songs to publishers, you should realise that while it is true that a simple piano or guitar accompaniment and a voice will carry a good song, executives in the music industry these days tend to want to hear a fuller arrangement.

Instrumentation

The instruments you use on a home recording will be determined by what you have access to, what you feel comfortable playing and what suits the song and/or genre in which you're working. For rock, you will need drums, bass, rhythm and lead guitar, and vocals. If you record more than one guitar part, you will need to differentiate them; this can be accomplished with one of the following combinations (see section 11):

- single coil/double coil
- front pickup/back pickup
- distorted/clean
- detuned/normal
- capoed/normal
- standard tuning/altered tuning
- strummed/fingerpicked
- 12-string/6-string
- acoustic/electric

Rock guitar is often played with distortion. Modern effects units have put amounts of distortion at the fingertips of guitarists that, in the 1960s, would have required huge stacks and enough volume to drown out the sound of most aircraft taking off. What's surprising, though, is that even on a hard rock recording a little distortion often goes further than you thought, so be prepared to use less on a rhythm part. Distortion acts like a sponge, soaking up frequencies and leaving less sonic space for everything else.

When you add other instruments, consider how they will sound when you come to mix the whole thing. Highly unusual sounds may detract from the vocal/melody line, so use them sparingly. Instruments can be divided broadly into those whose main function is to create the harmonic padding and those that have a supporting melodic interest. Strummed guitars, piano chords and sustained string or organ chords all function to provide the harmonic backdrop against which everything else happens. One such instrument on either side of the mix is a good approach – and it doesn't need to play all the time. A harmonic background can also be established with pared-down parts whose overall effect is to suggest a chord sequence.

When choosing instruments for an arrangement, consider:

Their natural sustain: Are they for stretching notes? Are they for short bursts?
Their pitch: Are they high, middle or low?
Their tone: Are they bright or muted, percussive or smooth?

In commercial music, certain instruments function as "emotional shorthand" – harmonica is for downhome sincerity; Spanish guitar indicates organic feeling; Irish pipes and South American pan pipes say "World Music".

Eight-track recording is an ideal compromise in terms of the opportunities it offers. Initially you may feel you have to pile on the instruments, fill all the tracks and even sub-mix to load on even more. Remember, though, that the more instruments you use, the harder it is to mix so they do not get in each other's way. Instruments with similar timbres can be difficult to separate in the final mix.

It is surprising how full a sound can be generated with just a few well-chosen parts. This is not to say that sparse arrangements are any better than full ones. It is partly a matter of taste; arranging styles go in and out of fashion. During the 1960s and 1970s, as recording technology went from two to four to eight tracks, and then to 16, 24, 32 and 48 tracks, songwriters and musicians responded accordingly, to make the most of such capabilities. Think of the production on a record such as The Police's 'Walking On The Moon' and compare it with The Beatles' 'Hey Jude' or a Phil Spector wall-of-sound single such as 'River Deep Mountain High'. They are very different approaches – but who would want to be without any of them?

Let's look at some typical arrangements that are possible on an 8-track without any "bouncing". In these examples, the keyboard part could be piano, organ, strings or any other sound from an electronic keyboard. Solid lines indicate a stereo part recorded in one go on two tracks.

TRACKS

1	2	3	4	5	6	7	8
vcl —— vcl		r/gtr —— r/gtr		dr —— dr		bass —— bass	

A "live" four-piece rock band sound, with all instruments and voice in stereo.

1	2	3	4	5	6	7	8
vcl —— vcl		r/gtr —— r/gtr		dr —— dr		bass	l/gtr

The same with bass stereo sacrificed for a lead guitar part.

1	2	3	4	5	6	7	8
b/vcl	vcl	r/gtr	a/gtr	dr —— dr		bass	keyb

Stereo rhythm guitar sacrificed for acoustic guitar

1	2	3	4	5	6	7	8
b/vcl	vcl	a/gtr	a/gtr	dr —— dr		bass	keyb

A nice combination of two acoustic guitars. Try this with two 12-strings or 12 + 6.

1	2	3	4	5	6	7	8
b/vcl	vc	a/gtr	a/gtr	violin	violin	viola	cello

A guitar ballad with a built-in string quartet.

1	2	3	4	5	6	7	8
l/gtr	vcl	r/gtr	a/gtr	dr —— dr		bass	keyb

1	2	3	4	5	6	7	8
b/vcl	vcl	r/gtr	l/gtr	dr —— dr		bass	keyb

1	2	3	4	5	6	7	8
b/vcl	vcl	r/gtr	sax	dr	bass	piano	organ

If you use a mono drum sound, then you have one more track to play with. Here's a pattern for a "soul revue" sound.

1	2	3	4	5	6	7	8
b/vcl	b/vcl	b/vcl	vcl	r/gtr	dr	bass	keyb

If you can sing harmony vocals, try this.

Bouncing

If you start "bouncing" tracks, all kinds of amazing things become possible – as long as you get the sub-mixes nicely balanced. Let's say you want to record a song with a three-part backing vocal but more instruments than in the previous example. The recording process would go like this:

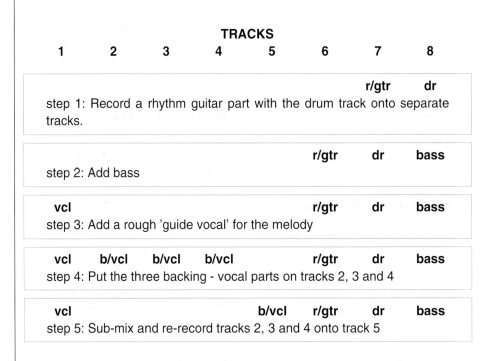

TRACKS

1	2	3	4	5	6	7	8
						r/gtr	dr

step 1: Record a rhythm guitar part with the drum track onto separate tracks.

1	2	3	4	5	6	7	8
					r/gtr	dr	bass

step 2: Add bass

1	2	3	4	5	6	7	8
vcl					r/gtr	dr	bass

step 3: Add a rough 'guide vocal' for the melody

1	2	3	4	5	6	7	8
vcl	b/vcl	b/vcl	b/vcl		r/gtr	dr	bass

step 4: Put the three backing - vocal parts on tracks 2, 3 and 4

1	2	3	4	5	6	7	8
vcl				b/vcl	r/gtr	dr	bass

step 5: Sub-mix and re-record tracks 2, 3 and 4 onto track 5

You now have a three-part harmony on track 5 and three empty tracks to add more guitars or keyboard-derived parts. To take an extreme example, you could record another two backing vocal parts on tracks 2 and 3 and then bounce them onto 4, adding as you do so a third backing vocal. This requires care in balancing the three parts – you must sing the last part so it blends with the two that are being bounced. If this works, you will have (presumably different) three-part harmonies on tracks 4 and 5, enabling you to place them left and right. That's a lot of vocal power.

Digital recording makes sub-mixing more effective because there isn't the same degradation of signal as with analogue recording. The situation is also helped by the facility of so-called "virtual tracks".

A Cheap String Orchestra

Many keyboards have "string" settings that imitate an orchestra's violin section. If you know how to write four-part harmony (and are patient), you can create your own string section. First, record single-line parts. Where there are two of the same instrument, try varying the vibrato, sustain or other characteristics between tracks. If necessary, use a click on track 8 to keep time. This can be erased later.

TRACKS

1	2	3	4	5	6	7	8
violin	violin	viola	viola	cello	cello	c/bass	

Bounce the whole lot onto track 8, taking care to get a good balance between the instruments. Then record them all again, with appropriate timbral or part differences on the first six tracks:

TRACKS

1	2	3	4	5	6	7	8
violin	violin	viola	viola	cello	cello		[full]

Bounce the individual instruments onto track 7, possibly adding another part as you do it. You now have seven string instruments on track 7 and seven on track 8, making it possibile to have a stereo mix of 14 orchestral instruments. And you still have six tracks left – either for adding more orchestral parts and creating your first "classical" piece, or for adding guitars, vocals and other instruments. You could also do this using orchestral instruments other than strings, following the same process of sub-mixing and repositioning on tracks 7 and 8.

Mixing and the Stereo Image

The choice of instruments and track alignment is also shaped by your sense of where things will go in the final production. One of the eccentric features of 1960s recordings, to modern ears, is the placing of the drums or vocals exclusively in one channel, left or right. In 'Don't Worry Baby', for example, a double-tracked lead vocal is on one side, the vocal harmonies are on the other side, and all the instrumentation is in the middle.

A standard mix puts the main vocal in the middle along with bass and drums. Even though they are in the same central position, these can be distinguished because they occupy different frequencies. Other instruments can then be panned left or right. If you have more than one guitar part, put them on opposite sides. If you have instruments dropping in and out at various points, you need to be careful that you don't make the mix "lop-sided" when one drops out. Try to avoid a situation where you have either left or right unoccupied for any length of time.

Mixing is too complicated an art to discuss here in any detail. For example, there is no set order in which instruments are supposed to be balanced. Try setting the level of the bass and drums first and then the lead vocal against the rhythm section. Then bring in the harmony instruments. Here are some other tips:

- Never mix on headphones. Use them only as a fine detail check or to scrutinize for unwanted background noises, hum etc. Obviously when you have a mix it's worth listening to it on headphones as well as through speakers.
- Sit equidistant between the speakers
- Don't mix at high volume levels. If it sounds balanced and exciting at a domestic listening level then it will sound great louder. High volume levels fatigue the ears and can fool you into thinking a mix is better than it is.
- The prominence of a part in a mix is influenced not only by its volume but by its frequency and the amount of reverb on it. Instead of pushing the fader up, try altering the e.q. Remember that e.q. can be subtracted as well as added.
- Try mixing in mono first. If the parts sound well defined in a mono mix

when you pan them out into stereo they will seem even better.

- Test a mix by listening from the next room with the door open, and by listening on different speaker systems and in varying locations.

Unusual Arrangements

Songs such as 'Rock On', 'Say You Don't Mind', and 'Barbara Ann' are worth analysis for their unusual arrangements. Sometimes, one instrument will stamp its sound on a mix and be part of what makes the song memorable. Think of the clavinet on 'Superstition', the bass harmonica on 'The Boxer', the wah-wah guitar on 'Shaft', the theremin on 'Good Vibrations', the sax on 'Baker Street', the synth on 'Baba O'Reilly', the harmonica on 'Join Together' or the accordion at the start of 'Constant Craving'. Artists like Beck and Gomez are worth listening to for the imagination they bring to arrangements.

The Drum Machine

For many songwriters, the drum machine is a necessary evil. It would be great to have real drums on our songs, but we either can't play drums, don't have the room or find that recording a kit at home is impractical due to space, expense and the neighbours. Enter the drum machine – a brilliant piece of kit (pun intended), even if it's no substitute for Keith Moon, Mitch Mitchell or John Bonham. If you are writing dance music, then the artificiality of the drum machine is part of the sound you want. But if you are writing pop, rock, soul, folk, blues or jazz songs, here are a few tips on how to make a drum machine sound more "human":

- Copy real drum patterns from records.
- Don't use the pre-set rhythms. Write your own.
- When you select drum sounds, make sure they "agree" with each other.
- Use quantization sparingly. Quantization is a handy technical feature that enables drum machines to move your tapped-in rhythm to the nearest beat or chosen division of a beat. But this is what makes drum machines sound mechanical: they play strict rhythm. Quantization is especially noticeable on handclaps.
- Use a variety of rhythms within a song, with plenty of small variations.
- Don't tell the machine to do things a drummer can't do. A drummer has only two arms and can, therefore, hit only two things at once. Don't program the machine to hit the snare, a crash cymbal and a side drum all at once.
- Avoid implausible bass drum patterns at faster tempos. The quicker the tempo, the sillier rapid bass drum patterns sound.
- If you want the drums to stop for a few bars, take care with the way they enter and exit. Use a fill to get in and a fill to get out.
- Don't put cymbal crashes only on the first beat of the bar.
- Change the parts of the kit within a song. For example, use a closed hi-hat in the verse and an open one in the chorus – this gives extra intensity to the latter.
- Flams on the snare – where the sticks hit a split-second apart – sound very "human".
- Time changes – going into half-time or double-time – also help to make the drum part less artificial.

Echo and reverb make drums sound more "alive". For a dance groove, write a simple drum pattern and then feed it through a delay until a coherent pattern of delays emerges. You can make the echoes quieter than the main drum part, if you like. When recording drums in stereo, try putting a fast echo on one side to thicken the sound.

Drum Pauses

The near-constant presence of a drum kit (real or electronic) in popular music can make us forget that a song could approach rhythm in a different manner. From time to time consider not having a continuous beat. In an orchestral setting tympani rolls, snare rolls and cymbal crashes occur only to mark special moments in the music, such as a crescendo or climax. Marking the beat percussively all the time would be considered vulgar in classical music – that's what the conductor is doing by waving his arms. If you compare the 1947 revision of Igor Stravinsky's ballet *Petrouchka* with the 1911 version, you will notice that he took out much of the percussion – presumably on the mature judgement that he had been over-emphatic in the original score. The Beach Boys' *Pet Sounds* album offers a fine example of percussion used in a less obvious way.

Even in a rock song, dramatic effects can be generated by taking out the beat for a few bars. Good examples are 'Summertime Blues', 'Something Else', 'Lucille', 'My Generation', Ash's 'Goldfinger', Dodgy's 'In A Room', Metallica's 'Enter Sandman', Led Zeppelin's 'What Is And What Should Never Be' and The Bluetones' 'Slight Return'. There's a wonderful pull-out and re-entry of the drums in 'Tumbling Dice'. The obvious place to delay the entry of the drums is on the intro, as in 'There She Goes', 'Bittersweet Symphony' and 'Over The Hills And Far Away'. 'In The Air Tonight' has a long-delayed entry which was the probable inspiration for Preston Hayman's spectacular snare-drum entry on Kate Bush's 'Leave It Open'. You can even bring in the drums on what sounds like a "wrong" beat, as on 'Start Me Up' and 'Marquee Moon'.

When considering alternatives, think of the tambourine that enters with a smack at the start of the verse on 'Dancing In The Street'. Listen to the interruption of a drum loop in Tori Amos's 'Caught A Lite Sneeze', where at 2:46 the drums are suddenly silenced. She sings "Right on time you get closer" and on the last word the drum loop is back in. Other arresting moments of silence occur in 'Novocaine For The Soul' (at 1:23), 'Single Girl' and 'Just' (at 2:22).

You can also use a drum machine to carry the early part of a song and bring in live drums later.

Roman numerals I VII
indicate chord
relationships within a key.

m *minor*

maj *major*

Song sections:

br *bridge*

c *coda*

ch *chorus*

hk *hook*

i *intro*

pch *pre-chorus*

v *verse*

Most of the chord-sequence examples
are standardized for comparison
into C *or* A minor.
Famous songs referred to in C major
or A minor *are not necessarily in*
the key of the original recordings.

To deepen your knowledge of songwriting, you should listen to well-written songs – here are some to consider. This chronological list is not the "greatest" of anything, but each of these 20 songs has an important lesson to teach the songwriter who's willing to learn. These brief discussions take us to the very edge of what can described as songwriting craft. At this edge we pass from the measurable nuts and bolts of songwriting to the mysterious domain of musical meaning - of why it is that one song which uses the same chords as thousands of others is far greater in terms of what it communicates. This is the domain which criticism tries to discuss, of course, but to pursue that road any further would take us outside the remit of a book on songwriting craft. Dave Marsh's *The Heart Of Rock And Soul* and Ian MacDonald's *Revolution In The Head* are essential reading if you want to understand the deeper meaning of songs.

1 Gene Pitney: 'Twenty Four Hours From Tulsa' (1963)

This is a fine example of a narrative lyric presented as a letter, as well as a song where ambiguous key relationships express an emotional conflict. The production has many classic early 1960s touches: high female voices; chopped, high guitar chords; light percussion; low-note guitar with tremolo; and the thrice-played brass motif, taken up twice by the strings for a five-bar intro. In the verse, each lyric phrase goes I-IImaj to V, establishing V as the key, only for the next line to take it back to the original key. Chord I represents the emotions he has for "home" (his wife), heard first as Pitney sings "dearest darling". The chorus introduces a I VI IV V progression in a stretched form in C and stops on the dominant, which is the key of the verse.

The coda settles on a C chord, the key of the past rather than the future. So, although he appears to be saying that he loves this new woman, the music insists on his regret that he cannot go home. Notice the dom9 chord at the end of the repeated "never", which cancels out the lover's key of G because it makes it harmonically subservient to the wife's key of C.

2 Roy Orbison: 'It's Over' (1964)

Orbison brought a new drama to pop with his song arrangements, and 'It's Over' is typical of his mini-epics, with its advanced (for the time) approach to arrangement and romantic lyrics. This is another song where the emotional distress of the speaker is mirrored by the presence of two keys.

A free-time intro announces the subject of the lyric ("Your baby doesn't love you anymore") before the foreboding, martial drum beat leads into the verse. Structurally, there are several different verses at work. The second is more complex and features a classic early 1960s chord change when F Am Dm Bb is followed by G and then C (IV IImaj V), creating momentary confusion as to whether the music has changed from F major to C major – or not. This key change is accomplished in the bridge, which starts on Em (a chord not found in F major), moves repeatedly from Em to F and then forward to G (chords III, IV and V in C major). The first climax comes with the establishment of C major at 1:32, the title line and a bar of 6/4. There are bars of 6/4 in the verse as well at the end of some lines. Notice how the melody creeps higher at the end, as the rhythm intensifies.

3 John Barry/Don Black: 'Goldfinger' (1965)

John Barry invented a distinct harmonic language for the James Bond films, full of strange chord changes, melodies with unusual notes and dissonant effects. Songs such as 'Thunderball', 'You Only Live Twice' and 'We Have All The Time In The World' all deserve study. 'Goldfinger' is structured ABABA and opens with a harmonically ambiguous and spacious I-bVI in E. This becomes the first change of the verse, which then compounds the ambiguity by going from C to Bm (the minor form of chord V in F.), leading to a brief change into A major:

Old key	I	bIV	Vm			IV	
	E	C	Bm	E	A	D#	B
New key			II	V	I	IIImaj	I

The stability of A major as a key is immediately undermined by the D#, which finds its way to B – which functions as chord V in E for the next phrase. The bridge section further confuses things by going to D#m, G#m and A#. The shifting harmonies express the untrustworthy nature of the villain.

4 The Beach Boys: 'God Only Knows' (1966)

'God Only Knows' may not match 'Good Vibrations' in the experimental stakes, but for sheer perfection of form it is perhaps even better. At a time when many songs seem to take take forever to get going, it is a powerful example of how inspiration and craft can evoke another world in a matter of seconds.

The short instrumental intro has a soaring horn melody that returns later in the song. A one-bar interruption to the quarter-note rhythm sets off the intro from the first verse. Our attention is immediately caught by the provocative lyric: "I may not always love you." The music has established a romantic atmosphere, and we are not expecting such an apparently negative statement. We listen to hear if the speaker will backtrack on this pronouncement – and, sure enough, he eclipses this blunt realism with a touching romantic promise.

'God Only Knows' does not have a separate chorus – the hook is beautifully incorporated into the verse itself. Notice the unexpected intervals in the melody (it keeps landing on notes that are not quite what we expect) and the inversions in the harmony. These inversions play a big role in making the progression so expressive. Verse 2 is prefaced by a one-bar link that is the same as the one that connected the intro and Verse 1, except it is played on different instruments. Strings thicken the arrangement of Verse 2.

No less than two verses and two hooks have passed by the time we get to 1:04-12. Here the song surprises us by changing its rhythm. This is a fine example of asymmetry. This makes the resumption of the verse form with "scat" vocals and the hook seem fresh. The coda is reached at 1:59. There is a brief lull in the

arrangement before the snare drum punches in and the ensemble surges at 2:16. The coda itself is a glorious three-way vocal counterpoint echoed by the swooping horn figure. 'God Only Knows' clocks in at a mere 2:45, but it makes us feel as though we have just had a week in paradise. No wonder they call Brian Wilson a genius.

5 The Kinks: 'Waterloo Sunset' (1967)

The Kinks had established themselves by 1967 as a first-class singles group with punchy numbers such as 'You Really Got Me' and 'All Day And All Of The Night', and satirical songs such as 'Sunny Afternoon' and 'Dedicated Follower Of Fashion'. Neither type anticipated the ethereal 'Waterloo Sunset'.

Musically, the song uses a descending bass line under a static V chord to create anticipation. Inversions play a significant part in adding a pastel colour to the I V IV progression, for the bass guitar makes it I iV iIV with sustained notes. The high melodic motif sung by the female backing vocalists is a striking regeneration of an arrangement technique that had been used conspicuously in pop in the early 1960s. A second descending sequence occurs on the F#m chord ("but I don't..."). The bridge introduces a more aggressive guitar part for contrast, with the F# chord implying that it is chord V of a new key, B major. Notice the quick B-E change on "sha-la", which contrasts with the smoother rate of chord change on the verse. The bridge concludes with the same downward bassline of the intro, having employed another descending line under the F#-B change. The psychedelic effect of the coda partly comes from the use of an unresolved A7 chord.

Lyrically, there's a fascinating tension between the detached speaker who, expressly unafraid, is mysteriously content to simply gaze at the sunset, and the lovers Terry and Julie, who meet each other every Friday night and "cross over the river". The lyric is deeply consoling because it offers not one but two ways out of loneliness. It is realistic and other-worldly at the same time. Ray Davies gives us details of London – the dirty river, taxis, the crowds, the Underground – and yet the city is transformed into something visionary.

6 The Mamas & The Papas: 'Dedicated To The One I Love' (1967)

In 1966-'68 the airwaves were blessed with the wind-blown harmonies of The Mamas & The Papas' on hit songs such as 'California Dreamin', 'Monday Monday', 'Dream A Little Dream Of Me' and 'Dedicated To The One I Love'. One member, John Phillips, also has a claim to fame as the writer of Scott MacKenzie's 'If You're Going To San Francisco'. So what has 'Dedicated To The One I Love' to teach us about pop songwriting?

Its obvious virtue is that of melody: 'Dedicated' has a beautiful tune and gorgeous harmonies. The arrangement is blessed by a quirky honky-tonk piano that lends character to what could have been out-and-out MOR. Most important of all, the song is continually inventive in a manner so different from the lazy mentality of much recent pop. It bursts with ideas, and you never know what is coming next. The delicate intro is almost a lullaby: a double-tracked vocal over two acoustic guitars. A D7sus4 chord takes us into the first chorus. Listen to the way the rhythm plays off four against the triplet swing of the 12/8 before the word "whisper". On the word "all" there's an unexpected chord, Eb7 (bVI), which suggests a key change that never happens.

The first verse contrasts two bars of melody with two bars that have plenty of blue notes. The lead-in to the second chorus uses an Am-A7 change that suggests we're going into D, but we actually land on D7sus4. Chorus 2 has a different last line, musically, than Chorus 1. After a four-bar honky-tonk piano solo, there's a

two-bar phrase of "There's one thing I want you to do" where each beat has a different chord. It's rare for pop songs to harmonize on separate beats. The melody going into the last chorus is pitched higher than you expect it over a D#7, which again creates the expectation of a key change. Chorus 3 has a different ending than the others do, and the coda features vocal counterpoint over a new sequence of Em C A G. And all of this in only three minutes! Too much variety to be commercial? 'Dedicated To The One I Love' was the 12th best-selling single of 1967 in the UK and a No. 2 hit in the US.

7 Jimi Hendrix: 'House Burning Down' (1968)

Hendrix tends to be thought of first as a guitarist and only second as a songwriter. 'House Burning Down' is, as usual, full of fittingly incendiary guitar work, and the phased tone of the middle lead break obviously inspired Ernie Isley to emulate it on 'That Lady'. The coda is stunning, as Hendrix's guitar goes whooshing off into the distance before apparently turning around and coming back. But 'House Burning Down' is a remarkable rock song not only for its lyric – a blend of UFO visitation and the smoking American cities of 1968 – but also for the fact that Hendrix had the audacity to link a galloping soul rhythm (in F minor) with a fox trot (in Ebm).

8 The Four Tops: 'I'm In A Different World' (1968)

Few songwriting teams can match the record of Holland-Dozier-Holland. 'I'm In A Different World' was one of the last hits they had with Motown and their last with The Four Tops. It has typical Motown features in terms of the arrangement and a characteristically impassioned, straining vocal from Levi Stubbs, though for once he has a happy love theme, a taste of the final redemption of the seraphic 'Still Water (Love)'. Most of all, it is an object lesson in how to use modulation to express the meaning of a lyric.

It starts without an intro of any kind, Levi's vocal coming in a fraction of a second after the instruments. The verse moves I-IV-II in Bb but changes to Gb when the title comes in for the first time over a II-V-I in that key. Stubbs sings that he is in a different world – and so is the music, because it has modulated. This leads to a bridge section ("Each time you call my name,,,") with a clever single-note guitar line (partly doubled by Jamerson's bass) that is reminiscent of the guitar line central to 'My Girl'. To get back to the verse and the key of Bb, the four-chord link goes Cbsus4 Cbsus2 Ab Db, momentarily making Db the key before dropping down to Bb.

'I'm In A Different World' is a song whose musical twists and unexpected turns mirror the shocked delight of the speaker, for whom life itself has turned so unexpectedly from dark to light.

9 Simon & Garfunkel: 'America' (1970)

'America' is a greater song than the more celebrated 'Bridge Over Troubled Water'. The latter plays to the gallery too much. Essentially a song of selfless love, there's something queasy about the self-glorification of the speaker in so religiose a manner. By contrast, the lyric of 'America' works from the concrete to the general. It is full of evocative images: the coach, the place names, the cigarette, the raincoat, the magazine, the moon, the bow tie. The apparent whimsy of the middle eight, where Simon gently evokes the paranoia of 1960s America, masks a deeper pathos. Maybe the man in the gabardine mac is a spy after all. And the hook – "All gone to look for America" – gives this song a breadth few popular songs attain. This is not just about lost love or lost lovers but a lost political ideal.

The song is played with a capo at the second fret, so the following discussion refers to chord shapes rather than actual pitch. In terms of the music, notice that the verse doesn't repeat the descending sequence but instead makes an unexpected shift to an A7. The last-line move on the word "moon" to a D and then C/G and G suggests a momentary key change to G, which is immediately cancelled out by a repeat of the descending sequence from C down to F. The D is also made less secure by virtue of being inverted (D/F#). Verse 2 has a slightly different form from Verse 1. The title hook (D G D Cmaj7) reaches for G major without getting a firm hold on it. The middle eight matches its lyrical change with an indeterminate bVII-Imaj7 sequence. Verse 3 is like Verse 1, but Verse 4 has some important extra touches, such as the organ entering and the harmonising of the second line as C Em Am instead of G/B, which deepens the sadness of the moment where he's lonely talking to her and she's asleep. Notice how the coda develops the intro's descending progression by extending it to a Dm chord.

10 The Carpenters: 'We've Only Just Begun' (1970)

There are *considerably* fewer songs that celebrate marriage as opposed to romance. 'Maybe I'm Amazed', 'Wonderful Tonight' and 'If I Should Fall Behind' are three famous examples. Such songs are lyrically difficult, because they risk sounding complacent and thus arousing hostility and/or envy in the listener. Take Streisand's 'Evergreen', which opens with the disastrous simile "Love soft as an easy chair".

Paul Williams's 'We've Only Just Begun' gets around this in two ways. The lovers' relationship is seen as something that will be experienced as a journey, so there are references to horizons, roads, ways, flying, walking and running. It is not a fixed state and is therefore less likely to arouse envy. Change and growth are emphasised: the couple choose, learn, watch, share, talk, work and find. Since they are active and at the start of something rather than the end, they win our sympathy.

Many trademarks of MOR are present in the arrangement, such as the block vocal harmonies (sometimes singing maj7 or maj9 chords), the use of orchestral instruments such as the plaintive woodwinds and the poignant min9 piano figure on the F#m chord (as on "promises"). Notice the dynamic contrast of the chorus, which is more rhythmic, with more prominent brass, drums, bass and tambourine. Here the sense of motion is more palpable. It is as if the verses express the inner side of the relationship and the active choruses its outer expression in the world.

The chorus also benefits from some unexpected key shifts. The verse is in A major (using chords I-VI) but a D-E-F# change establishes F# major as the new key:

Old key	I	IV	I	IV		
	A	D	A	D	E	F#
New key				bVI	bVII	I

The music changes from F# to B (I-IV) several times, establishing the new key, before transposing the I-IV change into the distant key of Bb. A semitone (half-step) slide from Eb (chord IV in Bb) to E takes us back to chord V of A major. The composer has one last surprise in store. After two A-D changes, the song resolves on a C# major chord (IIImaj in A), which cancels out the C#m chord in the verses and establishes a new key – perhaps hinting at a future state of fought-for happiness.

Karen Carpenter's vocal perfectionism sometimes resulted in a fatal discrepancy between the *way* she sang and what she was singing *about*. But 'We've Only Just Begun' finds a subject and a form that enable her unvarying control and glassy vibrato to signify the optimism and courage of the newlyweds. They have had the "white lace" and made the "promises" of the first line. They are entitled to their hope. They have earned it.

11 The Temptations: 'Ball Of Confusion' (1970)

Talk about 1960s protest and people will invariably mention Dylan and Baez. All too often Motown's last years in Detroit are forgotten, and if Motown is cited it's usually Marvin Gaye and *What's Going On* that get the plaudits. But the label also put out protest records such as Stevie Wonder's 'Heaven Help Us All', Edwin Starr's 'War' and The Temptations' 'Ball Of Confusion'.

'Ball Of Confusion' is a typical Norman Whitfield "groove" song, with a repetitious two-bar C pentatonic minor bass riff churning beneath the C major harmony. On top, guitars add strange licks with echo, notably on the dramatic intro with Dennis Edwards's arresting count-in (listen to the CD on headphones and you can hear the amps buzzing), and the brass section has the occasional jazzy flourish. Every now and then, there's an arpeggiated bridge using C, F and G, with a punchy James Brown-type link – but the rhythmic drive of the track is relentless. The music can be simple because of the aggression and the clever division of the lyric among the Temps' contrasting voices.

The lyric is an extraordinary set of snapshots of American society just after the riots of 1968 ("Cities aflame in the summertime") and the King and Kennedy assassinations. Race, poverty, taxes, back to nature, drugs, politics, religion, education, the moonshots, suicide, population growth, Vietnam ... it's all there, with daring combinations best caught in the line "Unemployment rising fast, The Beatles' new record's a gas". When did you last hear a line that hip?

12 10cc: 'I'm Not In Love' (1975)

10cc were a musically literate outfit with the ability to use pastiches of early pop and rock styles to make ingenious, witty singles such as 'The Dean And I' and 'Rubber Bullets'. 'I'm Not In Love' probably has more depth than any of their other hits and was certainly their boldest musical vision. The lyric was an excellent example of a speaker who is undermining the very thing he claims, as he invents various excuses to hide his love for the woman.

The song has a superb arrangement that defied the technological limitations of the day. The intro features a complex B11 to B change on electric piano and a sparse mix. The verse starts on A. The change from A to a sighing Am perfectly expresses the speaker's attempt to cover up his feelings giving way, as does the melancholy rise to C#m via G#. Notice the surprise when "It's because" lands on E, and the way the second bridge ("You wait a long time for me") is in G. For the amazing middle section, the band recorded a reputed 240 vocal parts on a 16-track. The effect resembles the work of the composer Ligeti, whose eerie vocal music was featured on the soundtrack of *2001 A Space Odyssey*. What is also striking is that 'I'm Not In Love' began life as a bossa nova, only later metamorphosing into the form by which it became a No. 1 hit. This shows that if a song isn't working, don't be afraid to try a drastic change of interpretation will transform it. (The same thing happened when George Martin told The Beatles to play 'Please Please Me' faster.)

13 Bruce Springsteen: 'Born To Run' (1975)

Springsteen's first three albums offer plenty of insights into lyric writing,

production and longer song structures. 'Born To Run' was the moment when he successfully revamped the best music of the pre-Beatles era. The Spectorish production starts with a six-note Duane Eddy-type guitar motif supported by a barrage of saxes, guitars and keyboards. The verse moves twice round an E-A-B change before bringing in a couple of minor chords. Listen for the bVII chord on the first "oh-oh", played as a sus4 and then resolved. There isn't a separate chorus, as the hook is part of the verse. Since the song is about journeying, it is fitting that the middle section after the sax break travels in harmony terms. From E major we go to a 16-bar sequence of sus4 chords and their resolutions: D, G, A and C. The sense of key is fluid throughout. We watch possible tonal centers rush by as though in a car seeing the sights. Then, with a crash, F is established as a new key for six bars; after a few bars there, the music ascends and then descends by semitones (half-steps), landing on a drawn-out B chord that thrusts the music back into the final verse. Springsteen repeats the hook several times, reharmonizing by adding a VI chord (C#m) before the coda.

At this time, Springsteen was very conscious of the effect of a song in concert and seems to have shaped his material for the stage. He adapted the old "soul revue" trick of having many mini-climaxes in a song. 'Born To Run' has a number of these peaks, so the energy of the track never drops.

14 Bebop Deluxe: 'Maid In Heaven' (1975)

Bebop Deluxe were a UK band who enjoyed moderate success at the tail-end of glam rock with a literate "take" on the Bowie/Queen sound. Led by singer-guitarist Bill Nelson, 'Maid In Heaven' is one of their two hit singles. It is a beautiful example of how exciting 1970s rock can be when it struggles out of its self-indulgence. 'Maid' starts with something of a false intro, an F D A progression that implies F is the key. A change to G in bar six, however, leads to the true key of D major and an eight-bar sequence with some fine lead over the top. The verse is a further ten bars – six vocal and four with a guitar arpeggio. After Verse 2, the song goes to a middle eight that pivots off an Em chord (displacing D and thereby adding interest) and links up with part of the intro (a crescendo on A) before two more verses, the last of which repeats the hook line "was made in heaven for you". The earlier descending arpeggio figure is then extended down a full octave. The coda is decorated by studio phasing, dynamic drums, expressive lead and a classic rock I V IV progression, before the whole thing finishes with a punched-out descending sequence going down the scale to chord I.

A bright, passionate, thumping little world in a mere 2:17, and for all its romance it still has the humanity to say, in the last verse, "take the rough with the smooth".

15 R.E.M.: 'Fall On Me' (1986)

This song was voted the best single of 1986 by *Creem* and is taken from the band's fourth album, *Life's Rich Pageant*. The lyrics are as impenetrable as ever with I.R.S-era R.E.M (the theme is apparently ecological), though enough of the images come through to carry a variety of emotions. The song is in C major but there's no sign of chord I until the pre-chorus, and there it is present only for two beats, displaced in a II V I IV progression. The verse consists of a melancholic Dm-Am change (II-VI). The middle eight is almost entirely on the minor chords II, III and VI, and there's an extended pre-chorus instead of a third verse to delay the last choruses by a fraction.

The real power of the song lies in the chorus, which is fueled by a powerful I II IV V turnaround. What lifts it into the sublime is the presence of an increasing number of vocal lines. If you listen carefully you'll hear four different vocal ideas on the final choruses. This is a powerful hook because no single voice can replicate it. The only way to satisfy the desire to hear it again is to play the record one more time. Yeah, I think I've got to play it again ...

16 Elvis Costello: 'I Want You' (1986)

'I Want You' is one of Costello's most dramatic arrangements. It has a false intro long enough to be a section unto itself, played in a country style using I IV V in A major. The second verse comes to an unexpected end on A G F#m. Appropriately for a song about emotional disjunctions, a sudden unrelated D#m chord on the electric hastens in the first verse proper in a new key. The main part of the song is built on a I III VI Vmaj turnaround in E minor: Em G C B7, occasionally interrupted by the D#m. The mix comprises a brittle spikey electric, sustained organ chords, an acoustic guitar, bass and drums. The playing gradually intensifies with the organ seeking higher voicings. At 3:21 there's a demented two-note guitar solo on two deliberately "wrong" notes. The music subsides, builds up and subsides again at about the five-minute mark. The long coda gradually fades to nothing – a kind of anti-climax.

The lyric obsessively alternates the title with the other lines. Costello's theme is jealousy and its self-torturing focus on the imagined details of a lover's betrayal. 'I Want You' falls short of the last degree of greatness. There's something melodramatic about it, almost as if the songwriter enjoys the conceit and prolongs the song as a consequence. Would it be any less effective if it were a minute or 90 seconds shorter? The speaker seems all too willing to embrace the pain he suffers. His imagination is voyeuristic, and the lyric (reinforced by Costello's close-miked vocal presence) implicates us as voyeurs if we get any pleasure out of this pain. But it's rivetting theatre.

17 Dire Straits: 'On Every Street' (1991)

Dire Straits are a frustrating band. It's easy to understand why their huge sales and the popularism of songs such as 'Twisting By The Pool', 'Money For Nothing' and 'Walk For Life' lead many to dismiss them as incapable of creating anything of depth – but don't let the image obscure how potent they can be.

In his vocal delivery, lyrics and guitar playing, Knopfler is a master of understatement, which in rock is an astonishing thing in itself. 'On Every Street' is a love song that conceals deep feeling behind sometimes offhand, oblique imagery. It has a powerful three-verse-plus-coda structure. The verses are melody driven, with frequent chord changes that rise with effort to C, the apparent key, and an interpolated 2/4 bar, indicating that rhythm does not have the upper hand. The hook has a sombre and unexpected Bb (bVII) chord, which lets the suppressed emotion through by shifting to Bbmaj7, reaches C with momentary hope and then dashes it with a drop to A minor on a tremoloed 1950s three-note guitar lick. Each verse is followed by a few bars of what will become the driving theme of the coda, the second statement having a rhythmic anomaly in it. Knopfler's trademark mournful guitar supplies tell-tale sighs throughout.

At 2:50, the guitars introduce a four-bar turnaround that is in C but never reaches the key chord and includes a telling D/F# inversion to preserve the shape of the bassline. The song rides out on a coda that is in strong dynamic contrast to the verses, with the drums entering for the first time. The use of a turnaround for the coda is more powerful because the verses did not have one. And how many guitarists could have resisted soloing loudly at this point? Knopfler judged rightly that the song did not need it.

18 Ash: 'Goldfinger' (1995)

The naff title (cue white Persian cat and "There's only *one* Goldfinger, Mr. Bond ...") is the only place where Ash's 'Goldfinger' disappoints. It has a good grasp of dynamics, which is essential to rock. It's loud and grungy but there are spaces, so the full sound doesn't get tiresome. In this age of desk-driven punch in/out beatboxes, it has tempo changes and a *real drummer* who *stops playing*, counts off two bars and then *re-enters* with a fill. Amazing. From an arrangement angle, notice how the backing vocals are kept till the last chorus.

'Goldfinger' creates interesting contrasts with keys. The band detuned by a semitone (half-step), but I'll pretend they didn't to make it simpler to describe the chord shapes. The instrumental chorus at the start is squarely in G, though it ends on an ambiguous B7sus4 (IIImaj). The guitar solo suggests E minor. B is the key for the verse, which is mostly a four-chord turnaround in B: B G#m C#m F# (I VI II V). I say "mostly" because there's a harmonically outrageous chromatic change from the F# to an F and then Bb, and then a leap back to C#m. This is topped off with a fine three-note guitar overdub that accentuates the sudden weirdness of the changes. Thousands of songs have been written using a I VI II V sequence, but Ash found a new angle on it.

19 Garbage: 'Stupid Girl' (1995)

'Stupid Girl' is carried by its arrangement. It's built on a I-IV change in F#, and both chords are dominant sevenths that provide a sulky edge. This change appears in the intro, verse, chorus and the instrumental bridge; the texture is varied to make the sections sound different.

On the intro, adorned only by a guitar pick-slide and other effects, four bars set the rhythm. The verse adds Shirley Manson's voice and a dancey bass riff with flattened blue notes for an almost R&B feel. An eight-bar pre-chorus cuts in with a couple of minor chords that provide harmonic contrast to the harder-edged strut of the F#7-B7 change. Listen for the way Garbage overdubbed a distorted vocal sample with reverse reverb, an effect guaranteed to make anyone sound like an extra from *The Exorcist*. On the chorus, the title hook is answered by a voice/guitar unison "ah-ah" (maybe a slight nod to 'Smells Like Teen Spirit'). The word "girl" is on a flattened blue note (A instead of A# against the F# chord). In Verse 2, Shirley sings lines that answer the main tune and in the last chorus adds a harmony. The bridge guitar figures include a bassy Duane Eddy-type phrase and a "stab" guitar chord on the opposite side of the mix. Listen for the bass dropping out during the bridge so that its re-entry is felt on the last choruses. 'Stupid Girl' has an effective sudden ending, the sort DJs don't dare talk over.

Sometimes you don't need lots of ideas – you just need to develop the one you've got.

20 Radiohead: 'Paranoid Android' (1997)

As with Ash, another naff title (pinched from U.K. radio comedy series *The Hitch-Hiker's Guide To The Galaxy*). The first time I heard this track on the radio, the DJ commented, after the abrupt ending, "Hmmm ... I'm not sure about that one." At that moment, it was clear Radiohead had done a great job. This track is disconcerting and does the unexpected.

Key-wise, it shifts between G minor, D minor and A minor in an ambiguous way. The opening acoustic Cm-Gm sequence cries out that it must be in some weird tuning, although it's actually standard. The music sounds like it's going into Am, but this happens only after the second verse. Next, a moment of arranging genius: most rock bands would have made the single-note riff a straight pentatonic minor figure. Instead, Radiohead introduce an Ab, implying an Am-Ab chord change, interspersed with a bVI bVII I. When the electric guitars come in the riff's power is unleashed, but the band don't overdo the headbanging – that heavy riff is played only a handful of times. This leaves you wanting more. After the first solo, the music enters its hymn-like third section, which starts on a Cm chord and changes key to D minor via an A7. Notice the feeling of dislocation when the music goes from A back to Cm, as they are distant chords.

The two solo breaks show how rock guitar returned to its roots in the 1990s, rejecting the over-technical widdling of the late 1980s for a less-is-more approach. The first break has what I would call "cultivated (apparent) incompetence".

Maybe the whole isn't quite equal to the sum of the parts (the song was apparently pieced together out of three fragments) but an impressive variety of emotion in one song by Oxford's finest.

FAMOUS SONGWRITERS SECTION 15
ON SONGWRITING

Musicians tend not to be a particularly articulate bunch of people. Those who write songs in the public eye sometimes have personal reasons for not wanting to give away too much about how they write or the meaning of what they have created. Nevertheless, almost all of them have, over the years, said things which offer fascinating glimpses into how they write and what they think the process is all about. Here - with all their contrasting opinions - are the songwriters speaking about the craft.

Paul Weller

When we finished *Setting Sons* (1980), I got the engineer to play the whole album backwards for me to listen to on cassette, and there was one little piece of music, of backward vocal, that I really liked the melody of. So I wrote the whole of 'Dreams Of Children' built around that, more or less made up on the spot. (1992)

I suppose in some ways I write in an old-fashioned way because I always have middle eights in my songs and not many people do any more. It's usually just a verse and chorus. Structure is really important. Some I've really had to work at, others come really quickly. Keeping the whole thing interesting – that's what it all comes down to. (1984)

Mike Mills (R.E.M.)

I asked everyone to sing a background part for the chorus [of 'Find The River']

without hearing any of the other guys. Mine was really emotional, and Bill's was totally the opposite, cool and low-key. They really worked together. That's the kind of thing that keeps it from being too processed – that let's you know it's not being machined to death, that there are human beings doing it. (1992)

Peter Buck (R.E.M.)

[On 'Country Feedback'] We didn't have a song. I walked in and I had four chords. I put them down with Bill playing bass. I put the feedback on it. John Keane put the pedal steel on it. Michael walked in and said, "Oh, I've got words for that." The next day he just sang it. The total recording time, not including the mix, was, like, 35 minutes. It's really nice if you can get it to flow like that.

Bruce Springsteen

The only trick to writing a new song is you have to have a new idea. And to have a new idea, you've got to be a bit of a new person, so that's where the challenge is. (1987)

The writing is more difficult now. On this album [*Born To Run*], I started slowly to find out who I am and where I wanted to be. It was like coming out of the shadow of various influences and trying to be me. You have to let out more of yourself all the time. You strip off the first layer, then the second, then the third. It gets harder because it gets more personal. (1975)

Neil Young

I try not to think about the songs that I write, I just try to write them. And I try not to edit them . . . I know there's a source where music comes through you and words come through you, and editing is really something you do to something that you've thought about. I think some of the things I write are mine, but I think some just come through me. My mind is working behind the scenes and puts these things together without me consciously thinking of it, and then when the time is right it all comes out. (1985)

I've written most of my best songs driving on a long journey, scribbling lyrics on cigarette packs while steering. (1990)

Bob Dylan

I just wanted a song to sing, and there came a point where I couldn't sing anything. So I had to write what I wanted to sing 'cause nobody else was writing what I wanted. I couldn't find it anywhere. If I could, I probably would never have started writing. (1984)

Since the late 1960s, maybe since *Sgt. Pepper* on, everybody started to spend more of their time in the studio, actually making up songs and building them in the studio. I've done a little bit of that, but I'd rather have some kind of song before I get there. It just seems to work out better that way. (1985)

Brian Wilson (The Beach Boys)

I think that 'Good Vibrations' was a contribution in that it was a pocket symphony. . . . It was a series of intricate harmonies and mood changes. We used a cello for the first time in rock'n'roll, so I think in that respect it was an innovation. (1976) When I've thought out a theme I go to the piano and sit playing "feels", which are rhythm patterns and fragments of ideas. Then the song starts to blossom and become a real thing. (1966)

Kurt Cobain (Nirvana)

When I write a song, the lyrics are the least important thing. I can go through two or three different subjects in a song, and the title can mean absolutely nothing at all. (1989)

I think of my new songs as pop songs, as they're arranged with the standard pop format: verse, chorus, verse, chorus, solo, bad solo. (1990)

Jimi Hendrix

On 'The Wind Cries Mary', the words came first, you know, the words came first and then the music was so easy to put there. The whole thing just fell in . . . it just melted together. (1968)

Paul McCartney

Sometimes I've got a guitar in my hands; sometimes I'm sitting at a piano. It depends on whatever instrument I'm at – I'll compose on it.

Every time is different, really. I like to keep it that way, too; I don't get any set formula. So that each time, I'm pulling it out of the air.

There's not much that takes years and years. If it takes that long, I normally abort it. . . . The best songs are written in one go. They're just done – inspiration comes quickly, it falls in place. (1990)

John Lennon

I remember in the early meetings with Dylan, he was always saying to me, "Listen to the words, man!" and I said, "I can't be bothered. I listen to the sound of it, the sound of the overall thing." Then I reversed that and started being a words man. I naturally play with words anyway, so I made a conscious effort to be wordy *a la* Dylan. But now I've relieved myself of that burden and I'm only interested in pure sound. All music is rehash. There are only a few notes. Just variations on a theme. (1980)

Keith Richards

If you try and add a melody to a riff rather than it evolving from it, it always sounds completely false, like the melody's been stuck on the top with a piece of cellotape. You don't create songs. They're not all your creation. You just sort of pluck them out of the air, if you're around and receptive, and then you say, "I kind of like this" and something about the songs says, "I'm worth the time and the trouble to keep playing me and find out." And if you hang on to their tail long enough, suddenly you get, "Ah, there I am, I'm ready." So you have to listen to the mechanics of the song all the time and be very receptive to what it's trying to tell you while you're making it. (1988)

Brian May

I like to live with the song for a while without touching the guitar at all. Then I can form an idea in my head of what I'd like to play, and then work it out on the guitar and take it into the studio pretty much complete. (1990)

Frank Zappa

Basically, what people want to hear in a song is: "I love you, you love me, I'm OK, you're OK, the leaves turned brown, they fell off the trees, the wind was blowing, it got cold, it rained, it stopped raining, you went away, my heart broke, you came back and my heart was OK." I think basically that is deep down what everybody wants to hear. (1974)

Damon Albarn (Blur)

I did all my grades on piano, but I write all my songs on acoustic guitar, which I can just about play 10 chords on. I do them all on an E shape, and put a finger

on the bottom E, so I've always got an E and B drone, whatever chord I do. That's all I do. I've limited myself massively, so the whole thing has become incredibly simple. (1991)

Eric Clapton

It's important for records to be as good as you can make them, you know? When I've written songs and made them into demos – for instance, on the *August* album I had one demo that we did clean up and polish a lot.

Mark Knopfler

Different keys on the guitar suggest different moods. I can't get any height on my voice, so I tend to choose keys that might not suit the song but happen to suit my non-existent range. Sometimes you pick the wrong key when you're recording – 'Why Worry' was recorded in E and you can hear it's in the wrong key. I'm straining to sing it, and I think on the last tour we changed it to D.

Morrissey

My lyrics are only obscure to the extent that they are not taken directly from the dictionary of writing songs. They are not slavish to the lyrical rulebook, so you'll never catch me singing, "Oh baby, baby, yeah." My only priority is to use lines and words in a way that hasn't been heard before. (1983)

Tori Amos

The songs just hang out, you know, they come in and move in. To me the songs already exist, I'm just an interpreter for them. Yes, because of my experiences they're going to come through my filter, and that's going to change how I see them. But they already exist in a certain form, and I'm just trying to take them to the third dimension – maybe the fourth, really, because I'd like to think my work taps into the fourth dimension, not just three dimensions.

I'm always trying to push the boundaries of form, but I don't anaylze it when I'm writing. (1996)

Marc Bolan

I play about for a couple of hours before I move into new dimensions where I'm being very creative. I record everything then. (1971)

I've suddenly tuned into that mental channel that makes a record a hit, and I feel at present as though I could write Number Ones for ever. Let's face it, the majority of pop hits that make it are a permutation on the 12-bar blues, and I've found one that works. (1970)

Matt Johnson (The The)

I think if a song sounds good on just an acoustic guitar, then it is good. That's a song as opposed to a track. A lot of modern records are just tracks, and if you take away the production then they cease to exist. (1993)

Glenn Tilbrook (Squeeze)

People often point out that some of our best-known stuff is musically quite tricky, it revolves around a lot of chord changes, but that was actually something I was striving to stop doing. I wasn't really conscious of doing it until other people mentioned it. I personally don't like songs that are too tricky, but it all depends on how it grabs you. The acid test for me is not whether it's tricky or not, it's whether it works when you play it on its own, just guitar or keyboards. I know that's an old chestnut, but it's true.

Joni Mitchell

[On altered tunings] You're twiddling and you find the tuning. Now the left hand has to learn where the chords are, because it's a whole new ballpark, right? So you're groping around, looking for where the chords are, using very simple shapes. Put it in a tuning and you've got four chords immediately: open, barre five, barre seven, and your higher octave, like half fingering on the 12th. Then you've got to find where your minors are and where the interesting colours are – that's the exciting part.

Jack Bruce (Cream)

I had this idea that you could have very heavy, wild, instrumental stuff but a lyrical, gentle vocal. Something like 'I Feel Free' – very rhythmic backing, very smooth voices on top. It would've been easy to scream something, but then it's one dimensional. (1993)

Kristin Hersh (Throwing Muses)

It's immature to think you're smarter than the music. For me, the only time I can write is when I see really clearly – and I'm so unselfconscious for that reason, I can hear what the songs are saying, and I let them say whatever they want regardless of how much it has to do with my situation. Not that you should make things up – it should resonate with you. You shouldn't pretend. (1995)

Toni Iommi (Black Sabbath)

I'd pick up the guitar, come up with a riff and go, "That sounds a bit evil." The words had to fit the mood. (1995)

Elvis Costello

Recently, I've started changing the keys. Steve [Naive] and I have been doing a version of 'Veronica' that brings back the feeling that was somewhat submerged by the brightness of the pop arrangement, by shifting the key. The verse is higher in register, in Eb, but then drops instead of ascending at the chorus, which closes the song into a more emotional feeling. (1996)

Kate Bush

How I wrote at least the last two albums was to go into the studio and write ideas onto tape – dump stuff onto tape, as it were, forget about it and then move onto the next area. But when I first started, I always used to write on the piano, and just the last couple of months I've felt at home again writing on the piano. It's such a different process, I find it quite shocking. It's like suddenly you've become the memory banks; instead of dumping it onto tape, it's staying in you. And each time you play the song, it changes. The sense of transformation is very subtle; each time you play it, something will change.

Richard Fairbrass (Right Said Fred)

We took a tea break, and the computer was playing this loop round and round, and right out of the blue – I can't tell you where it came from – I started singing "I'm too sexy for my shirt" and we all fell about laughing.

John Barry (film score writer)

It's quite an art to write a good bridge, 'cause it lifts you into another area. It's got to be a variant on what you've done before, but you have to come up with some surprise, so that when you get back to that last familiar strain it's almost like falling into something.

This list is not meant to be the greatest albums of all time, though some of these records would be included on such a list. Inclusion here is not primarily about great performances, profundity, commercial success, influence or the ability to evoke a period. I'm not attempting to present a perfect cross-section of popular music since 1960, nor are all musical genres represented. Instead, these albums show different directions in which the song has been taken. Careful listening to them will teach you an immeasurable amount about the popular song and what it is capable of, and what an elastic form it is. Lyrics, melodies, rhythms, hooks, song structures, arrangements, vocal and instrumental performances – they're all here, albeit in differing mixtures. If you can get your head round the songs on all these albums, then you're doing pretty well in songwriting awareness.

THE BEATLES: 1962-66/1967-70 (1973) Yes, their albums were great. But this is how the Fab Four reinvented the 45 single, from mop-top pop to hippie dreams and beyond.

BOB DYLAN: Blonde on Blonde (1966) Get tangled up in imagery as Dylan's folk muse dons a pair of cool shades and goes acid-rock.

THE BEACH BOYS: Pet Sounds (1966) The pop song as "pocket symphony". Check out the box set The Pet Sounds Sessions for real archaeological detail.

LOVE: Forever Changes (1967) Quirky, innovative lyrics and arrangements that juxtapose strings with 12-string guitars. Extraordinary titles and songs that are expressive and unpredictable.

BURT BACHARACH: The Look Of Love (1996) On the smoother side of things, there's nothing like a good compilation of Bacharach for an insight into melodic development and harmonic construction.

THE BAND: The Band (1969) Seasoned as a barrel of vintage whisky ó an unforgettable "take" on country rock in which fresh from their experiences with Dylan row upsteam of the musical currents of the late 1960s and re-connect with a panoramic American folk vision .

VARIOUS ARTISTS: Motown Chartbusters, Vols. I-V (1969-72) Okay, it's a cheat: five albums' worth of Hitsville USA classics from the company that charged rental space in the Billboard Top 100 during the 1960s. Great songs you can also dance to.

SIMON AND GARFUNKEL: Greatest Hits (1972) Probably the best deployment of two voices and acoustic guitars since the Everlys.

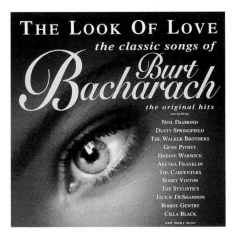

SECTION 16

RECOMMENDED ALBUMS FOR SONGWRITERS

LED ZEPPELIN: Untitled (1971)
If you want to write heavy rock, this is how you do it. Great guitar riffs and disciplined ensemble playing. 'Stairway' is a seamless venture into the longer structure, but don't miss the epic 'When The Levee Breaks', an object lesson in hard-hitting repetition, and the shadowy 'Battle Of Evermore, where Zep show that just because a song is acoustic doesn't mean it can't be intense.

BRUCE SPRINGSTEEN: The Wild, the Innocent and the E Street Shuffle (1973) Bruce's second album may not be as focused and popularist as its two successors, but it shares the same interest in long-scale song structures, haunting arrangements and lyrics that teem with characters and local colour. A unique rock-soul fusion.

JONI MITCHELL: Hejira (1976)
Classic singer-songwriting with fine, detailed lyrics set to open-tuned guitars and the fretless bass of Jaco Pastorius.

THE CARPENTERS: The Singles 1969-73 (1974) Music as melting ice cream. If MOR songwriting is your aim, these people wrote the textbook on smooth production.

QUEEN: Queen II (1974)
Their second album shows the progressive champs of multi-track overdubbing madness hitting their stride and stretching song structures. The level of arrangement detail on this record is astonishing. And who else but Mercury could have made so quintessentially English a rock song as 'The Fairy Feller's Master Stroke', named after a Victorian painting?

FLEETWOOD MAC: Rumours (1977)
Multi-platinum AOR, light and breezy, with a few bitter undertones like daggers under black lace. Listen for melodic guitar work, vocal harmonies and tight song structures.

ABBA: Gold (1992) Another commercial legend: mini-epics of marital tragedy that you could dance to. Take up thy handbag . . . and stuff your songs with hooks.

SIOUXSIE & THE BANSHEES: Ju Ju (1981) A punk band re-invents itself as African Gothic. This album is a lexicon of unusual musical approaches, from the weird spidery guitar lines to the tribal drumming, all serving to express a host of dark emotions pop normally keeps safely in the mouldier areas of the basement.

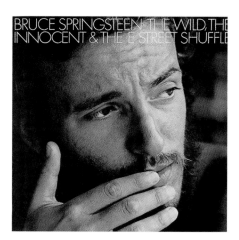

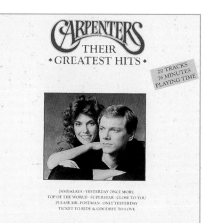

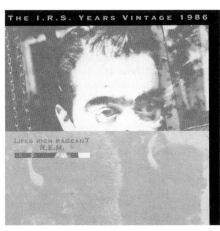

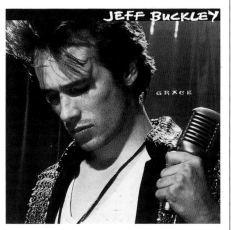

BOB MARLEY: Legend (1984) Marley's songwriting shows how reggae could reach a wider audience by combining religious and political themes with commercial melodies.

R.E.M.: Life's Rich Pageant (1986) The early R.E.M. blueprint of obscure lyrics, odd melodies, unconventional dual voices and jangle guitar is polished and reaches maturity on this record. You could call it classic 1980s alternative/"college" rock, but that sells it short. Few rock bands have so deserved the adjective "poetic".

KATE BUSH: The Sensual World (1989) A warmer album than its more popular predecessor, Hounds Of Love, this record is astonishing for the emotional depth of the songs and the amazing arrangements. Who else but Bush would have pitted her own vocals and Gilmour's rock guitar against Bulgarian harmony singing?

MADONNA: The Immaculate Conception (1990) Not even two double-albums could now gather up all of Madonna's chartbusters. Love her or loathe her, she and Patrick Leonard knew how to put a hit single together and maintained a remarkable run of success from the mid-1980s onward. This collection has the brighter, brassier early hits.

NIRVANA: Nevermind (1991) Grunge's finest hour, where pop hooks and verse/chorus structures collide, with unrestrained aesthetic glee, with a Big Guitar Racket.

JEFF BUCKLEY: Grace (1995) The singer-songwriter strikes back for the 1990s. Highly inventive mixture of styles, tremendous range of expression, clever arrangements, altered tunings, fine lyrics, terrific vocals.

BJORK: Post (1995) One example of how a female singer can find new ways forward by harnessing 1990s technology to an idiosyncratic muse.

RADIOHEAD: OK Computer (1996) Perhaps wanting a little in the lyric department (though in that respect these songs cover their tracks better than their 1970s equivalents), but a highly imaginative development of rock into new areas and textures.

INDEX OF SONGS

Page numbers in bold refer to the Gallery of Songs

INDEX OF ARTISTS

The page numbers locate titles of songs by the artist(s) in the head-word, but note that artists' names may not be given. The separate index of songs for may be consulted for these. Page numbers in bold refer to the 'Gallery of Songs', and to 'Songwriters on Songwriting'.

ACKNOWLEDGEMENTS

Thanks go to Tony, Nigel, Phil and Pen at Balafon Press for their work in the complicated task of bringing this book to fruition. I would also like to thank my guitar students over the past twenty years, who have brought new songs to my attention and sharpened my awareness of some of the points of songwriting craft discussed herein; in particular Paul Bridges, Ella Maitland, Hilmi Kocak, Martin Willbery, Roger Dalrymple, and Pardis Sabeti. For personal inspiration on the guitar I am indebted to Denys Stephens and Ian Jackson, and for musical instruction my music teachers at Humphry Davy Grammar, Penzance, Russell Jory and Elizabeth Duncan. Remembering further back, I thank my parents Dallas and Bryan for a childhood home that was full of music, popular and classical.